PICTURING ISLAM

KENNETH M. GEORGE

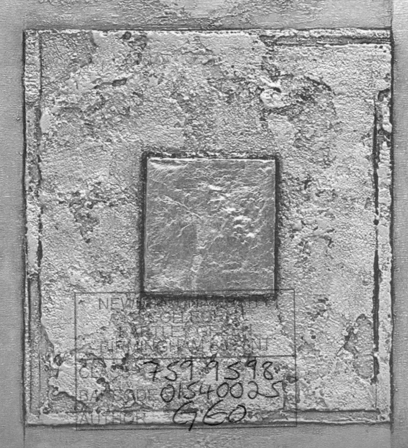

PICTURING ISLAM

ART AND ETHICS IN A MUSLIM LIFEWORLD

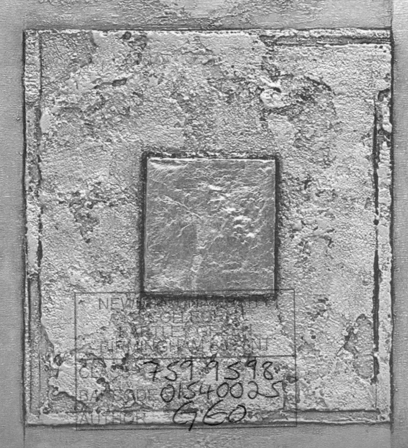

WILEY-BLACKWELL

A John Wiley & Sons, Ltd., Publication

This edition first published 2010
© 2010 Kenneth M. George

Blackwell Publishing was acquired by John Wiley & Sons in February 2007. Blackwell's publishing program has been merged with Wiley's global Scientific, Technical, and Medical business to form Wiley-Blackwell.

Registered Office
John Wiley & Sons Ltd, The Atrium, Southern Gate, Chichester, West Sussex, PO19 8SQ, United Kingdom

Editorial Offices
350 Main Street, Malden, MA 02148-5020, USA
9600 Garsington Road, Oxford, OX4 2DQ, UK
The Atrium, Southern Gate, Chichester, West Sussex, PO19 8SQ, UK

For details of our global editorial offices, for customer services, and for information about how to apply for permission to reuse the copyright material in this book please see our website at www.wiley.com/wiley-blackwell.

Library of Congress Cataloging-in-Publication Data

George, Kenneth M.
  Picturing Islam : art and ethics in a Muslim lifeworld / Kenneth M. George.
    p. cm.
  Includes bibliographical references and index.
  ISBN 978-1-4051-2958-9 (hardcover : alk. paper) – ISBN 978-1-4051-2957-2 (pbk. : alk. paper)
1. Pirous, A. D. (Abdul Djalil), 1932– 2. Muslim artists–Indonesia–Aceh–Biography. 3. Islam and art–Indonesia–Aceh. 4. Islam and culture–Indonesia–Aceh. 5. Islam and politics–Indonesia–Aceh. 6. Art and anthropology–Indonesia–Aceh. 7. Art and religion–Indonesia–Aceh. 8. Politics and culture–Indonesia–Aceh. I. Title.
  ND1026.8.P57G47 2010
  759.9598–dc22
  [B]
                    2009040194

A catalogue record for this book is available from the British Library.

Set in 10.5 on 13 pt Minion by Toppan Best-set Premedia Limited
Printed and bound in Malaysia by Vivar Printing Sdn Bhd

01   2010

For Pirous and Erna

CONTENTS

ILLUSTRATIONS

Plates

Figures

Paintings must be like miracles.

Mark Rothko

PREFACE

Picturing Islam is an ethnographic portrait of a postcolonial Muslim artist, Indonesian painter Abdul Djalil Pirous. My goal is to sketch a story of self-fashioning in the contemporary cauldron of politics, art, and religion. At root, this is a story about making art and a lifeworld "Islamic" as a way of coming to terms with political, cultural, and historical circumstances. It considers very generally, then, a question of enduring interest to anthropologists and others in the humanities and social sciences – the question of subjectivity, our experience of acting and being acted upon in our relations with others as we are caught up in the sway of powerful social and ideological forces. As Judith Butler (2005), Michel Foucault (1997, 2005), Paul Ricoeur (1992), and others have shown so persuasively, questions of subjectivity are also questions of ethics. We commonly look to art and religion for special insights into the ethics and aesthetics of self-fashioning, despite all our trouble in defining art and religion, or the risks we may take in giving them privileged attention. My long collaboration with Pirous has given me a chance to reflect on the hopes and perils of self-fashioning in a Muslim lifeworld. How Pirous has pictured Islam is not just about his relationship to God, but also about his artistic and ethical being and location in this world.

My aim here, then, has been to write an accessible ethnographic account that will find use in a broad range of classroom discussions in anthropology, religious studies, Asian studies, and art history. *Picturing Islam* is not a primer on that religion, or on the Qur'an, but a portrait of how Islamic ideas and dispositions might settle into the experiential and expressive lifeworld of a believer, or make their way into art. It is a study of lived religion. At the same time, I have tried to show in this book how ethnography might be used to "confront art history with the present tense" (Belting 2003: 192). In that spirit, this book is a modest contribution to a global art history that includes Southeast Asian art and Islamic art as part of its theoretical, historical, and critical venture.

Framing the book as I did around an empirical look at art and ethics in the work of a Muslim painter, and wanting to keep it to a manageable length, I left many theoretical and comparative questions unaddressed. Colleagues interested in subjectivity, the anthropology of art, or art history and visual culture may want to glance at the Afterword.

I will be especially glad if Muslim readers find this book useful or pleasurable. If they find errors of understanding in this book, the errors are mine, despite Pirous's generous and unflagging effort to help me see clearly.

ACKNOWLEDGMENTS

Picturing Islam would not have come together as it did without the intellectual push from four colleagues: Charles Hallisey, who drew me into conversations about ethics and lived religion; James Siegel, whose work and conversations about subjectivity, language, cameras, and the political unconscious in Aceh and Indonesia suggested ways I might dwell with materials; Nora Taylor, who reassured me that an ethnography of a single artist might actually be a very welcome intervention in art history; and Kirin Narayan, who knows better than most the joys, risks, and power of bringing friends and family into ethnographic writing. Charlie, Jim, Nora, and Kirin bear no responsibility for this book's shortcomings, many of which stem from my not always following their example or advice. I thank them for their inspiring support.

Conversations with other colleagues and friends have enriched this book in countless ways too. I am especially grateful for helpful insights and suggestions from Abdul Hadi W. M., Warwick Anderson, Lorraine Aragon, Iftikhar Dadi, Veena Das, Kevin Dwyer, Susan Friedman, Anna Gade, Hildred Geertz, Byron Good and Mary-Jo DelVecchio Good, Ramachandra Guha, Michael Herzfeld, Charles Hirschkind, James B. Hoesterey, Pradeep Jeganathan, Carla Jones, Webb Keane, Arthur Kleinman, B. Venkat Mani, Vida Mazulis, Birgit Meyer, Sarah Murray, Fred Myers, Paul Nadasdy, Hamid Naficy, Ashis Nandy, Sally Ness, Terry O'Nell, Kevin "Will" Owen, Christopher Pinney, Allen and Mary "Polly" Roberts, Kathryn Robinson, Setiawan Sabana, T. K. Sabapathy, Patricia Spyer, Mary Steedly, Sunaryo, Stanley J. Tambiah, Julia Thomas, Fadjar Thufail, Aarthe Vaddi, James and Rubie Watson, Andrew Willford, Jessica Winegar, Aram Yengoyan, Yustiono, and Merwan Yusuf. I am indebted, as well, to Lindsay French, Charles Hallisey, Carla Jones, Nancy Smith-Hefner, and Andrew Willford who at the request of Wiley-Blackwell gave generously of their time to advise and encourage me about the direction of the book while it was still a half-written manuscript. Their insights and queries were instrumental to my giving the book its full and final shape.

There is no way I can measure my gratitude to Abdul Djalil Pirous and his wife Erna Garnasih Pirous. Their family and circle of friends have always welcomed me with abundant kindness and conversation, and all of them have shown uncommon generosity in letting me share and write about their lives in as much detail as I have. Pirous and Erna have never told me so, but over the years I am sure I must have made slights, blunders, and intrusions that hurt, angered, or embarrassed someone. I hope they will forgive the flaws and lapses of their friend and resident ethnographer. I want them to take pleasure and pride in this book, confident that the intimate lessons they have given me over the years about art, Islam, and goodness will prove useful for others.

Closer to home, I thank Didi Contractor, Maya Narayan, and Devendra Contractor for their unflagging interest and support. Cheers from my brothers Phil and Andy, my sister Lois, and their families have meant much to me too.

Which leaves Kirin, my wife, companion, and mutual muse. Kirin appears rather late in this book, but has been a miracle of goodness and inspiration since page one. I once knew writing as a desperately lonely burden. Kirin has helped me see writing otherwise, as a way to care for myself and for us both. For that and for all the light she continues to throw into my world she has my unending affection.

Funding for the field research that led to this book came from several sources. I gratefully acknowledge support from the Aga Khan Trust for Culture; the Social Science Research Council; the Wenner-Gren Foundation for Anthropological Research; the University of Oregon's Center for Asian and Pacific Studies; and the University of Wisconsin-Madison's Center for Southeast Asian Studies. Fellowships from the National Endowment for the Humanities; the Institute for Advanced Study; the John Simon Guggenheim Foundation; and the Vilas Associates Program at the University of Wisconsin-Madison gave me release time from teaching, making it possible for me to conduct library research and to draft some of the analyses that went into this book. My thanks also go to my Indonesian sponsors at Lembaga Ilmu Pengetahuan Indonesia (LIPI, the Indonesian Institute of Science); Yayasan Festival Istiqal (the Istiqlal Festival Foundation); and Fakultas Seni Rupa dan Desain, Institut Teknologi Bandung (the Department of Fine Arts and Design at the Bandung Institute of Technology).

Some passages in this book appeared in my previously published work. I thank the publishers of the following journals and books for permission to reprint passages or excerpts from:

"Ethics, Iconoclasm, and Qur'anic Art in Indonesia." *Cultural Anthropology* 24(4): 589–621 (2009). Wiley-Blackwell and the American Anthropological Association.

"Ethical Pleasure, Visual Dzikir, and Artistic Subjectivity in Contemporary Indonesia." *Material Religion* 4(2): 172–93 (2008). Berg Publishers, an imprint of A&C Black Publishers Ltd.

"Art and Identity Politics: Nation, Religion, Ethnicity, Elsewhere." In *Asian and Pacific Cosmopolitans: Self and Subject in Motion*, edited by Kathryn Robinson, pp. 37–59. New York: Palgrave (2007). Palgrave Macmillan Publishers.

"Picturing Aceh: Violence, Religion, and a Painter's Tale." In *Spirited Politics: Religion and Public Life in Contemporary Southeast Asia*, edited by Andrew C. Willford and Kenneth M. George, pp. 185–208. Ithaca, NY: Southeast Asian Publications Series, Cornell University (2005). Southeast Asia Program, Cornell University.

"Violence, Culture, & the Indonesian Public Sphere: Reworking the Geertzian Legacy." In *Violence: Culture, Performance and Expression*, edited by Neil L. Whitehead, pp. 25–54. Santa Fe: SAR Press (2004). School for Advanced Research.

"Conversations with Pirous." In *A. D. Pirous: Vision, Faith, and a Journey in Indonesian Art, 1955–2002*. Bandung: Yayasan Serambi Pirous (2002). Yayasan Serambi Pirous.

Signature Work: Bandung, 1994. *Ethnos* 64(2): 212–31 (1999). Taylor & Francis Group.

Designs on Indonesia's Muslim Communities. *Journal of Asian Studies* 57(3): 693–713 (1998). Cambridge University Press and the Association for Asian Studies.

I am deeply indebted to Ilham Khoiri and Dar Charif for their help in translating the Qur'anic Arabic in Pirous's calligraphic paintings. I thank Fadjar Thufail, Atka Savitri, Amy Farber, and Bart Ryan for help in transcribing my Indonesian interview materials, and Noah Theriault for help with the index. Over the years I have worked on this project I have had the help of some wonderful graduate research assistants. They are: James B. Hoesterey, Erica James, Kate Lingley, Jennifer Munger, Susan Rottmann, and Fadjar Thufail. I thank them all, and want them to know how proud I am of their accomplishments.

I am so very lucky to have had the professional assistance of the Pirous family "Dream Team." The digital reproductions of Pirous's paintings and family photos were prepared with the superb care of Rihan Meurila Pirous, Eka Sofyan Rizal, and their colleagues at dialogue+design and at paprieka. Mida Meutia Pirous and Dudy Wiyancoko kept me supplied with archival data from Yayasan Serambi Pirous. Dudy and Iwan Meulia Pirous also reviewed this manuscript and offered helpful tips and insights.

Last, I owe unending thanks to Jane Huber, Blackwell's former senior acquisitions editor for anthropology, for her unflagging interest and confidence in this project. I am deeply grateful as well to senior editor Rosalie Robertson, editorial assistant Julia Kirk, production editor Elaine Willis, and project manager Helen Gray at Wiley-Blackwell for their steady counsel and outstanding care in helping bring this book to completion and into the world.

In memory

Since late 2002, I have lost six colleagues and friends whose personal and intellectual company helped guide me as I moved forward with this project. I want to remember them here: anthropologists Begoña Aretxaga, Daphne Berdahl, and Clifford Geertz; painter Umi Dachlan; art writer Mamannoor; and the always kind Masjoeti Daeng Soetigna.

NOTE ON QUR'ANIC VERSE

Ilham Khoiri and A. D. Pirous identified the Qur'anic passages that appear in the paintings discussed in this book. I have rendered these Qur'anic passages in English, adapting and mixing translations prepared by Abdullah Yusuf Ali (2005), Ahmed Ali (1994), M. A. S. Abdel Haleem (2004), and Michael Sells (1999). I use the abbreviation QS followed by a number when identifying a Qur'anic sura, or chapter (e.g., QS 112 is Qur'anic Sura 112, *Al-Ikhlas*). Sura names and their translations are taken from Ali or Sells.

Khoiri and Pirous also transliterated the Jawi in these Qur'anic paintings into Romanized Indonesian-Malay.

GUIDE TO INDONESIAN SPELLING AND PRONUNCIATION

I use conventional Indonesian spellings for Indonesian, Arabic (without diacritics), and Acehnese terms. Some personal names reflect an idiosyncratic mixing of modern and colonial-era spellings. Here are the rough approximations for pronouncing consonants and vowels.

Consonants: as in English with the following differences:

< ' > is a glottal stop, as in "Uh' oh!"
< c > like the first "ch" in "*ch*urch"
< kh > as in the German "Ach!"
< sy > as in "Syah" or "Shah." Also written < sh >
< dz > like < z >, but with the tongue on the alveolar ridge above the teeth

Vowels:

< i > as the vowel in "f*ee*d"
< a > as the vowel in "p*o*t"
< o > as the vowel in "b*oa*t"
< u > as the vowel in "b*oo*t"
< oe > = < u > (colonial era spelling, usually in names)
< oo > = < u > (in personal names)
< ou > = < u > (as used by Pirous)
< ö > = < o > (approximate)
< e > as in the first vowel in "*a*bout"
< é > as the vowel in "m*ai*d"
< eu > as the vowel in "h*e*r" but with rounded lips

INTRODUCTION: PICTURING ISLAM

"This isn't *da'wah*. I'm not campaigning for religion. I am making art. What you see here, all these paintings, these are my spiritual notes." My friend Pirous grew animated, eager to refute the complaints of the clerics and critics who had questioned his motives in making "Islamic art." It was early March 1994, and we had spent much of the afternoon at his private hillside gallery, Serambi Pirous, sorting through paintings for the gallery's long-planned opening, timed to coincide later in the week with the artist's birthday, but designed too as a special Ramadhan gathering of family, friends, and colleagues. With sunset and the muezzin's call to *maghrib* prayers echoing from mosques and radios, we put aside some paintings that still needed hanging, broke the daylong fast with sweets made from palm sugar and coconut milk, and headed back to his nearby home. Our car crept through narrow, crowded lanes of motorbikes and mosque-bound pedestrians. A bend in the road gave me a panoramic glimpse of Bandung's sprawling neighborhoods and urban ridgetops, all aswarm with the lamps and headlights of the city's two and half million inhabitants. We pulled into Pirous's driveway. Pirous climbed upstairs to the rear of the house to pray, while I lingered in the entryway, as I sometimes did, to study one of his signature Qur'anic paintings.

Pirous and his wife Erna had designed and built this house in the early 1980s. Featured in several of the popular architecture and design magazines that cater to Indonesia's urban elite, the house served as their home and studio, as well as a showcase for some of Pirous and Erna's best paintings. The main doorway had brought me – like all their guests – squarely before the ochre- and sienna-colored expanse of *At the Beginning, the Voice said "Recite" (Sebermula Suara Itu, "Iqra"),*

1

Figure 0.1 A. D. Pirous, 2001. Photograph courtesy of Yayasan Serambi Pirous.

a "calligraphic painting" that features the first five verses of Qur'anic Sura 96, *Al-'Alaq* ("The Embryo"). Take a look at Plate 1. Many Indonesian Muslims place decorative plaques featuring short and familiar Qur'anic inscriptions near the main threshold of their homes – the *Basmallah* ("In the Name of God the Compassionate the Caring") and the "Verse of the Throne" (QS 2: 255) are favorites. Pirous's painting is a grand and arresting variation on this customary use of calligraphic art. Pirous once told me that he kept this painting for himself, and placed it at the doorway, "because it builds the spirit of the house." It renders in unblemished

2

Qur'anic (or Classical) Arabic one of the first revelations given to the Prophet Muhammad. Opening with the *Basmallah*, the passage reads, from right to left:

> In the Name of God the Compassionate the Caring
> Recite in the name of your Lord who created
> Humankind from an embryo
> Recite, for your Lord is all-giving
> Who taught by means of the pen
> Taught man what he did not know before

This Qur'anic passage reminds the faithful of their capacity for language, thought, and learning – the gift of knowledge and reason from the pen of God. The passage appears written in raised letters on an immense slab, a visual allusion, perhaps, to what Islamic traditions describe as a concealed primordial tablet, the eternal, already-inscribed, "uncreated" Qur'an. Yet the tablet looks broken or divided at the painting's midsection, a "break" that visually marks a shift in language. The Qur'anic passage is repeated on the lower panel, but translated and inscribed in Jawi – Indonesian-Malay written in Arabic script. Two languages, one "message." Five gold-lipped holes – are they punctures? leaks? – pockmark a fragmented plate near the top of the painting. Are they a painterly reference to the "five pillars" of Islam? To the five hours reserved for daily prayer and witness to God?

After a few minutes of reflection, I pulled myself away from the painting, slipped off my shoes, and wandered upstairs to the living room. Not long after, Pirous came down. Freshened by prayer and evening bath, Pirous settled into a chair and earnestly resumed our conversation about the mingling of religion and art and the dilemmas one has to face in making "Islamic art" in Indonesia. A massive painting loomed high on the wall behind us as we talked: *For the Sparkling Morning Light* (*Demi Cahaya Pagi yang Cemerlang*; Plate 2). The cracked, magenta tablet in the center of the painting displays all of QS 93 *Ad-Duha* ("The Early Hours of Morning") in Qur'anic Arabic and turquoise. The first few verses reassure the faithful in the face of adversity:

> In the Name of God the Compassionate the Caring
> By the morning's bright light
> By the night when it is still
> Your Lord has not abandoned you and does not hate you
> What comes after will be better for you than what came before

Pirous went on to tell me about some of those who harbored suspicions about his calligraphic paintings and who had scolded him for using art for *da'wah*, proselytizing or spreading the faith. Like all our conversations, this one was a playground of languages. Pirous darted back and forth between Indonesian and English. His hands joined the conversation too, his fingers and palms speaking animatedly about his exasperation.

The religious leaders and *ulama* (Islamic scholars) here never talk about art and culture. They are blind to art. They don't know what is meant by modern art. And they don't recognize it as a form of knowledge or its relationship to Islam. They don't know anything about that.

A smile broke out behind his mustache and goatee, and his eyes brightened with earnest conviction.

Whatever I say in my art expresses my belief, and my faith in values for this life, because for me, religion has two faces: There is a face in the form of religious teaching. But there is also a face that is in the form of art, the face of culture, where my life is at peace, and where I can learn more about Islam. Like I say, I am an ordinary Muslim. I just want to be a good Muslim.

Lifeworlds

Picturing Islam is about Indonesian artist Abdul Djalil Pirous and the many years he has spent making "Islamic art." It tells a story about an artist with an anthropological and art historical twist. Pirous has long been celebrated as a pioneer of contemporary Indonesian Islamic art, and there is no shortage of newspaper articles, reviews, exhibition catalogues, and book chapters about him, read mostly in Indonesia, but found in Europe, the United States, Australia, and other places in Asia too. As for me, I see in his art a vast canvas of global social and cultural forces. These forces result in the mingling of religion, art, nationality, and selfhood, sometimes with great promise and potential, other times with considerable panic and peril. The story is not Pirous's alone, but could be told by (or about) many postcolonial artists throughout the Muslim world. The details might be different, but the dilemmas would be similar. At root, it is a story about making art and a lifeworld "Islamic."

The term "lifeworld" belongs to a long tradition of phenomenological philosophy and sociology. I use it in this book as shorthand for the ongoing circumstances in which we find ourselves, culturally, politically, historically, and experientially. Each of us is thrown, with others, into a lifeworld through which we must find our way, refashioning its horizons as imaginatively and as pragmatically as we can. What I find so useful about the term is that it helps us avoid portraying people in the confines of an all-encompassing language or culture. Today's lifeworlds are both intimate and global in dimension. They are the interconnected, lived-in spaces that bring people – with their thoughts, experiences, and sense of self – into reciprocal touch with global currents, seldom through a single language or culture but more commonly through a vast field of cultural-linguistic alternatives and pluralities. Although lifeworlds are situationally imposed on us, and prejudiced by sedimented cultural traditions, they are, in no small way, open-ended, uncertain, politically inflected works in progress – fragile, blinding, prone to turmoil and repression, and yet creative, aspiring, and exalting in possibility and power.

Taking an anthropological view, I think of a lifeworld as an informal and every-day realm of thought, feeling, and subjectively meaningful activity. People dwell in their lifeworlds, but not freely or unproblematically so. Every person's lifeworld is complexly cultural, inescapably political, and very bound up with the public sphere. Each is filled with the contradictions and predicaments that come with seeking identities and solidarities, with finding meaning and dispelling illusion. All are vulnerable to the political-economic intrusions and enticements of states and markets. All are richly storied. As we have seen, a story that matters a great deal to Pirous is about his being or becoming a good Muslim through making art. (One could ask, of course, whether he is also keen to become a good artist by being a devout Muslim, but I will set that question aside for now.) This involves his pursu-ing religious and ethical goals in the largely secular and market-driven world of contemporary art, but also convincing a Muslim public that making art is a worth-while and ethical project. As Pirous explained to me that evening at his home in early 1994, the very idea of a Qur'anic painting has made some Muslim religious authorities very uneasy. As we will see, an expressly Islamic art does not always find ready or wide embrace in contemporary art venues. For now, however, my larger point is this: A lifeworld is not set apart from collectivities and publics, but is the very place in which collectivities and publics work their magic – and exact their demands – on a person's sensibility, judgment, ambition, and thought.

It is my view that Pirous's paintings, and the stories that accompany and sur-round them, are a bridge between the public and the private aspects of his lifeworld. Taking cue from Hannah Arendt (1958) and anthropologist Michael Jackson (2006), I consider these art works and art stories a "subjective in-between" – a highly political arena for the intermingling of experience and recognition. Jackson so elegantly summarizes Arendt, I quote him here:

> Every person is at once a 'who' and a 'what' – a subject who actively participates in the making and unmaking of his or her world, and a subject who suffers and is sub-jected to actions by others, as well as by forces that lie largely outside of his or her control. This oscillation between being an actor and being acted upon is felt in every human encounter. (2006: 13)

I ask readers to think of Pirous's paintings and his stories about them as points of human encounter. As he makes his way in his lifeworld, his works and ideas belong not just to him, but to others as well. They are the places where he is in expressive dialogue with predecessors and peers, with his nation, with ideas about art, and with God. These paintings and stories thus give us a glimpse of Pirous caring and accounting for himself in relation to others, showing us how making art is an ethical venture too.

In the pages ahead, I tell how Pirous was thrown into a lifeworld from which he would respond to the call of Indonesian nationalism and the Indonesian

5

Figure 0.2 Pirous at work in his home studio, Bandung, 2001. Photograph courtesy of Yayasan Serambi Pirous.

nation-state, the global currents of postcolonial art, and, of course, Islam. Many would recognize in this chorus the call of modernity, especially for a remaking of the self and its relationships with others. In that respect, it was a call to moral action and ethical conduct: to assent to citizenship and sacrifice for the nation-state; to assent to expressivity and sacrifice for art; and to assent to the teachings of Islam and surrender to God. The call of Indonesia, art, and Islam brought with them, of course, all sorts of predicaments and possibilities. How Pirous has reconciled and lived with those forces and predicaments is the theme of this book.

Our Collaboration

To write about Pirous's lifeworld also gives me a way to discus my ethnographic collaboration with him. My friendship with Pirous began nearly twenty-five years ago, in 1985. By that time, he had distinguished himself as a leading proponent and spokesman for a fledgling Islamic arts movement in his home country of Indonesia. His solo retrospective show in Jakarta that year won critical acclaim and earned him an invitation from the US Embassy to visit museums, galleries, art schools, and studios across the United States. I was working on my Ph.D. in cultural anthropology and had just returned home after three straight years of field research in a very

6

remote mountain district on the Indonesian island of Sulawesi. Scrawny, out of money, out of touch, dressed in dated, ill-fitting clothes, and clueless about the CDs, videos, and computers that had moved into nearly every home while I was gone, I was in sore need of a makeover and cultural upgrade while I figured out a way to finish my thesis. My Indonesian was pretty good, however, and so I began contract work for the State Department as a translator-escort for official Indonesian visitors to this country. In early November 1985, I began a six-week tour with Pirous, taking him to centers of art activity in places such as New York, Chicago, Houston, Santa Fe, Los Angeles, and San Francisco. (Erna joined us for the last two weeks of the tour.) Serving as his escort and sidekick, I not only fattened up and found some polish on this upscale tour, but also found myself drawn into a transcultural art world both wondrous and unfamiliar to me. I especially recall our conversations about Euro-American art history, a field in which I had no background or experience. As we walked through galleries and museums, I learned about the art of "the West" for the first time – but through the eyes and experience of someone from Asia ("the East", or, for some of us, "the world South") – thus reversing the patterns of authority and learning that we associate with imperialism.

This was not Pirous's first visit to the US. He had studied in the US fifteen years earlier, and came this time expecting to see an intensely innovative art scene, but one uninterested in expressions of faith or spirituality. Three shows brought him immense pleasure and surprise. The Metropolitan Museum of Art in New York was holding the blockbuster exhibit *India!* as part of the countrywide Festival of India. The crowds flocking to a show so steeped in religion and ethnicity left a huge impression on him. The high point of his whole tour, as I remember him saying at the time, was our hour at the Rothko Chapel in Houston, a meditative, interfaith sanctuary featuring fourteen massive, but very intimate, abstract canvases by Mark Rothko, and Barnett Newman's *The Broken Obelisk*, a monument sculpted in honor of Martin Luther King, Jr. Yet, in looking back, I also recall our encounter with an installation at the New Mexico Museum of Fine Arts in Santa Fe. It was *Tent of Meeting* by artist Michele Zackheim. Enclosing 1,000 square feet, the free-standing tent took inspiration from Zackheim's trip to Jerusalem, her climb up Mount Sinai, and her meeting with an Arab Bedouin seer, Saleh Umbarak Seliman Reneiman. Incorporating Judaic, Christian, and Islamic iconography, *Tent of Meeting* celebrated the unifying themes of the Abrahamic religions. Pirous was exceptionally moved by it, and I know it made a lasting impression on him.

As he was about to return home, Pirous gave me a copy of the catalogue to his 1985 retrospective show in Jakarta, inscribed with a heartfelt message in Indonesian: "As souvenir and keepsake of our month wandering in the world of art. Art and friendship are things that are strong and deeply intimate." There is a page in that catalogue that has always held my gaze, and I kept coming back to it again and again, as I do now. It shows a reproduction of Pirous's first Qur'anic work, an etching called *Surat Ichlas*, a reference to QS 112, *Al-Ikhlas* ("Pure Faith," or "Sincerity"). I could not read the Arabic, but was drawn to the squall of calligraphy and the etching's colors – turquoise, teal, scarlet, and tarnished copper. It appears in this book as Plate 3. The calligraphic figures in turquoise and teal contain all four verses of *Al-Ikhlas*, considered by Muslims to be the most famous Qur'anic statement of *tauhid* (God's divine unity and one-ness), and of the sincerity with which it should be acknowledged:

> In the Name of God the Compassionate the Caring
> Say, "He is God, the one, the eternal
> God the refuge
> Not begetting, unbegotten
> There is no one comparable to Him."

At the foot of the etching, in a band of red, is inscribed QS 2 (*Al-Baqarah*) verse 256, a verse about freely surrendering oneself to God:

> There is no compulsion in matters of faith.
> True guidance stands clear from error.
> Whoever turns away from the forces of evil
> and believes in God, will surely hold fast
> to a handle that is strong and unbreakable,
> for God hears all and knows every thing.

There is an important story Pirous tells about this etching, one that I will discuss later. Here I want to say that in the countless times I have lost myself in this image, its colors, its composition, and its calligraphy, it has begun to take on a life of its own. I no doubt project something of myself into the picture, and yet I feel touched by it, beckoned to something Pirous wanted to reveal in material form.

My curiosity about Islam and art owe much to being beckoned by my friendship with Pirous and by images such as *Surat Ichlas*. Indonesia, as many readers may know, is a predominantly Islamic nation, and boasts a community of nearly 220 million Muslims – more than those living in any other country, or in the entire Arab Middle East for that matter. Though I had lived with Muslim families and friends from time to time during my three years in highland Sulawesi, my work there focused on followers of a minority ancestral religion known as *ada' mappurondo* (George 1996). Deep in the mountain forests, and well beyond the call of a muezzin or a mosque drum summoning Muslims to prayer, I listened instead to the songs of spirit-possessed women and the boastful speeches of men who came of age in acts of sacrificial violence. I studied taboos and the language of omen birds, not the Qur'an. Pirous's friendship and artwork seemed an invitation for me to expand my understanding of Indonesia by spending time with Muslim artists and intellectuals in two of the country's major cities, Jakarta and Bandung. After years of work on the verbal arts of a highly localized and out-of-the-way ritual tradition, I saw something fresh, a chance to explore the intimate and global dimensions of a major world religion and its visual culture.

I often make friendships through research; here I had a chance to bring research to a friendship. Pirous wrote to me in 1991 about Festival Istiqlal, a festival of Indonesian Islamic art that he was helping stage in Jakarta. Over 6 million visitors attended the month-long festival, and he noted that a second was immediately planned to coincide with the fiftieth anniversary of Indonesia's independence in 1995. An art event of this popularity and magnitude looked especially significant to me. When I expressed my interest in studying the festival and Pirous's own work, he and Erna wrote back to say they would be happy to host me for a few months. With the support of the Aga Khan Foundation and other fellowships I left for Bandung in February 1994, to sit in on festival planning sessions and to get better acquainted with Pirous's art.

What I envisioned as a year-long project turned into a decade-long ethnographic collaboration, and through it our friendship and understanding have deepened. We did not have identical tasks or goals in collaborating. My goal was finding the "big picture" in the ethnographic details of a lifeworld – finding issues of general or comparative interest to anthropologists, art historians, and others in terms of understanding the cultural politics of art and religion. For Pirous, on the other hand, the project had more appeal as a way to stir public interest in his painting and Islamic art more generally, both nationally and internationally. Our collaboration, of course, has had a history of its own. It has unfolded over time, and changed in terms of direction, depth, and styles. We have worked not so much in unison, as in concert.

I belong to a cohort of scholars who began their research on Indonesia during the "New Order" – the years when the country was ruled under the strangling grip of President Soeharto and the political and military circles who had come to power in 1965–66. The regime set many of the limits and prospects for painters like Pirous, and for researchers as well. Our conversations about art and culture thus took a dramatic turn with the sudden collapse of the Soeharto regime in May 1998, an event that led many to believe a long era of authoritarian rule in Indonesia might be over. Three years later, the September 11 attack on the World Trade Center stunned us with worry, paranoia, and despair. Sticking with the collaboration has been a way for us to refuse the divisions of violence and turmoil. At the same time, it lets us acknowledge, too, the ways art, religion, and fieldwork have been drawn ever more deeply into the cauldron of world politics. Knowing my familiarity with his artwork and everyday routines, and with the changing political climate in Indonesia, Pirous asked me to write a long biographical essay about him for his career retrospective show at Jakarta's National Gallery in 2002. I also joined the show's curatorial team and spent three months helping with publications, a video documentary, translation, public relations, and curatorial decisions. Writing that essay and working on the show meant writing for someone other than Western scholars. My work had to appeal to art collectors, gallery goers, art critics, and journalists, most from an urban Muslim background. Then again, in 2003, Pirous asked me to write the catalogue essay for his solo show, *Words of Faith*, held at the

National Art Gallery in Kuala Lumpur, Malaysia, in conjunction with the Tenth Organization of Islamic Countries Summit Conference.

Writing those two essays for predominantly Muslim audiences helped me more deeply understand Pirous's work. But they also challenged me to acknowledge the cultural, political, and religious limits of my understanding. I am keenly aware that I write as someone set apart and on unequal footing with respect to today's Muslim art worlds. I am neither Muslim nor artist. I am not an insider. But I hardly subscribe to the idea that you have to be an insider to be capable of writing ethically and discerningly about a community. Curiosity should never limit itself to the horizons of our religious and ethnic identity. Curiosity should take us beyond ourselves and into partnership and debate with others.

Representing Muslim Artists and Islamic Art

"To live in any culture," writes W. J. T. Mitchell, "is to live in a visual culture" (2005: 349). He reminds us about the deeply social, cultural, and political character of visual images and visual practices. At the same time, he invites us to consider the visual construction of our lived-in worlds – how images, image-making, and seeing shape our political, economic, religious, and cultural fields of experience. No society is without visual culture, and part of what distinguishes one social world from another are the different ways images are created, managed, and experienced in each.

Still, we need to be careful in terms of what we do with these differences, or how we portray them, for they *link* social worlds together, even as they divide them. I am thinking here of some popular and scholarly works that depict Islamic communities as austere and hostile to art and images. Though admired for traditions of poetry and verbal imagery, Muslims and Muslim communities are often pictured as aniconic (avoiding images), iconophobic (afraid of images), or iconoclastic (denouncing or destroying images), especially when it comes to human figures and figuration, or pictures of living things. For example, the very influential Dutch Orientalist, Christian Snouck Hurgronje, visited both Mecca and Pirous's homeland in Sumatra in the late nineteenth century; he found these Muslim communities rather artless, and declared that "Islam is but little favorable to the awakening or development of the artistic sense" (Snouck Hurgronje 1906: 65). In the late twentieth century, art historian Oleg Grabar has done much to stir our regard for Islamic art works and aesthetics. Yet even he has written that "Islamic culture finds its means of self-representation in hearing and acting rather than in seeing" (Grabar 1983: 31), a view echoed by other leading historians of Islamic art (e.g., Blair and Bloom 2003: 153). Islamic thought, it seems, gives little or no privilege to the images and events widely reported in the media – the global Muslim outcry over images of the Prophet in the so-called "Danish cartoon controversy," or the Taliban's destruction of the Buddha monuments at Bamiyan and its prohibition against the display of photographs and images in public – reinforce the idea that Islamic culture, wherever it is found, is hostile to representational art and image-making. Muslims and Muslim communities come across in these portraits as backward, repressive, and aesthetically impoverished. Their purported trouble with images spells trouble for others.

Everything I know about Pirous and his work – and I have been his friend for over twenty years – convinces me that this popular understanding of Islamic attitudes misses the picture. What I have learned from my time with Pirous is that Islamic art and Islamic aesthetics are not settled matters, but arenas of intense debate, conflict, and, of course, creativity. Iconoclasm in Islamic societies, like iconoclasm in Western and largely Christian contexts, typically springs from crises and changes in politics and rule. As Finbarr Barry Flood has so succinctly put it, there is no "timeless theology of images" in the Islamic world, but instead a rich history of "aesthetic appreciation, awe, fascination, [and] revulsion" (2002: 650, 652). Muslims ceaselessly rethink and rework their arts as they respond to the shifting currents of culture, politics, and history, and as they negotiate their varied allegiances to – and identifications with – nation, ethnicity, kin, and ideology. This book shows how one contemporary Muslim artist – Pirous – has pictured Islam as a personal *and* public pathway for aesthetic and ethical pursuits. It shows, too, how he has tried to picture Islam in his own art – giving Islam an image, you could say, yet also giving Indonesia's Muslims a glimpse of their community and the transnational "living space of Islam" (*dar-al-Islam*) as a reawakened and spiritually oriented art world. Doing so comes with problems and worries: complaints from clerics, puzzled looks from gallery-goers, stresses of self-censorship, to name but a few. It also comes with troubling betrayals, hurts, and exclusions – reminders that the traffic in art is a worldly, and sometimes cruel and disillusioning pursuit.

Figure 0.3 Making a preparatory work for a painting, 2001. Photograph courtesy of Yayasan Serambi Pirous.

11

I recall a complaint I heard well over a dozen years ago. I was having lunch with a Muslim acquaintance from South Asia, his parents, and two of his colleagues. Conversation had turned to the way Muslims are portrayed in both scholarly and popular media. His mother was surely not alone in feeling exasperation over everyday stereotypes of Muslim life. "I am sick and tired of the endless photos of Muslims praying or going to mosque," she vented. "Don't they think we do anything else?" I think it fair to say that commentators from the non-Muslim West have typically placed emphasis on the ritual and theological life of Muslims, rather than on other aspects of their everyday lifeworlds. Veiling, marriage customs, and food taboos, of course, have had long and frequent mention, and the last twenty years have witnessed an outcry and widespread reportage over women's prospects for justice under *syari'ah* law in the Islamic courts of places such as India, Nigeria, and Pakistan (an issue sharply debated by Muslims themselves). These matters notwithstanding, the general failure to take interest in the broad spectrum of everyday Muslim life suggests that Western media see in Islamic communities an excessive religiosity, and, more recently, a tendency to religiously inspired violence or cruelty. I took my lunch companion's complaint very seriously. Although religion may be basic to Muslim identity, it does not deserve exaggerated emphasis in our portrayal of Muslim lives. Rather, we should try to learn how and when Muslims turn to religion to understand their everyday circumstances and labors, and when they do not. In this book, then, I won't have much to say about the principles and tenets of Islam except as they come to bear on Pirous's art and its reception in public. Nor will I give much attention to the way my friend fulfills his religious duties. My emphasis, instead, will be on how Pirous finds his way around the terrain of Islamic culture through making art.

I worry that some may feel that my writing this book about Pirous and Islamic art runs the danger of taking us right back to the political-intellectual tradition of Orientalism. In that tradition, colonial-era scholars in Europe and the United States represented "the Orient" – Asia and the Middle East – as a mysterious social region, inclined to spiritualism, eroticism, and irrationality, and untouched by modernity. This, of course, amounted to a "looking down" on Asian cultures, even when celebrating "Eastern" spiritual, cultural, or civilizational glories (a view that went hand-in-glove with colonialism). The Muslim Orient came in for special scrutiny and took form in the scholarly literature as a place resistant to change and rational thought – the basic engines of progress. The Muslim Orient settled into the Euro-American imagination as an intriguing spectre, absolutely different from the West. And it has lingered there, almost unchanged, well into our postcolonial era.

The late Edward Said, the foremost critic of Orientalism in our time, remarked that "Orientalists are neither interested in nor capable of discussing individuals" (Said 1978: 154). They think of humanity in large collective terms such as "Muslims" and "Asians." There is always the danger of trying to show in Pirous the whole of Islam and Islamic culture writ small. I do feel, nonetheless, that our transcultural friendship and ethnographic collaboration over the years promises a way around or through the dangers of Orientalist thought. Friendship, per se, doesn't free us from the workings of power, and neither does collaboration. (Friendship and collaboration, it seems to me, succeed only when we are alert to power, not blind to it.) As Said has shown (1978: 160–61), the transcultural friendship between Muslim and non-Muslim may be betrayed if the latter writes for others and conceals (perhaps in the name of "objectivity") the way that friendship gave shape and direction to knowing about Muslim lifeways. Keeping friendship at the heart of my stories about Pirous means showing how he has revealed himself and his ideas about Islamic art in conversation with me.

Dwelling in a lifeworld, and doing an ethnography of one, imply our "being with" others. I have spent countless hours "being with" Pirous's paintings and etchings during my collaboration with him. Like the artist, these art works also tell me something about what it means to dwell in a Muslim lifeworld, and I should not betray the "friendship" I have with these paintings any more than I should betray my companion in this study. The paintings and graphic works featured in this book (and which figure so significantly in my fieldwork) come mostly from the artist's personal collection. Unlike hundreds of other paintings and prints that Pirous has made, these works have never yet been for sale, and so have been kept out of circulation and exchange among collectors and investors. These are his "spiritual notes" – the paintings that he keeps at home or on display in his gallery. They are the ones that travel to major shows and help sustain his reputation. They are his favorites, the storied ones he can't yet let go.

More than one person complained to me that Pirous seldom sold his best work. I know that his reluctance to let certain paintings go routinely thwarted the desires of collectors, and had a dampening effect on the pricing of his work. Not a few collectors and curators saw in Pirous an unreasonable stubbornness about keeping favorite paintings to himself. But I would not fault him for holding on to the works, so deeply are they bound up in his lifeworld. Though objects, they are not "mere" objects, but "friendly" and "companionable" ones that are deeply emblematic and revealing of Pirous's subjectivity, of his sense of being a "who" and a "what." I will have more to say about this later in the book. My obligation here is to let readers know that I have relied on a select set of works that have a special relationship with Pirous.

There is a risk that we might too easily equate his life and these works. As Thomas Crow (1999: 1–2) reminds us, looking at a painting and telling a life story are profoundly different activities. If we look for parallels and points of contact between a life story and a work of art, Crow warns, we risk redundancy; surprises are needed to make the exercise work. I can probably trade on the fact that Pirous and Islamic art may seem rather exotic to many readers. Besides, I recall something he said to me as we worked shoulder to shoulder sorting through canvases for his 2002 show in Jakarta: "Good paintings are always full of surprises." Take a look again at the turquoise Qur'anic calligraphy in *For the Sparkling Morning Light* and *Surat Ichlas* (Plates 2 and 3). Do you look at these words and works with a different eye when I tell you that "Pirous" (pronounced *peer'-oos*) is the Arabic, Persian, and Indonesian-Malay word for turquoise? What would you make of an artist who paints verse from the Qur'an in his own colorful name?

1

BECOMING A MUSLIM CITIZEN AND ARTIST

"Pirous, I've got a question for you." It was a September morning in 1995, and we were finishing up breakfast in the dining room of one of Jakarta's boutique hotels before driving over to the Istiqlal Mosque to meet with festival planners. I knew Pirous was going to have a busy day ahead of him. This was not a good time to distract him with an interview. But fleeting moments of conversation often told me much about his work or his ideas. "Tell me. Were you born Muslim or did you become Muslim?"

Pirous put down his cup of tea and gave me an astonished look, the kind someone does when a matter seems so obvious that questions about it come across as mindless. He shook off his perplexed surprise, and said, "Born Muslim."

People who wish to become Muslim do so by uttering the *syahadat* ("profession of faith"), saying in Arabic, "*asyhadu an la ilaha illa Allah, wa asyhadu anna Muhammadan rasulullah*" ("I affirm there is no God but Allah and that Muhammad is His messenger"). Surrender of oneself to Allah, the very core of what it means to be Muslim, begins with these words, and finds daily expression in them because they are repeated as part of obligatory ritual prayers (*salat*). On that morning in Jakarta, I was wondering what it means to say one is "born Muslim." Being Muslim involves – as a matter of obligation – uttering the *syahadat*, performing *salat* and reciting the Qur'an in Arabic, fasting (*puasa*) during the month of Ramadhan, giving alms (*zakat*), and, if capable, going on the pilgrimage to Mecca (*hajj*). *No one* is born doing (or having done) these things, or any of the things we associate with Islamic faith and culture. So for someone to say that she or he is "born Muslim" seems to me more like a statement about one's social and religious destiny, a conviction that one was *destined* to be *raised* (and thereby *become*) Muslim. It is a way of saying that fate has thrown one into a Muslim lifeworld.

15

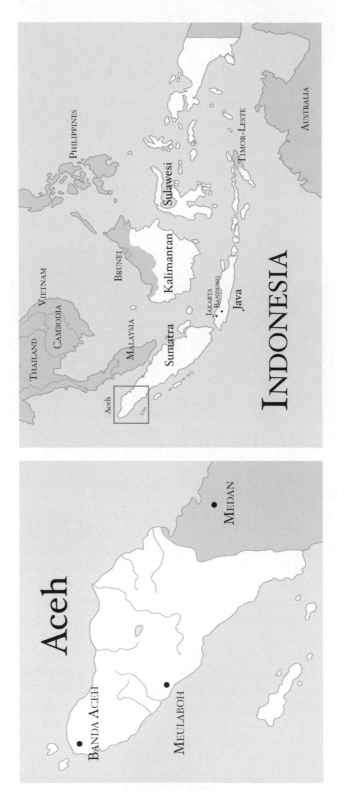

Figure 1.1 Maps of Aceh and Indonesia. Drawn by Jennifer H. Munger.

Declarations about religion, in many countries, are declarations of ethnicity and ethnic belonging. Pirous was born in Aceh, a region located on the northern tip of Sumatra, and long known as Serambi Mekah, "Mecca's Veranda" (see the maps in Figure 1.1). It was in and around Aceh that Islam first put down roots in the Indonesian archipelago roughly 900 years ago. Maritime commerce with India, Persia, Arab principalities, and the Ottoman Empire brought Muslim teachers, traders, and migrants to Aceh's ports. As the Acehnese grew in political stature over the centuries, they developed a fervent attachment to Islam too. Even today, the Acehnese are known throughout Indonesia for their intense religiosity. Like most Indonesian Muslims, they do not speak Arabic as their native language or as a language of everyday communication. But they do devote themselves to mastering the language for Qur'anic recitation, and many Acehnese have become leading scholars of Islamic thought and Arabic-language manuscripts over the centuries.

Telling me that he was "born Muslim" doesn't have much to do with Pirous's being a good Muslim or being a good Indonesian. Telling me that he was "born Muslim," however, is a good Acehnese reply to my question, and perhaps the only reply a good Acehnese properly should give. Members of other ethnic groups in Indonesia might have answered my question in the same way – Bugis and Makassans from Sulawesi, or perhaps the Madurese. Like other Indonesians, then, telling me that he was "born Muslim" is, for Pirous, a declaration about an unquestioned religious destiny and ethnic belonging. It is a declaration of identity.

Although he was destined to become one of Indonesia's most distinguished painters, my friend was not "born Indonesian." Rather, he was born in 1932 in the coastal town of Meulaboh, Aceh, as a colonial subject of the Netherlands East Indies. European powers had sailed Aceh's waters for almost 400 years, and the Dutch East India Company – the world's first multinational corporation – had held sway throughout the Indies archipelago through treaties, monopolies, colonial settlements, and armed conquest. Aceh managed to stay independent, but once the Netherlands took over administrative and then direct rule of the company's territories in the nineteenth century, Aceh came under intense pressure from the colonizers. Throughout the nineteenth century, indigenous groups in Sumatra and Java led prolonged revolts against the Dutch under the banner of Islam. Armed Acehnese resistance (1873–1914) was exceptionally fierce and never wholly quelled. The Dutch prevailed, and though they were to begin a more progressive period of so-called "ethical" colonial dominion (1901–41), they kept a watchful eye on Islamic affairs and discouraged the use of Arabic script for writing local languages.

The Japanese occupation of the Indies during World War II (1942–45) dislodged the Dutch from their colony for a few years. With the war's end, nationalist groups seized the moment and began their struggle for independence. So, it was on August 17, 1945, when Sukarno and Hatta declared the colony as a free and autonomous new nation, that an Indonesian identity was thrust upon Pirous. He embraced it, just as he has embraced the religious and ethnic identities that were his heritage. As we will see, managing and exploring these identities, coming to understand them, and bringing them to bear on his art have been a significant part of his life's work.

17

When I arrived in Bandung in late February 1994, I did not know all that much about Pirous's upbringing. Settling in with Pirous and his family as their house-guest, I hesitated about starting up the life history interviews I had planned. The time did not seem right: the rhythms of the fasting month of Ramadhan were in full sway, and getting Serambi Pirous in shape for its opening preoccupied us much of the time. The holy celebrations of Idul Fitri (also known as Lebaran) came right on the heels of the gallery opening, bringing the fasting month to an end, and ushering in three days of family visitations and endless meals, as relatives and friends ask each other for forgiveness for any conduct – in thought or deed – that might have caused offense.

The household quieted as soon as Idul Fitri came to a close. With the fast and the Lebaran holidays behind us, Pirous and I found that evenings were the best part of the day for our conversations about his life and career. We took our time, lingering over stories and questions. Sometimes Erna, or their daughters or son would listen in, hearing stories from him for the first time. Erna (b. 1941) had been born and raised in a Sundanese family in Kuningan, West Java, and had spent most of her school years around Bandung. Though she had been to the city of Banda Aceh, she had little firsthand knowledge of small-town life in northern Sumatra. Unlike their Acehnese father and Sundanese mother, the Pirous children, Mida, Iwan, and Rihan, grew up quite Indonesian and urbane. All in their early twenties, Aceh was for them a rather distant place which none had visited. Though very aware of their Acehnese roots on their father's side, they seemed more familiar with the Sundanese ambience of Bandung, and would even switch out of Indonesian from time to time to speak in Sundanese with Erna or her mother, Masjoeti Daeng Soetigna.

Pirous was of course a very practiced interviewee and storyteller from years of meeting with magazine, newspaper, and television reporters. No doubt I worked at a slower pace than reporters, however, and to different ends. As the lifeworld of a young artist came into view for me, Pirous himself was surprised by the depth and span of his reawakened memories. "You know," he confessed after a few evenings, "I didn't realize I knew or could remember this much."

Beginnings

Being born "Acehnese," one is pushed forward, out of one's family, thus out of one's ancestry, to find a place elsewhere. (James T. Siegel, *The Rope of God*)

People in Aceh would say that Pirous got off to an auspicious start. He was born at noon on Friday, March 11, 1932. The Friday noon hour is of course the time set aside for weekly worship in the *ummat*, a time when Muslims gather together to make their obligatory midday prayers at the mosque or prayer-room and to listen to sermons. His father, Mouna "Piroes" Noor Muhammad, asked the religious

18

Figure 1.2 "Boss Piroes." Mouna Piroes Noor Muhammad (wearing a white jacket and holding a rifle) at his rubber plantation outside of Meulaboh, Aceh, 1921. Photograph courtesy of Yayasan Serambi Pirous.

teacher who boarded with the family, Fakih Nurdin, to name his infant son. And so young Pirous came into the world bearing the name Abdul Djalil Syaifuddin.

Mouna Noor Muhammad was the grandson of a Gujarati trader from India, and was given the nickname "Piroes" because of the unusual turquoise (*pirus*) birthmark on his left arm, a mark many saw as a sign of spiritual significance and potency (*pirus* also means "triumphant" in Persian and "fearless" in Arabic). Raised elsewhere on the northwest coast of Sumatra, "Piroes" was a newcomer in Aceh, and, indeed, his natal family maintained their ties to their other homeland in India. He ultimately settled in Meulaboh, took a much younger Acehnese woman as his wife, and began work, first as a manager of a German-Dutch provisioning store and then as owner of a thriving rubber estate and rubber export business.

Marrying a young woman from Meulaboh was surely crucial to Mouna Noor Muhammad's prospects in the town. It was customary in Aceh for a woman's parent's to give her a house at marriage – usually near or next door to those belonging to the bride's parents, her married sisters, and her mother's sisters – and newlywed husbands were in practice expected to move in with their spouse. Moving in with his wife and near his wife's kin, Mouna Noor Muhammad gained a home and started a family, and relied on his wife's broader family to help raise the children. Like all Acehnese, these children would trace their descent through both their

19

mother and father, but would have different expectations in life: Acehnese girls tended to live out their lives in these tightly bound mother-sister-daughter groups, while Acehnese boys at adolescence would begin to gravitate to the *meunasah* – the local meeting hall and male dormitory – ultimately to marry into and take residence with other families.

By the time Djalil, the fifth of six children, was born, the family was quite comfortable and well-to-do. Mouna Noor Muhammad himself was known locally as *Tauke Piroes* – "Boss Piroes." His social origins – in the eyes of Acehnese neighbors and local colonial administrators – marked him as an outsider, a trader from *Asia Muka* (the "Face of Asia" – today's India, Pakistan, Sri Lanka, and Bangladesh). Undaunted, he took advantage of his outsiderhood and served as head of Meulaboh's *Asia Muka* community (several of whom were siblings or cousins). The family's rising commercial and social fortunes placed them among the dominant class elite, and made it possible for Djalil's father to invest some of his wealth and reputation in religious work. As Pirous recalls it, his father was not drawn to the mystical Islamic *tarékat* (or "Sufi brotherhoods," such as Khalwatiyyah or Naksyabandiyyah), nor did he make the pilgrimage. He instead used his wealth and position to promote Muslim institutions in Meulaboh itself: He built a prayer-room (*surau*) for public worship, funded a *madrasah* (religious school), and brought several religious teachers, or *ulama*, to town.

Mouna Noor Muhammad's ethnic background, prosperity, and civic-religious work distinguish him from those Acehnese who affiliated with the resistance movement that had struggled tenaciously against the Dutch since 1873. Yet, given his familial ties to India and the political-economic atmosphere of the late colonial period in Aceh, Djalil's father was surely familiar with reformist Islam and the call to religious struggle, or *jihad*, in resisting colonial domination. Secret recitations of the banned epic poem, *Hikayat Prang Sabil* (*The Chronicle of the Holy War*), which celebrated acts of Acehnese martyrdom, would have had special allure to many in and around Meulaboh (Siegel 1979). Although currents of anti-colonial feeling were astir, Pirous himself recalls the hometown of his childhood as "very peaceful, very clean, and very Muslim." At the same time, young Pirous's imaginative horizons stretched well beyond Meulaboh and Aceh. His father's storied ties to India gave Pirous an imagined but unvisited homeland and family abroad. Around 1939, he began to frequent the town's movie-house, where Gene Autry and Flash Gordon films (subtitled in Dutch) sparked a lifelong interest in foreign cinema. By this time Pirous was already enrolled in Meulaboh's elite, Dutch-run elementary school and had begun religious instruction in reciting the Qur'an and writing Arabic. He was an avid reader, and, as he approached his teens, he devoured translations of Western books in the school library – among them, *The Count of Monte Christo* by Alexander Dumas, and Karl Friedrich May's novels about the American West and his fictional Apache hero, Winnetou.

As Pirous tells it, it was his Acehnese mother, Hamidah, and his older brother, Zainal Arifin, who led him to the arts. Hamidah was from Meulaboh and did not trace her descent beyond her natal town. She was no less religious than her husband,

Figure 1.3 Hamidah, Pirous's mother, early 1950s. Photograph courtesy of Yayasan Serambi Pirous.

Figure 1.4 "Mopizar." Mouna Piroes Zainal Arifin, Medan, Sumatra, early 1950s. Photograph courtesy of Yayasan Serambi Pirous.

but, unlike him, Hamidah was drawn toward mystical spiritual practices. She pursued *dzikir*, or mindfulness of God, through special meditation and chants – such as reciting the twenty exalted qualities of God, or the ninety-nine "beautiful names" of God (*Asma Ul Husna*). Hamidah and her husband also had very different views about art. Mouna Noor Muhammad was the more austere of the two and frowned on art as something that conflicted with Islam. Art was a distraction from more important things. Hamidah saw it as a part of everyday life. As Pirous told me: "My mother was truly an artist. My father didn't have a drop of artistic blood, but my mother had it strong and my older brother Arifin, too. They were the ones who stirred my ambitions." Hamidah was adept in several of the Islamic arts. She was especially skilled in Qur'anic recitation and in storytelling, and made a practice of writing down Acehnese and Malay-language stories in Arabic script. She also enjoyed a reputation for making sumptuous, gold-embroidered velvets, felts, and silks for ceremonial occasions such as weddings and circumcisions. Among these are the *kasab*, the geometric patterns which Pirous would later appropriate as icons of his ethnic roots. Making a *kasab* could take a year or two of labor, sometimes more, and Hamidah was assisted by her children in preparing patterns, stretching fabric, and so on. It often fell to Pirous to mix inks and prepare varnishes, and, to this day, Pirous can detail every step and technique in preparing the *kasab*.

Pirous's enchanted reverence for the artistry his mother brought to stories and fabric found its most explicit expression in a 1982 serigraph called *Sura Isra II: Homage to Mother* (*Sura Isra II: Penghormatan buat Ibunda*). Look at Plate 4. It features brightly colored vertical borders patterned directly after Acehnese ceremonial curtains called *tabir*; an image of the winged *bouraq*, the Prophet Muhammad's legendary mount; and a two-dimensional reproduction of a red and gold *kasab* made by Hamidah herself (Plate 5), but inscribed with the Qur'anic verse traditionally associated with the Prophet's night journey and ascension to Heaven on the *bouraq* (QS 17 *Bani Isra'il*: 1) in place of the arabesque embroidered in his mother's work. Pirous's eyes gleamed as he talked about making the serigraph:

> This is something taken directly from the craft treasures of Aceh. It is from a piece of embroidery that my mother prepared from gold thread and scarlet velvet. This image of the *bouraq* makes visual the story, the sura, about the Prophet Muhammad's night journey from this world to heaven, from the Haram Mosque [in Mecca] to the Al-Aksa Mosque in Jerusalem and to the sky above. My mother always told me stories about how fast [that *bouraq*] could fly. In one jump it could leap as far as you could see. It was like lightning! So all of this is to make a fantastic story very visual and concrete. This was a story from my mother. That's why I made it. All of this is a homage, a homage to my mother.

When speaking to curators, art journalists, and scholars, Pirous generally points to his mother Hamidah as a driving force and inspiration in his becoming an artist. Yet in our unhurried evening talks, the painter told me many affectionate and admiring stories about his brother, Zainal Arifin. Arifin made use of his drawing and storytelling skills at the local movie-house, where he would sketch cartoon stories on glass plates and use a lantern to project the cartoons onto the screen. The kids in town, including the young Djalil, were delighted. As Pirous reminisced for me one evening:

Arifin was really good at drawing and it got so that he was well known for it. And as his little brother, I was very proud. I wished that I could paint and draw like that too. I later heard him when he asked my father whether he could go to the Kayutanam art school in West Sumatra. He was very disappointed. My father didn't consent because his outlook was extremely conventional and very tied to his religion. It was like saying that working as a painter was wrong. In fact, my father proposed that he enter the school for religious studies in Medan. But that didn't suit him. He had an artist's soul.

If Pirous learned something about the eye and hand from his mother as they prepared her *kasab* together at home, he learned from Arifin and Arifin's drawings what the eye and hand could be good for in public: connecting with people through art. Hamidah's hand and eye probably nurtured in Pirous an appreciation for pattern, color, and design. Arifin's drawings, on the other hand, showed Pirous that art could bring him friends, camaraderie, and reputation not unlike that which his father enjoyed in trade and religious good works.

Judging by the stories that he shared with me over the course of several evenings, the cultural world of his Acehnese boyhood was neither narrow nor impoverished, but was instead rich with embroidered fabrics, their inks, their bands of color, and their geometric patterns; with Qur'anic recitations and elaborate calligraphies; with tales of the Prophet and stories of the tigers that prowled near his father's plantation; with curries and Indian cottons; with glimpses of Flash Gordon's Mars and Karl May's American West; with cartoons, libraries, movie-houses, mosques, and *madrasah*; with intermingling streams of Acehnese, Malay, Dutch, Arabic, and Gujarati; with verses from the *Hikayat Prang Sabil* and strains of jazz; with sandals, sarongs, shoes, and trousers. The Acehnese he knew did not stand alone in the world, but also shared their homeland with Javanese plantation workers, European merchants, Chinese shop owners, Arab teachers, and Gujarati traders.

Although Islam was already the "religious tradition" in Meulaboh in the 1930s, there was nothing un-modern about it. In fact, we need to think of it as a modernizing force during those years in the Aceh. One of the best descriptions of the era is from James Siegel (2000). As he explains, reformist Islam posed significant change for Acehnese thought and social relations, and by 1930 had met with popular acceptance. Modernist *ulama* seeking moral and ethical reform put stress on religious obligations (*ibadah*), prayer, and reason (*akal*) as the mechanisms for perfecting interior experience and achieving self-possession. Religious teaching advocated the unity and harmony of men regardless of the groups to which they belonged. Modernist ideas about human nature and the self thus came to prominence in interpreting social roles, surpassing the attachments of kinship or local village society. The new way of thinking about self and society also meant that Acehnese Muslims had new ways of thinking about their place in the world.

Reformist ideas did not have their origin in Aceh, but in late nineteenth-century Cairo and Mecca, centers of learning for students and pilgrims from throughout the Muslim world. European imperialism was at its peak and Muslims in Asia,

Africa, and the Middle East were acutely aware of their status as second-class colonial citizens. Reformist Islam went hand-in-glove with anti-colonial sentiments and nationalist struggle, and stressed the unity and common cause of Muslims everywhere. Those in Cairo and Mecca knew full well about the Dutch annexation of Aceh in 1873. Michael Laffan (2007: 691) tells us that Muslims there saw this as one more episode in "a series of showdowns between an aggressive West and a victimized, largely Muslim East," and feared that Aceh and Southeast Asia more generally would be "another Andalusia" lost to the West. However, the idea of Islamic unity and the experience of colonial subordination did not diminish the sense among Southeast Asian students and pilgrims that they were set apart culturally and ethnically from Arabs. Teachers, students, and pilgrims who returned to Aceh from the Middle East no doubt saw religious and moral reform first and foremost as a path toward Acehnese independence.

Growing up in the "very Muslim" atmosphere of 1930s Meulaboh meant that Pirous knew a lifeworld that included both modernist and mystical strains of religious practice. It is too simple to insist that his father was a self-possessed, *madrasah*-founding reformist and his mother a sensual Sufi mystic. Yet the affectionate memories of their son make clear that the colorful stories and embroidered fabrics with which Hamidah enriched their home touched Pirous no less powerfully than the civic and ethical energies of "Boss Piroes" who frowned on art as pursuit that distracted one from prayer, religious duty, and reason. What these dual – and maybe dueling – influences may have augured for Pirous's art is a matter I will come back to later. Key here is seeing in the push and pull of parental nurture a domestic stage for the play of ideas about religion and art.

Becoming an Artist-Citizen

As World War II came to a close in 1945, the Dutch planned to resume control of their former Asian colony. Nationalist leaders Sukarno and Hatta declared Indonesia a new sovereign nation, and called for unsparing support for the revolution that would bring the country independence. Pirous remembers his family's evacuation into the hill country above town, and watching Meulaboh burn as nationalist forces struggled to resist the return of the Dutch. Having seen everything he had built burned down, the aged and ailing Mouna Noor Muhammad remarked despairingly to his son, "I don't know what *merdeka* (independence) means." The words may strike us as odd given the resentment most Acehnese felt toward the Dutch. Yet we need to keep in mind that "Boss Piroes" had found a way to prosper during a lifetime of Dutch rule. The promise of independence was probably little comfort to an old man watching the work of a lifetime swallowed up in the chaos of revolution. Young Pirous had a different view of things but even he recalled that Aceh's place in a sovereign Indonesian nation was by no means clear at the start of the Revolution:

24

What did independence truly mean? The only thing we knew was that we had been ruled by the Dutch, then ruled by the Japanese, and now we wanted to have our own government. One day a plane suddenly appeared overhead dropping leaflets and I picked one up and there was the text of the declaration (by Sukarno and Hatta): "Our independence." "So that the people live as one." And so on. I still didn't understand what it really meant, though in time I did. If we talked about independence we talked about Indonesian independence, not independence for the Acehnese.

Dropping a people's identity papers on them from an airplane may not be the most effective way to recruit citizens, but that was how things started for Pirous: writing from the sky. Although he continued his schooling in Meulaboh, Pirous was swept up in the fervor and romance of the Indonesian Revolution. Modernist Islamic youth groups under the leadership of Daud Beureuèh urged everyone in Aceh to join the struggle for national independence. At age sixteen Pirous joined the Indonesian Student Army (Tentara Pelajar Indonesia) and served in a local after-dark propaganda unit making silkscreened posters, handbills, and leaflets that promoted the nationalist campaign. This was the first time Pirous would use his art skills in public for public ends. It was through art, *Bahasa Indonesia* (the official national language, based on Malay), and anti-colonial struggle that Pirous began shaping himself, and understanding himself, as an Indonesian citizen.

Indonesia cemented its sovereignty in 1949. In 1950, at the age of eighteen, Pirous left Aceh for the North Sumatran city of Medan to join his older brothers Arifin and Idris, and to continue his studies at that city's first-rate middle schools and high schools. Already married, Arifin was now working in theater and illustration under the name "Mopizar" (for *Mouna Piroes Zainal Arifin*), publishing cartoons and painting movie posters, in addition to selling custom portraits, decorative paintings, and Lebaran (Idul Fitri) cards. Idris took up framing, and Pirous put his own hand and eye to work to earn money while in school. "I did souvenir drawings, decorated certificates, ornaments, and I made portraits of leaders like Sukarno, Gandhi, Haji Agus Salim, Nehru, and Kartini." Thus Pirous left Aceh just as Indonesia found recognition as an independent nation. Born Acehnese, he was now Indonesian and taking part in the social and cultural energies of an urban post-colonial world. He would never again live in Aceh.

In Medan his artwork brought him friends, and they would ask him to illustrate their books of poems or stories. It also gave him a reputation: he took part in North Sumatra's student art competition and submitted three pictures – one of an old ruined boot, one of a large bucket, and one of a landscape. He won first, second, and third prizes. His middle-school art teacher, Hasan Siregar – himself a self-taught painter – urged him to consider art school. As he worked in watercolor, tempera, charcoal, pencil, ink, and oil paints, his pictures remained "naturalistic," copied from nature or photographs. Then, in 1952, about the time he was twenty, an exhibition featuring contemporary work by Zaini, Mardian, Handrio, Nashar, Widayat, and Sudjojono – modernist painters from Jakarta, Yogyakarta, and the Revolution – came to Medan. The exhibition gave Pirous a glimpse of an art world unlike the one in which he was honing his skills, and sharpened his desire for formal

Figure 1.5 Pirous with his Uncle Ahmad on the eve of leaving Meulaboh for Bandung, 1955. Photograph courtesy of Yayasan Serambi Pirous.

art training. There were a few works that really perplexed him. Trading on his knowledge of Steven Spielberg movies he quipped to me, "It was a close encounter of the third kind. It really took me by surprise compared to what I had been doing. This was something that was beyond my imagination, and I just knew that I had to go further." Shortly after that exhibition, he followed the example of his brother Arifin and adopted a name with the panache befitting an artist: "A. D. Piroes." Three years of high-school art classes followed, and, as his graduation neared, Pirous applied to the rival art academies at Bandung and Yogyakarta. He left for Bandung, West Java, in 1955 to start his studies at the Academy of Art at the Bandung Institute of Technology (or ITB) under the supervision of Dutch cubist, Ries Mulder. It was the same year that Indonesia and the city hosted the Asian-African Conference of newly independent and largely "non-aligned" nations that had emerged from colonial rule after World War II.

Indonesia, of course, was still a fledgling nation. Comprising thousands of islands, hundreds of ethnic groups, hundreds of ethnic languages, dozens of political parties (including the largest Communist party in Asia outside of China), four major world religions (Buddhism, Christianity, Hinduism, and Islam) and a vast range of indigenous or syncretic religions, Indonesia nonetheless wished to place itself on the world stage as a modern, secular, and self-governing political community with a unique social and cultural identity. To the frustration of some Muslims, Indonesia did not become an Islamic state. The very question of how the Constitution would reflect and accommodate Islamic principles came in for sharp debate, and sparked revolts. Separatist rebellions aimed at establishing an "Indonesian Islamic State" began as early as 1949 in West Java, Sulawesi, and

Sumatra. In North Sumatra, Daud Beureuèh broke with the national government in 1953 and attempted to establish Aceh as an independent Islamic state that would conform to *syari'ah* law. These rebellions simmered into the early 1960s, as did "regional" uprisings aimed against the overwhelming dominance of Java and the Javanese in Indonesian affairs.

In the sphere of democratic parliamentary politics, Islamic modernists – especially those from places other than Java – rallied to the party known as Masyumi, but failed to find a secure place in coalition governments after the party's disappointing showing in the 1955 elections, Indonesia's first. The outcome of the elections, the turmoil of the rebellions, and growing ties to China led President Sukarno to abolish Western-style parliamentary democracy. In its place he established "Guided Democracy." Resting on an ideological blend of nationalism, Islam, and communism, Sukarno's new government sought to appease military factions, Islamic groups, and communists. Masyumi and other Muslim parties opposed Sukarno's plan but got nowhere. By 1959, Masyumi was banned. Those wanting an Islamic state or a strongly Islamic constitution had been effectively thwarted.

In a sense, nearly everyone was a nationalist in 1950s Indonesia. The country's political leadership and intellectual elite had long encouraged nationalist thinking, so that people would frame their understandings and aspirations in terms of belonging to the new Indonesian nation. Just as modernist Islam offered new ways of thinking about self and society, so too did nationalism. National citizenship and national culture were to trump attachments to family, ethnicity, language, and region, and come center stage as the most crucial terms for personal allegiance, collective solidarity, reckoning cultural pasts (i.e., tradition, heritage), and working toward cultural and political futures. But essences and the true nature of things are elusive and illusory, more fabrication than "fact." No one could really say what lay at the heart of the nation. The nation was up for grabs. The time was one of struggle – struggle to invent the ideological, cultural, and religious foundations of the nation.

Questions about the cultural foundations for Indonesia go back to the debates and polemics of the 1930s. Some, like Sutan Takdir Alisjahbana, argued that there was nothing "Indonesian" about the past, and that no ethnic culture should be imposed on the national whole. Indonesian culture needed to be created, went the argument, and should draw from both Asian and Western societies if it was to assert its modernity and compatibility with international culture. Other public intellectuals saw in Javanese, Malay, and island ethnic traditions the very cultural resources and values the nation needed to become "Indonesian." An embrace of Western culture was unnecessary, and perhaps dangerous; it should be avoided. The Revolution-era writer Chairil Anwar, whose poetry was well known to Pirous, offered yet another approach. He brought together a group of intellectuals who were interested in "world culture" and its universalist associations. Frowning on East–West dichotomies, they declared that "We are the true inheritors of world culture, and we shall develop this culture in our own way. ... The important thing is for us to find man" (Kratz 2000: 182, trans. mine).

Artists, among others, were caught up in the polemics, and stridently so, during the 1950s and 1960s. It was a time of manifestos, and unbending moral and proprietary claims to the nation. The declaration of Anwar's group, which came to be associated with "universal humanism" and the bourgeois orientation of the West, was met by the manifesto of the leftist Institute for People's Culture (LEKRA), which called on artists and writers to resist imperialism and to serve the cultural needs of the Indonesian people. For LEKRA, "universal humanism" and "art for art's sake" did not offer a progressive political stand on art and culture (as "socialist realism" appeared to do), and would only lead to subjectivism and a "politics of the unpolitical" conducive to Western domination. The 1950s and 1960s also saw the brief rise of Islamic cultural organizations. Most, like the Indonesian Institute for Muslim Artists and Cultural Experts (LESBUMI) and the Institute for Islamic Literature (LEKIS), catered to writers, rather than to those working in the visual arts. A couple of manifestos are of interest, however. A key Muslim student organization (Indonesian Islamic Students, PII) declared in 1956 that: "Islam does not ban the arts, it even encourages them and fills them with meaning. Islamic art is art that 'breathes' [i.e., is inspired by] Islam. ... National art is the field of growth for Islamic art. The art of the Indonesian nation has to at least try to be in accordance with Islamic art. For Islamic art to come into being, Muslims who wish to make art must perfect themselves as true Muslims" (Kratz 1986: 71). Several years later, in 1962, the reformist Council of Islamic Art and Culture (MASBI) stated that Islamic culture should be based on *tauhid* (God's unity). To be Islamic, art should reflect devotion to God, cultivate ethical conduct in line with Islamic teachings, and benefit the inner and outer welfare of human beings. In spirit, these Muslim declarations were much in accord with the views of universal humanists, the difference being that these Muslim organizations saw Islam and Islamic civilization – rather than the secular or subjectivist pursuit of the human – as the source of universal values. In contrast to the socialist realist stance of LEKRA and the bourgeois modernist outlook of the universal humanists, the views of these Islamic organizations failed to generate much of a following or to resolve theological debates about art and religion. Despite the official call from the Minister for Religious Affairs in 1956 for Muslims to bring order to "the jungle of Islamic art and culture" (Kratz 1986: 72), the groups found no way to "overcome the fragmentization and uncertainty within the Muslim community" (Maier 1987: 11).

No surprise then that when Pirous arrived in Bandung in 1955, he found himself stepping into sharp ideological debates over the direction of the Indonesian art world. Unlike some other academies, the Bandung school was staffed by Dutch and Dutch-trained artists and was very international in outlook. Just the year before, it had been pilloried as "the Slave of the Western Laboratory" for producing "bloodless, formal, self-absorbed, and bourgeois art" (Soemardjo 1954). Pirous appeared unfazed and adapted quite quickly to the international and universal humanist approaches. We can find telltale signs of a subjectivist and universalist sensibility in the small details of his life. Just as he started his formal art training, Indonesian orthography (or spelling) was officially revised so that the vocal sound once rendered as "oe" would be written as "u." The young painter, however, did not like the "look" of "Pirus," or so he told me years later. To suit his graphic tastes, he wrote his name as "Pirous." Had the nation not intervened, he still might be signing his name as "Piroes." What, then, should we make of the superfluous "o" in "Pirous"? (A graphic sign that for years led me to mispronounce my friend's name.) Is there anything behind it? A signature, of course, is intimate *and* public – part touch, part expressivity, part legibility, part adornment. The habit of seeing an "o" in his signature might have been tough to overcome. Perhaps the "o" lingers as a reminder of his father. Why would the "look" of a signature matter anywhere except on the surface of an artwork, where it plays a part in the authenticity and reputation of painterly touch? Considering its life on the surface of hundreds of paintings, I think of the superfluous "o" as an orthographic ornament that embellishes and internationalizes the name, giving it a French or (a Romanized) Persian "look." In this sense, the painter's signature and artistic subjectivity go beyond the limits of the nation, orthographically.

The earliest sample of "A. D. Pirous" that I know is tucked in a book. While browsing in Pirous's library in early 2002, I came across a 1957 paperback copy of Henri Pirenne's *Mohammed and Charlemagne* (in English). The bastard page is inscribed in ink and is in Pirous's hand. It reads, "States are as men, they grow out of the character of men – Plato." On the title page that follows, Pirous has placed his signature in brown pencil and beneath that the date, "4/58." The inscription reads as aphorism and lesson to the artist himself, for who else other than Pirous would likely peruse this very volume, kept in his private library? I perhaps make too much of the passage, yet I think it gives us an revealing glimpse into Pirous's thinking when he, his nation, his art, and his new signature were very young. In April 1958, Indonesia was thirteen years old. Pirous had just turned twenty-six a month earlier, and was working hard to master modernist styles of painting. In quoting or paraphrasing Plato, Pirous seems to be talking to himself, not only about the Prophet or Charlemagne, but about the young Indonesian nation-state and his place in it. The inscription is not accidental; it is deliberate and ideological "reported speech," a quote he has written down in anticipation of returning to it for further reflection (cf., Foucault 1997: 211, 273). Whether he means to admonish or inspire, his choice of aphorism – "States are as men, they grow out of the character of men" – ties the welfare of the nation-state to the conduct and thought of those individuals who are its citizens. It is a draft sentence for the constitution of the postcolonial artist-citizen. With it, Pirous is fashioning himself, giving himself purpose and shape, not only for his own well-being, but for the welfare of his companions, too, in the shared, civic venture of being Indonesian.

These telltale signs of subjectivity – these signs of being a who and a what – no doubt reflect, too, the aesthetic modernism that Pirous had begun to absorb in his training with Dutch and Dutch-trained painters at the art academy. Anxieties about art modernisms were extremely significant in the cultural debates of the 1950s, and have continued to inform critical art historical assessments of Indonesian art right up through the present. "Modernism" has never been a unified set of ideas and practices, nor has it been always centered in the West; it has always been plural in terms of its debates, contradictions, and proponents. As in other parts of Asia, modernism and modern art became part of the late and lingering colonial art world in the Netherlands East Indies, and then endured as an arena of decolonizing struggle and tense debate with respect to cultural nationalism and fears of Western imperialism after Indonesian independence. In many important respects, then, the first fifty years of Indonesian art could be described as an attempt to inhabit and domesticate – that is, make "Indonesian" – the modernist legacy. Debate, plurality, and internal contradictions notwithstanding, modernism was predicated – as Frederic Jameson (1983: 114) has put it – "on the invention of a personal, private style, as unmistakable as your fingerprint, as incomparable as your own body," and in this way was "linked to the conception of a unique self and private identity … which could be expected to generate its own vision of the world." Modernism brought with it, too, a preoccupation with aesthetic standards and originality that not only played a part in distinguishing high art from traditional and mass art, but also in subjecting an artist to the demands of self-expression. Indeed, abstract, formal, and non-objective images were thought to reveal the artist's inner being, and painting, in particular, enjoyed a privileged status as the most direct inscription of artistic subjectivity.

Modernism appeared in Indonesia as a set of local dilemmas rather than as a set of globalized certainties. Writing about India, Geeta Kapur (1996) has argued that the mingling of nationalism and modernism in the early postcolonial period recruited artist-citizens for contradictory pursuits. On the one hand, the painter-citizen aspired to a unique and innovative artistic individuality and subjectivity. The modern and singular artistic self had a desire and an obligation to become visible in expression. On the other hand, the painter-citizen sought an identity as a representative of a people and a nation. Indeed, to be modern, the country aspiring to nationhood needed modern artists whose work would be emblematic of the nation. This was surely true of Indonesian artists of the time as well. Commitment to a nation, to a self, and to an "idealized notion of the artist immersed in an undivided community" were key (Kapur 1996: 60).

Arriving in Bandung, Pirous brought with him years of practice in religious iconography and lettering, a strong graphic sense, a capacity to imitate or copy with precision (which Pirous sometimes describes as "naturalistic"), and a familiarity with commercial and decorative arts. He also had considerable experience in using his skills for group or public endeavors. What the twenty-three year old encountered was a program aimed at inspiring students with modernist and international approaches to art, most notably cubist and abstract styles and the ideologies that went along with them. As the painters at Bandung saw it, there was a universal "visual language" that transcended the borders of parochialized national art worlds. If they could master it, it promised them the means to develop a singular form of expression in the international sphere. If liberal international styles and values could find root in Indonesia, the reasoning went, they would in turn take on an Indonesian character. Thus the Bandung painters favored icons of the self rendered in abstraction (a style seen as an icon of "the modern"). Indonesian-ness, per se, was not a problem. As Pirous put it in one of our evening talks:

> We were always Indonesians. We all live in the same world with this language of visual communication. This was the extraordinary strength of the Euro-American mainstream. If we wanted to enter that stream, we used the language. If you didn't use the language, you were out of the mainstream. You were marginalized. It is clear the Bandung School was more international than national. But we weren't Americans, we weren't Dutch. We had a culture rooted in this country.

I hear in Pirous's recollections a proud refusal to be a second-class citizen in a world of modern international art, and a readiness to engage that realm on its own terms, however dominated it might be by Western values, ideologies, and institutions. I also hear in Pirous's account the voice of the talented Acehnese youth whose alert fascination with foreign films and books inclined him to take interest in a world lying beyond the borders of Aceh and Indonesia. This is the same youth whose father was part of the *Asia Muka* community in Meulaboh, and so something of an outsider to Acehnese society. It is also the same youth whose class background brought him more closely in touch with bourgeois tastes and outlook than some of his Acehnese peers. In short, I hear the words of someone already long-

Figure 1.6 Ries Mulder teaching his course on "Art Appreciation," Bandung, 1955. Pirous sits furthest to the right. Photograph courtesy of Yayasan Serambi Pirous.

31

accustomed to thinking about his place in the world beyond regional and national borders.

For Pirous, finding a unique painterly self meant breaking way from the "naturalist" or "realist" habit of copying the world around him. It also had to do with colonial subjection and anti-colonial struggle. In Medan, he had no worries about personal vision and style. That changed as he began his formal studies with his Dutch teacher, Ries Mulder. There is, of course, considerable political and cultural irony (and strain!) in a postcolonial art student trying to find a unique painterly self under the tutelage of a former colonial master. Ries Mulder could be arrogant and cruel. If his lessons about cubist geometries, colors, abstraction, and vision for a time eluded Pirous, his demeaning insults did not. The condescending Mulder knew no Indonesian and so wounded his student in English or in Dutch – "This is shit! Shit!" or "Hey Pirous, not bad, perhaps you could find work with Disney." Several years of these stinging insults led Pirous to withdraw to the solitude of his home and to the nurturing and informal atmosphere of a local art collective, Sanggar Seniman ("The Artists' Studio"). There he began an intense struggle with materials and textures, sometimes scorching and scratching his canvases:

> Mulder was too hard on me. ... It was always "this is bad, this is bad" to the point I got furious. So I left it all behind. I locked myself up at home and painted for months. Forget all those theories. I took a painting, spilled paint all over it, rubbed it, everything. I burned it. Rrgrrrgrrrg. I looked at it burning, then I put it out and scratched it. ... Suddenly I found something, a way to get at a special richness in using colors, and the form was beginning to be abstract. I was startled! I painted on a large piece of jute. It was good! A picture of chickens. Very wild, very abstract, but still figurative.

It was 1960, and Mulder already had been asked to return home to the Netherlands the year before. Pirous put this work, *Cocks in the Garden* (*Ayam di Kebun*), on show in an exhibit run by Sanggar Seniman in Bandung. A Canadian collector who worked for UNESCO spotted it and purchased it for about $30. Pirous was thrilled. He had sold his first painting, and for a good price.

Disciplined training in a "new visual language" at Bandung was for Pirous a process of forgetting and denial as well. Much of the art that he had worked on earlier in life – his mother's *kasab*, the portraits of nationalist leaders, the illuminated birth certificates – were no longer talked about as such; it was merely craft or kitsch in light of the philosophy and styles at the center of the Bandung program. As Pirous pursued a unique painterly style and identity, he moved more and more deeply into an art world shaped by the values, tastes, and prerogatives of Western critics, museums, and collectors. Most collectors of high-end art in Indonesia at this time were foreigners associated with embassies. Pirous recalls his being invited to the home of Jozias Leaö, the Chargé d'Affaires for Brazil: "For the first time in my life I saw international paintings, in his home in Jakarta! Paintings by Georges Bracques, Picasso, young painters from Europe, that's what I saw at his house! Paintings that I had seen in books. And when he went home, he took a very valuable collection of Indonesian paintings with him!" In Bandung's circles, making it as an Indonesian artist was about succeeding with these elite, and largely foreign, collectors. Indeed, "making it" was perhaps best captured in a remark made by Affandi – a self-trained artist and the best-known Indonesian painter of the era. Invited to Bandung to address the artists-in-training, he offered students a gustatory analogy of success: "If you are a beginning painter," Pirous remembers him saying, "you probably will live on rice wrapped up in banana leaves. But if you become a famous painter, you can eat *rijstafel*." The unknown eats simple local fare, but the successful painter eats the European version of an Indonesian feast. As we saw above, it was only upon selling an abstract painting for the first time – to a Canadian collector – that Pirous felt he had arrived at a singular personal style. Pirous threw himself into painting and activities at Sanggar Seniman for the next two years, becoming one of its leaders and helping organize its first-ever open-air exhibition. That exhibit, too, was a critical and commercial success, bringing Pirous steady sales among foreign collectors.

I have condensed here a much more complex and nuanced story about artistic influence in the early postcolonial period. What I want to stress is that Pirous's formal training at Bandung shows one way in which a colonizing modernism – in terms of its discourses and institutional structures – was occupied and domesticated. Though subjected to aesthetic modernism, Pirous was able to find within it a place for the self-defining work that afforded him a sense of independence from his Dutch teacher. It was the source of his humiliation and subsequent emancipation. For Pirous, then, aesthetic modernism and its peculiar discourses of painterly subjectivity became a way to be an Indonesian artist in a global world of art.

The Darkening Sky

Sanento Yuliman (Buchari and Yuliman 1985) has described in considerable detail the style and direction of Pirous's earliest paintings (1959–65). The young painter worked almost exclusively in oils, and from sketches. The work tended toward "lyric expression" – thematic or symbolic representations of nature, landscapes, everyday people, and everyday objects. Experimenting in color, line, strokes, and texture, he produced paintings that give the impression of shallow space and reflect a preference for order and dynamism. For a few years the paintings did quite well; they sold, and a couple even made it into officially arranged shows in Hanoi and Rio de Janeiro.

Pirous became a staff-assistant at the academy in 1960, but, absorbed in his own painting, he did not make progress toward his degree. None of our conversations suggest that he took special note of the manifestos on Islamic art. Yet he did not, or could not, ignore changes in the country's political climate. As Sukarno moved the nation further to the communist left and against the neo-colonialism of the West in the early 1960s, LEKRA's confidence and influence grew. So did its strident

33

Figure 1.7   Pirous with wife and painter Erna Garnasih Pirous, Bandung, 1968. Photograph courtesy of Yayasan Serambi Pirous.

rhetoric and its capacity to intimidate. On Independence Day, August 17, 1963, twenty-one writers and artists seeking a more open ideological climate for their work signed and made public what is known as the "Cultural Manifesto" (Manifesto Kebudayaan, or Manikebu). Arguing that art should not be sacrificed for political ends, the authors took exception to principles of socialist realism (and so to LEKRA's policy). The manifesto circulated in Bandung, where several of the younger artists added their signatures on January 28, 1964. Pirous was the second to sign. The ninth signatory was student-painter Erna Garnasih, who would later become Pirous's wife, in 1966. Not long afterward, Sukarno banned the manifesto, making it plain that there were considerable political risks in adopting a pro-Manikebu outlook or in painting in styles that LEKRA deemed imperialistic, neo-colonial, or bourgeois. Threatened by growing ideological pressures to conform to socialist realism, Pirous retreated from public exhibition and just painted at home. "I was afraid," he confessed to me.

Whether by coincidence, or in a calculated effort to protect Pirous at a time of intense political scrutiny, the chair of Fine Arts and Design at ITB insisted that Pirous finish his undergraduate thesis if he wished to keep working at the academy. Abandoning an earlier line of study on children's art, Pirous instead interviewed painters who had used their talents for the Indonesian Revolution – as he once did – and compared their past work to art works created in Indonesia's ongoing "confrontation" with neo-colonialism. Six months of oral historical research and photographic study yielded *Poster Art as a Tool of Propaganda in National Struggle* (*Seni Pariwara Sebagai Alat Propaganda Perdjoangan*), submitted in late 1964. Pirous subsequently joined the academy as a permanent member of the faculty.

The deadly political maneuvering that took place on the night of September 30, 1965, brought the Sukarno years to their close. Military factions under the command of Major General Soeharto assumed control of Jakarta and began a campaign to inflame smoldering class and religious tensions. The Indonesian left was purged in a terrible fury of mass violence and arrests during the course of the next six months. Hundreds of thousands were murdered, and hundreds of thousands were jailed. As Soeharto fashioned his regime, the leftist cultural institute, LEKRA, was outlawed, and many of the painters it supported were killed, imprisoned, or left without prospects for exhibiting their work. No longer in risk of censure, the international and humanist painters associated with the Bandung academy mounted a major comeback show under government sponsorship at Jakarta's Balai Budaya ("Cultural Pavilion") in December, 1966. Called simply "Eleven Bandung Artists" (*Sebelas Seniman Bandung*), it included seven paintings by Pirous. He quickly became a rising star in the Bandung and Jakarta art circles.

Like most of the other artists and writers who signed the "Cultural Manifesto", Pirous did not foresee the authoritarian future that was in store for Indonesia with Soeharto's rise to power. The immediate political changes in the country were for Pirous and many of his colleagues very liberating. He began to paint furiously. Climbing into public view, he began, too, a furious refashioning of self. For example, the brochure for a 1967 show in Bangkok had this to say about the artist:

> A. D. Pirous, without a doubt a modern artist, could sometimes be termed an impressionist. Then again, when expressionism takes over there are signs of abstraction. … Although Pirous moves in many fields of artistic expression, it is not possible to compare his style with an existing mannerism. Pirous is unaffected by the examples of past creations; he relies on his own self for true and individualistic expression.

The passage strikes me as overreaching, and strained, though fully in line with modernist emphases on finding a unique subjectivity. It paints a romantic picture: an artist uninfluenced by precursors, peers, or a cultural milieu as sources of inspiration. Nothing less than pure and incomparable, self-conscious expression.

Pirous had his first "solo" show at Jakarta's Balai Budaya in October 1968. He completed fifty-four paintings that year, and in them we can discern a confident shift in his work. He paints without sketches; improvisation has taken over. Lyric self-expression is all. Figuration matters less, and imagined landscapes preoccupy him. Shallow space flattens further onto the surface of the painting. He experiments with textures by dripping, splashing, and brushing thin mixtures of oil paint and turpentine onto canvas. He goes for a kind of playfulness and tension between materials and the eye, trying to create thick visual texture with thin paint, sometimes in contrast with ridges of impasto. I have long been drawn to the moody palette, drips, and thinned paints of the horizonless landscapes in *An Isolated Place* (*Daerah Terpencil*) and *The Night Landscape I* (*Pemandangan Malam I*). But the bright hopes vested in the boundless panorama of planes, spills, and impasto smears

Figure 1.8 "Without a doubt, a modern artist." Pirous with his paintings in a publicity shot taken for his first "solo" show in Jakarta, October, 1968. Photograph courtesy of Yayasan Serambi Pirous.

in *The Sun after September 1965* (*Mentari Setelah September 1965*) deserve comment (see Figure 1.9).

The Sun after September 1965 was especially significant for Pirous at the time, and he positioned it as the visual focus of the exhibition space at his 1968 Jakarta show. Talking to me in 1994, he said:

> This one was a primadonna on the walls. This was the centerpoint of all my paintings, my focus. All these paintings were there as an expression of thankfulness about the situation [made] possible after '65, okay? *September* here, was the focus of the room,

Figure 1.9 *The Sun after September 1965*. 1968. 135 × 150 cm, oil on canvas. Photograph courtesy of Yayasan Serambi Pirous.

the biggest painting in that space. It's a commemoration of this, this sun that is carrying happiness after '65.

The title of the painting alludes, of course, to the sudden end of Indonesia's embrace with the communist left. Yet the painted image and Pirous's remarks about it appear to me oblivious to the terrifying, deadly violence in the months after September, 1965. They turn away from the tragedy and suffering and point instead to the horizonless possibilities for a "self"-pursuing modern artist who has begun to taste the fruits of critical and commercial success. Here, the "sun" (whether it is the disc-like form to the upper left of the canvas, or the light distributed throughout the image) is placed as a deliberate and self-conscious icon of personal happiness and grateful relief.

Some who know this painting see it as propaganda for the regime that had begun to coalesce as Indonesia's authoritarian "New Order." Others have seen it as protest against the same regime (George 1997). No surprise. After all, how could a painting achieve a timeless, privileged, and singular meaning? Paintings, like all works of art, have social and historical lives, gathering up sometimes very divergent stories and interpretations along the way. This painting invites people to take sides, so long as we know its title. I keep coming back to the painting – in catalogues, in the dark storage room at Serambi Pirous, in the nook of a museum show – and the story Pirous has told me about it. I would not call the painting or his story propaganda, but rather, the residue of a time when Pirous shared with others a buoyant set of hopes and expectations in the aftermath of a violent social upheaval, an upheaval that also extinguished the light and lives of those who saw things differently. To borrow from Raymond Williams (1977), we might say the painting and Pirous's story describe an emergent "structure of feeling" – the lived and felt paths of experience for a cohort of urban Muslim artists passing together through a particular moment of social and aesthetic transformation. The political storm of 1965–66 gave his art fresh public chances. Modernist abstraction and universal humanism had come into favor, and set down conditions in which he could strive for maximal self-expression and self-promotion.

For early postcolonial artists like Pirous, the realization of a signature modern style served as proof of their nation's sovereignty and progress, just as it proved their personal maturation as artists. The artist and the nation were making it on the global stage, asserting their distinctiveness and their parity with others in the world. Recognition depended on those others, of course. Pirous never found recognition from Mulder, but gained it in having his work purchased by collectors belonging to foreign diplomatic circles in Jakarta, figures, I should point out, whose very job in Jakarta was to "recognize" Indonesia's status as a sovereign state in the family of nations. All the works for sale at his solo show were snapped up, and cultural officers from the Danish, Dutch, and US embassies offered fellowships to study abroad. Those gestures of recognition from foreign collectors gave Pirous purchase on his own expressivity and artistic identity.

For Pirous, as for most any modernist, to paint was to show oneself, to put oneself into view, before others of course, but also to oneself. That his works of self-expression brought pleasure to others reaffirmed his mastery of modernist orthodoxy and his stature as an artist whose work appealed to connoisseurs from abroad. Borrowing a page from Michel Foucault (1997), we may think of painting and its public display as an ethical path, a means through which someone becomes a who and a what, finding relationships with oneself and others, with self-reflection, and with the painted images that objectify and refract one's subjectivity. It is a way of deciphering and achieving a way of being, though not without risk or vulnerability. By the end of 1968, at age thirty-six, Pirous had found for the moment a place of happiness and confidence within the seemingly universal and decidedly secularist visual language of aesthetic modernism. Islam may have offered him happiness and purpose in other pursuits, but not visibly so in his art.

2

REVELATIONS AND COMPULSIONS

Friday, March 11, 1994. Pirous's sixty-second birthday had arrived, and with it the long-planned opening for Serambi Pirous. "This is going to be a *soft opening* for my gallery," chuckled Pirous, using an expression he had picked up at meetings of the local Rotary Club. "It is for my friends and family." Soft openings are supposed to be on the quiet and informal side, with none of the fanfare of a grand opening. All the same, he and Erna had something special planned for the eighty guests they had invited to the gallery that evening: *tarawih* prayers and a ceremonial meal of welcome and thanksgiving. By sunset, the kitchen at Serambi Pirous was brimming with snacks and sweets, platters of mounded rice cooked in turmeric and coconut milk, and bowls filled with savory curries or spicy vegetables and tempeh. Pirous sported a rich, earth-toned batik shirt and a black felt *péci*, the cap of Muslim origin usually worn by Indonesian men when ceremonies, religious events, or circumstances call for formal attire.

The gallery atrium boasted a few of Pirous's well-known Qur'anic paintings. The four monumental panels of *O God, Listen to Us, I–IV* towered on the west wall, their verses imploring God for divine guidance, grace, and favor. My friend had proudly featured these panels in several shows in the early 1990s (and many times since!), yet I confess I had trouble finding surprise or pleasure in them; even today I am stubbornly judgmental about their muddy, sulfurous colors. Stepping into the atrium back in 1994, I always gravitated to the saturated red, violet, turquoise, and gold of *Which of God's Blessings Do You Still Deny?* – named "Best Painting" at the Second Indonesian Biennale in Jakarta in 1976 – or to the etched copper plaques and strong horizontal energies of the mixed media painting called *17 Names for God*. The upper floor of the gallery housed dozens of paintings and prints, most of

39

them calligraphic works with Qur'anic themes, or abstract meditations on form, line, and color. I recall only one work on display that dated from before 1970, *Valleyscape*, an oil painting inspired by the view of the urban hamlets opposite the gallery and clinging to the slopes above the Cikapundung River.

Scores of guests came to admire the gallery just after the twilight hour for *maghrib* prayers. Most were friends and associates from the Bandung Institute of Technology. "Very German," one of Pirous's colleagues murmured to me, as his eyes swept across the gallery, appraising its design. Acquaintances huddled together companionably to study a painting or to run their hands over the gallery's smooth teak beams. Not long after the last guest arrived, Pirous and his elder brother, Idris, circulated among the gathering, inviting everyone to go to the upper floor to ready themselves for *salat tarawih* – a special (but non-obligatory) session of evening prayer and Qur'anic recitation reserved for Ramadhan. Facing west to Mecca, Pirous's nephew, Epi, began the *adzan*, the Muslim call to prayer. In prayer, the guests moved in near unison, making their bows, prostrations, and recitations in each *raka'at* (the units of prayer that make up *salat*) so as to comport themselves with the gestural code of Islamic ritual. As anthropologists Charles Hirschkind (2006) and Saba Mahmood (2005) have rightly stressed, the gestural and recitational acts of the *raka'at* are a way for Muslims to deepen their ethical sensibilities. Outward bodily and verbal comportment in prayer, say the faithful, work inward and lead one to a rightly disposed heart and mind.

As the guests absorbed themselves in prayer, I retreated to the margins of the gathering. It was very striking to watch gallery space become a place of prayer, like a mosque or a chapel-sized *surau*. I was reminded of an Indonesian poem – one of Pirous's favorites at the time – written by Taufiq Ismail, "Looking for a Mosque" (*Mencari Sebuah Masjid*). In that poem, Taufiq writes of a search for a mosque said to be the most glorious and soaringly beautiful one ever built. The poem's narrator wanders the world yearningly and fruitlessly in his or her search, until one day a stranger approaches and points to a humble garden clearing, saying, "This is the mosque you have been seeking." Tears flowing, the narrator realizes that nearly each and every corner of our world, and especially those small places shaped through our own labors, are a creation of unrivaled design and blessing, and so perfectly suited to turning one's mind to God. Most any spot of one's choosing – a garden or a gallery – may be turned into a place of prayer. With my friend's "spiritual notes" in eye-catching display on its walls, Serambi Pirous offered an especially congenial atmosphere for *salat tarawih*. The paintings seemed to comport with prayer, and a rightly disposed heart.

As soon as the *tarawih* recitations came to a close, the guests filed downstairs to the atrium, where a delicious feast awaited them. Erna, Pirous's daughters Mida and Rihan, his son Iwan, and Mida's fiancé, Dudy Wiyancoko, attended to the festivities, making sure guests had full plates and comfortable places to sit on mats or chairs. The meal marked the evening as a very propitious one – Pirous's birthday, the gallery's opening, and an occasion resonant with the providential blessings of *Laylat al-Qadr*, the "Night of Power," which fell the evening before, on the twenty-seventh day of Ramadhan. *Laylat al-Qadr* is the anniversary of the night the angel Gabriel first revealed the Qur'an to the Prophet Muhammad. It was most auspicious, then, and quite fitting with the spiritual mood of *Laylat al-Qadr*, for Pirous to reveal his gallery and private collection of Qur'anic and meditative paintings the following day.

Food and art are things to be shared, and so are feelings of gratitude and pride. As his guests finished their meal, Pirous delivered a humor-filled but heartfelt after-dinner speech, sincere in his gratitude for his guests' friendship and professional support, and beaming with pride in his new gallery. As the evening's culminating gesture of hospitality and affability, Pirous announced a drawing. Conversation bubbled as guests' names were collected on slips of paper and, when that was done, Idris and Dudy came forward with a framed work, cloaked in brown wrapping paper. Peeling away the paper, Pirous unveiled a calligraphic print, an etching in deep brown and ochre entitled *The Journey of Humankind*, its verses taken freely from the Qur'an and some *hadith* (reported sayings of the Prophet Muhammad) and interspersed with arabesque designs.

Fate saw to it that a professor of engineering, a colleague known to be rather uninterested in arts and culture, came up as the winning name. He stepped forward to collect his prize amid merry applause and a cascade of laughter. As the chuckling in the room subsided, Pirous pointed out several passages on the etching and translated them in Indonesian for the prizewinner and the other guests:

> Allah created humankind from an embryo.
> The best you can do is to be useful to others.
> To Him you will return.

This print, Pirous told the gathering, summed up his philosophy of life, and what he saw as the larger purpose behind his art. Offering a few further reflections on art and good deeds, he turned over the print to his colleague to a round of applause. With that, the gathering began to disperse, as some guests lingered with one another for conversation and coffee, and others took their leave.

The evening was a success in every way and left a satisfied glow on Pirous's face. Looking back on the opening, and knowing the meticulous care and oversight that Pirous brings to all his shows, I am mindful of the works he left out of view that night: a storage room crowded with paintings dating before 1970 – the lyrical, abstract work that propelled him to the forefront of Indonesia's art scene nearly three decades before. I still saw abstract painterly gestures in the "spiritual notes" that he put on show for the gallery's opening, but have come to realize how much the collection on display that night involved the "shelving" of an earlier expressivist identity in favor of the reflective and religiously inflected subjectivity of a painter concerned with making Islamic art.

This chapter tells the story of Pirous's "conversion experience" – the moment he began to picture Islam as a global cultural force. This was an artistic conversion or awakening, not a religious one. Pirous, we should remember, was "born Muslim"

41

and has never gone through a lapse of faith or religious identity, even when Bandung's emblematic modernism pushed him deeply into secular and cosmopolitan pursuits. Bandung gave him a glimpse of a globalizing art world, but one whose horizons were largely shaped by Euro-American institutions and ideas. The cultural and aesthetic riches of Islam remained obscure or altogether out of view. Oblivious to the Orientalist views within Euro-American art circles that looked upon Indonesian modern art as "derivative" and "inauthentic," Pirous saw eager and unconstrained artistic selfhood as the way to mark his place in what he thought was a broad and inclusively international art world. Judging by his stories of his early Bandung years, he saw little of relevance or appeal in Islam that would help him on the path toward the boundless self-expression that would make him a world artist.

That all changed when he found himself elsewhere and adrift, not in the galleries of the "East" – in Bandung, Jakarta, or anywhere in Asia – but in the museums of the "West," right in New York, on Manhattan's Upper East Side.

Self and the Spectre of Comparison

… the colonized [painter] always considers the colonizer as a model or as an antithesis. He continues to struggle against him. He was torn between what he was and what he wanted to become, and now is torn between what he wanted to be and what he is making of himself. (Albert Memmi, *The Colonizer and the Colonized*)

While the European artist is allowed to investigate other cultures and enrich their own work and perspective, it is expected that the artist from another culture only works in the background and with the artistic traditions connected to his or her place of origin. … If the foreign artist does not conform to this separation, he is considered inauthentic, westernized, and an imitator copyist of "what we do." The universal is ours, the local is yours. (Sebastián López, "Identity: Reality or Fiction?")

The success of his solo exhibit in Jakarta in late 1968 brought Pirous a two-year Rockefeller Fellowship to study graphics in the United States at the Rochester Institute of Technology, beginning in September 1969. Every time he went to New York City to visit museums, he would ask his sponsor where he could see contemporary Asian art, especially Indonesian contemporary art. As Pirous tells it, he always would get the same answer: "No way. There is no category for that yet. If you are talking about folk art, traditional art, primitive art, ethnic art, okay. But if you are talking about modern, contemporary art, no way." Indonesia, and indeed, most other countries in Asia had yet to be acknowledged by curators and art writers as nations capable of producing modern art. "If you went door to door in the galleries," remembers Pirous, "you could see modern paintings from Japan, or from India, but displayed as the personal works of individual artists, not as a category or classification in art. So, I felt very bad at the time." Indeed, Pirous must have felt tricked: The West had given Pirous and other Asian artists a supposedly new and universal visual language of modernism, but did not want to listen when these artists used it to join in the conversation.

The painful and growing realization that modern Indonesian art did not count for much in the galleries and museums of the West plunged Pirous into a period of brooding search and reflection. Visiting the Metropolitan Museum of Art in the early winter of 1970, he experienced what he has described to me and to others as a moment of intimate self-recognition upon seeing the museum's collection of Islamic art. Let me use his words to describe what happened just beforehand. The story begins with him feeling the currents of a globalized modernity:

When I went to America, I already had an attitude. "I am one of this world's artists!" My outlook in Indonesia was like that. I wanted to be a modern painter. I studied the Americans, the Dutch, the French. I already was a world painter. I liked abstract expressionism. I liked Paul Klee. I felt close to Jackson Pollock, very close to Willem de Kooning. But when I got to New York and as I walked along Fifth Avenue or along Madison Avenue, I suddenly felt: "Now Pirous, who are you? Yes, you are a modern painter, but are you a modern *Indonesian* painter? What's the proof that you are a modern Indonesian painter?" When I was in Indonesia I never asked questions liked that. Really, until that moment I felt that making art didn't need to be discussed that much. You just did it with an open mind, and invited the world into yours. You didn't have to be worried about whether you were Indonesian or not. It turned out that that wasn't completely true. If we want to become cosmopolitans, we have to become Indonesians first. If you want to be an internationalist, you have to be a nationalist first. You have to prove you are an Indonesian, your Indonesian characteristics. So I didn't have an answer at the time.

When I asked him what prompted his self-questioning, Pirous replied, "Distance, distance, not just physical, but a way of thinking." Yet he also let on about an exhibit that threw him into self-reflection:

What I still remember very well is an exhibition from Japan. Modern contemporary Japan. Very abstract. I felt the blood of the Japanese very strongly in their works. So I asked myself, "Well, Pirous, do you have such blood we can call Indonesian blood?" There wasn't any! I started groping.

I went again to New York City, visiting galleries. There, quite unexpectedly, I got the answer! The works of Islamic art at the Metropolitan, and also at other small commercial galleries: sometimes plates, sometimes ceramic fragments, sometimes manuscripts, miniature paintings, or calligraphic writings. Suddenly I thought, "Well this is very close to me!" This actually was around me when I was born. It was in Aceh. It was in my village, in my mother herself. This is a part of my own body, a part of my own blood. Why didn't I see it before? How come I didn't feel it before?

I asked why not.

> Because of my education! I studied at the school in Bandung. My teachers were Dutch. They taught about Jacques Villon, not about this. And that's what I got. I didn't know it was something that would harm me. This was the consequence of colonialism for the whole of Indonesia. And not only for Indonesia, but for all Asian nations that were subject to colonialism. When I was there in New York, and I happened to see and encounter that Islamic heritage, I said, "Wah! This is it!" Suddenly it came back again. "*This, this* is my property, *this* is my treasure."

Brimming with excitement, he hurried back to the studios upstate and set about making his first Qur'anic work, the calligraphic etching *Surat Ichlas* (Plate 3).

Pirous's story is in many respects typical of those told by other colonial and postcolonial painters. He plainly succumbed to what Benedict Anderson (1998) has called "the spectre of comparisons" – the haunting double-vision acquired through seeing oneself and one's circumstances in light of the world's communications – as he visited New York and went through the self-transforming experience in viewing the standing Islamic art exhibit at the Metropolitan Museum of Art. He came away a cultural nationalist. As he said twenty-five years later, "You have to be a nationalist first before you can become a cosmopolitan." He also came away convinced that Indonesian aesthetic identity rested in Islamic civilization and culture. With that he began a decades-long exploration and recuperation of "Islamic" aesthetics.

Remembering how an art show in Medan and a glimpse of an original Picasso had such profound impact on him earlier in life, I am not surprised by the self-recognition and creative ardor that Pirous experienced in 1970. Once-familiar possibilities of expression, long ignored during his training in modernism, returned to enthrall him. They reoriented his eye and his imagination, and suggested a way to express a self-conscious "Indonesian-ness" in his art. Already an Indonesian Muslim who made modern art, he started down the road of becoming a Muslim who made contemporary Indonesian Islamic art. A new set of questions had to be answered: What made an object or a set of practices "Islamic," "art," and "Indonesian"? What made them "Acehnese"? What made them "modern"?

It is clear that the museum exhibit succeeded in overturning some of the modernist hierarchies of value to which Pirous had grown accustomed. This was the first time he had encountered Islamic art in the very sort of institution that bestowed value and legitimacy to modern painting. Here he saw Islamic art elevated to the same civilizational plane as Western painting and grasped that it need not be treated as a subordinate form of aesthetic expression, even if its display in the museum hinted that it was a "lesser" form. We have to keep in mind that Pirous was encountering a particular version of Islamic art, a collection defined as such largely by Western specialists and curators, not by Muslims of Asian or Middle Eastern heritage. Museum specialists were careful not to mingle this collection with either

Western or modern painting (or with much "Asian" art for that matter): Islamic art remained "ethnic" and "other." These contradictory expressions of parity and alterity, in my view, did not cancel each other out, but led Pirous to new ways of thinking about himself and prospective directions for his art. This moment of self-recognition and creative possibility thus came as a potential form of emancipation from the language of Euro-American modernism, the aesthetic and political ideology that had spurred him away from the arts of his upbringing and yet had marginalized or excluded Asian modernisms.

Looking back through his story of that winter in New York City, we see Pirous searching for a distinctiveness that would help him grasp a more secure place in a global world of art and its commerce of ideas and objects. It is a story of essences and identity, and yet the terms of the search appear in accord with modernist ideas about nationality, ethnicity, and authenticity. A national visuality mattered most to Pirous. After all, he did not ask his sponsor where he could find contemporary "Acehnese" art, but rather "Indonesian" art. Wanting to feel "Indonesian blood," he instead feels emptiness, an absence of authenticity. The recuperative transfusion comes with the museum visit and feeling a kinship with some of the arts that he associates with his youth and with his mother. The sources of authenticity lie in the past and in his Acehnese birthplace, whose Islamic religiosity and romantically conjured communitarian values set it off from the West. But modernist discourses of authenticity such as this dated back as far as the early Cubist period and before. Neither is it a surprise that authenticity is conflated in Pirous's mind with the figure of his mother. After all, it was very common for modernist discourse to feminize and to make ethnic the figure of the "other." In this way, it reserved modern art as a refined, masculine pursuit with global aspirations and horizons.

From Pirous's vantage point in 1970, the Acehnese art he recalled from boyhood looked neither ethnic nor primitive, but civilizational and museum-class, a local expression of something global in scale. Although Aceh is a culturally and politically distinctive region in Indonesia, it is certainly easy to see that for Pirous, and many others, Acehnese-ness could be counted as an expression of Indonesian-ness. For Pirous, the culture of Aceh and Indonesia more broadly had much in common, especially in light of their Islamic foundations. Indeed, Islamic arts found throughout the country's provinces could be construed as a significant part of Indonesia's national heritage, and no less important than the Hindu-Buddhist traditions that linger today most visibly in Java and Bali. Asserting a civilizational status for the Indonesian Muslim arts of the past (even though "Indonesia" did not pre-date 1945), meant that there was an indigenous heritage worth recuperating for the purposes of the present.

We see then how Pirous's views tied nationalism, religion, and ethnicity together. Looking at *Surat Ichlas*, however, we may not see anything either "Indonesian" or "Acehnese" about such art. This was, Pirous tells me, a complaint from an art critic in a Singapore newspaper twenty years later: "Where is Indonesia in such work? Pirous's art is really international art. He doesn't speak about Indonesia. He speaks about Islam. There are no signs of the national there." Let's put aside for the moment the question of why one would desire or want to privilege "signs of the national" to begin with, as if a work of art needed a passport. The dilemma Pirous describes is a persistent one, because national or ethnic identities are not ready-mades in the visual language of modernism or Islamic aesthetics. Since 1970, Pirous has routinely resorted to iconographies and narratives that he hopes will keep his painterly identity "Indonesian." He has been "possessed," if you will, by a nationalist ethno-aesthetics, even as he works with ideas and approaches explored by Muslims in other times and places around Asia and the Middle East. The epiphany in New York was, perhaps, nothing other than his being thrice hailed, summoned by faith, the nation-state, and by a global art market that was – at the time – obsessed with iconographic or gestural assertions of national and regional identities in the postcolonies. Yet this has meant, too, that domesticating Islamic aesthetics – making them Indonesian, and making them his – has been Pirous's foremost problem since 1970.

Pirous's story is, in light of that problem, interesting for what it leaves unmentioned about that moment of recognition at the Metropolitan Museum of Art. He describes his artistic "blood" as a national substance, Indonesian, and even as an ethno-religious substance – Acehnese and Muslim. Harder to make out is how he feels this "blood" gives him ties to *dar-al Islam*, the worldwide Muslim community. His feelings of solidarity with *dar-al Islam* go unrevealed in this telling. Judging from his conversations with me in 1994, a sense of belonging to a global Islamic community did not seem to have been especially relevant to his ambitions for gaining recognition as a world artist in 1970. Then, again, those feelings of solidarity may have posed a threat too dangerous to acknowledge in a story told to me, or to others.

In finding possibilities for his own artistic subjectivity in Islamic aesthetics, Pirous helped put a new twist to the principal tension Kapur saw in Indian post-colonial art, and which I similarly see in much Indonesian work. The strain of working toward a unique painterly identity, while standing in as a representative of a nation, in Pirous's work now could be rethought and perhaps resolved through the mediating practices and discourses of Islamic art. To embrace Islamic art at the moment he did was to revolt against the modernist precursors with whom he was familiar, and gave him the challenge of finding an innovative space within the realm of secular modernism by adhering to an aesthetic tradition long colored by theological debates. The gesture was at once a revolt against Western-dominated modernism, and a submission to Islam. This revolt, I should be careful to point out, did not involve a wholesale rejection of aesthetic modernism in favor of Islamic art principles but resulted in a hybrid genre of painting, incorporating something of both. As I hope I have made clear, he saw an embrace of Islamic art as an embrace of the Indonesian nation-state. It was a shift in moral and civic vision that led him to claim an Islamic heritage for the nation at large, a move that politically and aesthetically ties together the transcendental discourses of nation and faith.

1 *At the Beginning, the Voice Said "Recite."* 1982. 180 × 135 cm, fiberglass, gold leaf, acrylic on panel and canvas. Courtesy of the artist and Yayasan Serambi Pirous.

2 *For the Sparkling Morning Light.* 1982. 160 × 200 cm, fiberglass, gold leaf, acrylic on panel and canvas. Courtesy of the artist and Yayasan Serambi Pirous.

Surat Ichlas. 1970. 40 × 50 cm, color etching. Courtesy of the artist and Yayasan Serambi Pirous.

4 *Sura Isra II: Homage to Mother.* 1982. 80 × 54 cm, serigraph. Courtesy of the artist and Yayasan Serambi Pirous.

5 A *kasab* designed and embroidered by Pirous's mother, Hamidah, in 1941. Photograph courtesy of the artist and Yayasan Serambi Pirous.

6 *White Writing.* 1972. 100 × 180 cm, marble paste, acrylic on canvas. Courtesy of the artist and Yayasan Serambi Pirous.

7 *The Night Journey.* 1976. 145 × 115 cm, marble paste, acrylic on canvas. Courtesy of the artist and Yayasan Serambi Pirous.

8 *And God the Utmost.* 1978.
30 × 30 cm, marble paste, gold leaf,
acrylic on canvas. Courtesy of the
artist and Yayasan Serambi Pirous.

9 *Prayer XII/Homage to Tanöh Abée.* 1981. 84 × 56 cm, serigraph. Courtesy of the artist
and Yayasan Serambi Pirous.

10 *A Forest of Pens, a Sea of Ink, the Beautiful Names of God Never Cease Being Written.* 1985. 120 × 100 cm, marble paste, gold leaf, acrylic on canvas. Courtesy of the artist and Yayasan Serambi Pirous.

11 *Green Valley.* 2000. 135 × 150 cm, marble paste, gold leaf, acrylic on canvas. Courtesy of the artist and Yayasan Serambi Pirous.

12 *The Horizon on the Southern Plain.* 1998. 140 × 190 cm, marble paste, gold leaf, acrylic on canvas. Courtesy of the artist and Yayasan Serambi Pirous.

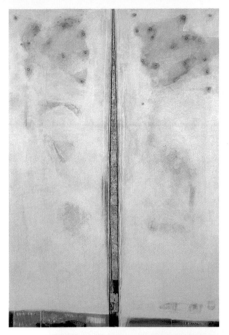

13   *It Pierces the Sky*. 1997. 145 × 95 cm, marble paste, gold leaf, acrylic on canvas. By permission of Elmy and Stan Maringka. Photograph courtesy of Yayasan Serambi Pirous.

14   *The Night That is More Perfect than 1000 Months*. 2000. 150 × 95 cm, marble paste, gold leaf, acrylic on canvas. Courtesy of the artist and Yayasan Serambi Pirous.

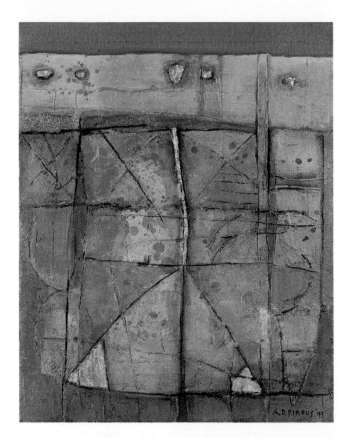

15 *Triangle with an Ascending Vertical Gold Line.* 1993. 46 × 35 cm, marble paste, gold leaf, acrylic on canvas. Courtesy of the artist and Yayasan Serambi Pirous.

16 *Meditation on a Circle with a Vertical Line.* 2000. 45 × 35 cm, marble paste, gold leaf, acrylic on canvas. Courtesy of the artist and Yayasan Serambi Pirous.

Pillars of the Sky. 1996. 125 × 145 cm, marble paste, gold leaf, acrylic on canvas. Courtesy of the artist and yasan Serambi Pirous.

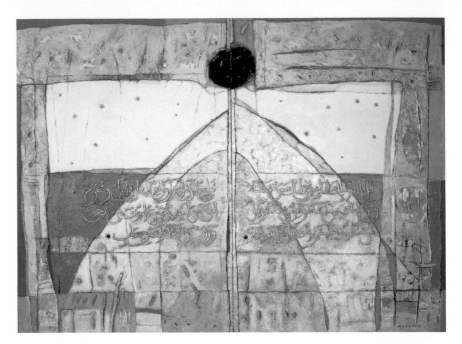

18 *An Admonition to the Leader: Concerning the Transient Palace and the Beginning and End of Life.* 1995. 175 × 260 cm, marble paste, gold leaf, acrylic on canvas. Courtesy of the artist and Yayasan Serambi Pirous.

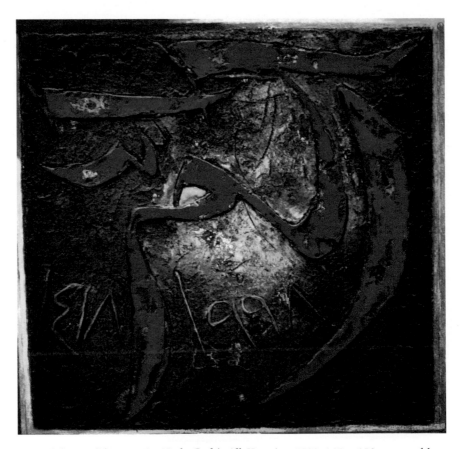

19 Detail from *Alif Lam Mim/Only God is All-Knowing.* 1998. 145 × 150 cm, marble paste, acrylic on canvas. By permission of the artist and Yayasan Serambi Pirous. Photograph by Kenneth M. George, 2002.

Once There was a Holy War in Aceh: Homage to the Intrepid Hero Teuku Oemar, 1854–1899. 1998. 45 × 150 cm, mixed media on canvas. Courtesy of the artist and Yayasan Serambi Pirous.

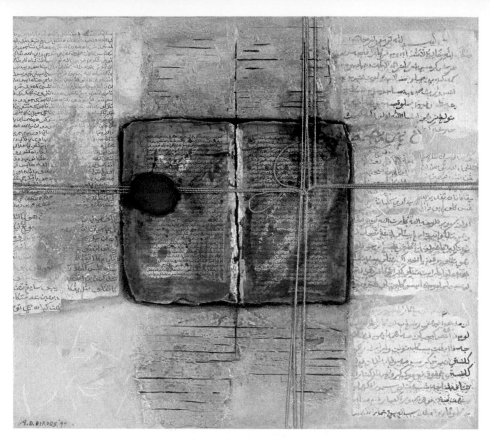

21 *The Shackling of the Book of the Holy War, II.* 1999. 72 × 77 cm, mixed media on canvas. Courtesy of the artist and Yayasan Serambi Pirous.

22 The painter brooding over *They Who are Buried without Names.* 2001. 122 × 122 cm, marble paste, colored sands, acrylic on canvas. By permission of the artist and Yayasan Serambi Pirous. Photograph by Kenneth M. George, 2002.

A People's Fate is in Their Own Hands. 2001. 140 × 190 cm, marble paste, gold leaf, acrylic on canvas. By permission of the artist and Yayasan Serambi Pirous. Photograph by Kenneth M. George, 2002.

24 *Meditation Toward the Enlightened Spirit, I.* 2000. 70 × 72 cm, marble paste, gold leaf, acrylic on canvas. By permission of Kenneth M. George and Kirin Narayan. Photograph courtesy of Yayasan Serambi Pirous.

25 Allah. Detail from *17 Names for God.* 1980. 140 × 120 cm, marble paste, acrylic on canvas and etched copper on panel. By permission of the artist and Yayasan Serambi Pirous. Photograph by Kenneth M. George, 2002.

Making Spirit Matter

Seyyed Hossein Nasr (1987), among others, has argued that Qur'anic calligraphy enjoys a special privilege in Islam as the visual embodiment of divine revelation, as "the geometry of the spirit," and as a talisman with a power and agency all its own. It is, he says, the progenitor of traditional Islamic visual arts and the most characteristic feature of Islamic civilization, culture, and discipline. Pirous's first "Islamic" work – the etching *Surat Ichlas* – seems to me an artistic and spiritual gesture much in keeping with Nasr's remark, and a "spiritual note" that marks a turning point in the way Pirous thinks of himself as a who and a what. His artistic subjectivity from this moment forward takes on religious inflection. For this reason, I want to give this work some deeper reflection.

Surat Ichlas makes a visual recitation of Sura 112, Al-Ikhlas, in full. The etching means to be seen and read – it is a speech act and an art act. I can't say where one begins with this work. For the Muslim gallery-goer, the work might invite a silent reading, or a murmured re-oralization of its Qur'anic passage. He or she would recognize it as the most famous Qur'anic statement about *tauhid*, God's one-ness. For a few moments, their eyes would travel across the image, following the script from right to left and from top to bottom. But they would also take in the picture whole. For the non-Muslim, or for those unable to utter or read Arabic, the writing remains inscrutable. (Most, I believe, would grasp the Arabic as writing, and not as something else.) They are left with a picture only.

As Michael Sells (1999: 137) explains, this sura describes God as eternal but also as one approached for refuge, and what I know about Pirous's life persuades me that the picture gestures in that direction. I think of it as a spiritual note about the artist taking creative and cultural refuge in his faith after a period of disappointment, resentment, and emptiness:

> In the Name of God the Compassionate the Caring
> Say: "He is God, the one, the eternal,
> God the refuge.
> Not begetting, unbegotten.
> There is no one comparable to Him."

Islamic theological tradition also associates this sura with sincerity, construed as the pure and earnest affirmation of God's unity by the one reciting the verse. The color of this passage in the etching – something between teal and turquoise – strikes me as an unmistakable icon of the artist's personal agency and intentionality. At the very least, the bluish calligraphy hints that it is Pirous that is making the visual recitation of Al-Ikhlas, and thereby affirming God's unity. The Qur'anic passage at the foot of the etching, Sura 2 (Al-Baqarah) verse 256, seems to me a kind of scrawled footnote or marginalia offering commentary on the picture as a whole. Our eyes don't come to it immediately, but find it after taking in the calligraphy of

Al-Iklhas, which rises from the surface of the image to swirl above a background of tarnished copper. The passage from Sura 2 emphasizes the voluntary character of one's sincere surrender to God, and the solace and strength that comes with surrender:

> There is no compulsion in matters of faith.
> True guidance stands clear from error.
> Whoever turns away from the forces of evil
> and believes in God, will surely hold fast
> to a handle that is strong and unbreakable,
> for God hears all and knows every thing.

Finally, the etching is doubly signed: Pirous's signature appears on the ribbon of red in very small Arabic script, just after the verse from Al-Baqarah, and then again in Roman script in the lower right corner of each print.

Pictures and Qur'anic passages, of course, lend themselves to multiple interpretations. I asked Pirous about the verses of Al-Ikhlas, but he did not have anything to say about faith as a refuge. He instead pressed the notion of God's eternal character. Sura Al-Ikhlas, he told me,

> is a statement that is very important for a Muslim in recognizing the difference between self and God. The self has but a transitory existence compared to the existence of God, which is eternal. The oneness of God goes beyond anyone and can't be compared to anything. So there is a great contrast between humankind, with all of our flaws, and God, with all of God's magnificence. God is one. Begetting no one and begotten by no one. Without beginning, without end. Very abstract, belief in one God. So this is a statement about *tauhid*.

"Abstract," I have learned over the years, is for Pirous an exceptionally positive term, one that connotes marvel, rationality, transcendence, and truth, both in art and in faith. Just as abstract painting relinquishes representation of this world in favor of pure expression and imaginative vision, so does belief in God take one beyond the limits of worldly existence. I have never heard Pirous talk about the Indonesian nation-state or his commitment to it as "abstract." Neither does he describe Acehnese-ness or his sense of ethnic belonging as "abstract." But by depicting the "truths" of artistic vision and faith as abstract, he would place them beyond the unruly realm of worldly politics and worldly attachments – beyond compromise, beyond compulsion, beyond worldly awareness. Declaring something like art or religion as non-political is, of course, a thoroughly political if wishful gesture. For this reason, "abstract" appears to me as a loaded term, commonly used by Pirous (and many others, to be sure) in making claims about truth and worldly political placement.

To come back to *Surat Ichlas*, the etching suggests to me further doublings, beyond the matter of the artist's signature. Its visual recitation of Qur'anic passages are not so much an "outpouring of inner feeling" as a sincere gesture of submission and surrender in which a believer consciously conforms to God's one-ness, God's commands, and a sacred text (cf. Siegel 2000: 114–15). It is a consummate display of reason and self-control, the sort of rational being Indonesian Muslims call *akal*. There is here, in the passage from Al-Ikhlas, a giving or a submission of oneself to the abstractness of *tauhid*. But let's consider, too, the matter of form: the calligraphy itself is an abstraction, in the sense that it adheres not to real objects in nature but represents through shape, line, and color emotional and symbolic values. As Pirous explained in 1987 to a reporter from the Indonesian magazine *Tawakal* (*Trust in God*):

> I actually became a painter grounded in Western method and knowledge. I am an abstract painter. The moment I saw calligraphic forms [in New York], I suddenly felt close and in touch. Calligraphy is an abstraction ... forms focused on the symbolic but carried out with expressive values and significance.

In short, Pirous's first Qur'anic work shows a doubled surrender to the abstract, in which abstract form carries the burden and promise of revealing abstract spiritual truths.

There is yet another reason why I have dwelt so long on this work. *Surat Ichlas* is not a painting; it's a print. It is Pirous's earliest Qur'anic etching. These are exceedingly few, and *Surat Ichlas* is the only one made in the US. Pirous's grasp of "Islamic art" in the winter of 1970 comes precisely at the moment when he is *not* painting, but exploring for the first time high-viscosity etching techniques that had been developed only a few years before by Stanley William Hayter, the abstract expressionist and printmaker who founded Atelier 17 in Paris. This was a new and innovative approach to engraving that involved the acid-bath etching of a single metal plate – usually made of copper or zinc – and the careful application and wiping away of several colored inks, each with a different viscosity or syrupy-ness, so as to fill the incised recesses of the plate with layers of pure or mixed color. When the plate is brought into contact with paper, all the colors print at once. Although the technique demands planning and extreme care and attention, it yields exceptionally appealing textures and visual qualities.

Pirous's immersion in new graphic and printmaking techniques in 1969–70 gives further clues about that moment of self-recognition at the Metropolitan Museum of Art. As I have said, his weeks or months of self-questioning took place during a period when he was not painting. He has never told me so, but I have a hunch that he missed losing himself and expressing himself in the act of painting. That is not to say he wasn't busy: He was learning about inks, plates, acids, rubber rollers, paper, and various ways to handle them – all unfamiliar materials and techniques, and none especially conducive to the improvisatory and expressive play he knew in painting. Unlike painting, making an etching required planning and discipline. It might have felt to Pirous as if his self-expression had been put in check. At the same time, the plunge into printmaking techniques and materials in Rochester, New York, must have brought back memories of his youth in Aceh,

49

when he helped his mother with inks and dyes for making *kasab*, or worked with stencils and silkscreens in making nationalist propaganda posters. The feel of materials from his youth, I like to think, were indelibly etched into his memory but covered up by the experience of painting. Printmaking, I would like to suggest, brought those embodied memories to the surface, and it remained only for a museum exhibit to lend them legitimacy and aesthetic affiliation. The decisive turn in his artistic subjectivity toward Islam and Islamic aesthetics surely helped restore the self-esteem that had been battered by the condescension and neglect that befell him as an Indonesian modernist in the West. We would be wrong, however, to see it only as a spiritual recovery. The feel of materials was part of his self-questioning and recuperation.

The Influence of Peers

Were I to end it there, the story of Pirous's turn to Islamic aesthetics might seem singular and unheralded. Wijdan Ali (1989, 1997) and Iftikhar Dadi (2006) find comparable stories in the rise of modern Islamic art throughout the Middle East, Africa, and South Asia, going back as far as the 1950s. Ali observes that all modern Islamic artists known to her enjoyed training in Western aesthetics and that most sought an identity forged from traditional heritage and Euro-American modernity. Dadi, meanwhile, calls attention to the way many of these postcolonial Muslim painters pursued subjective projects in dialogue with nationalism, aesthetic modernism, and cosmopolitanism, especially during the 1950s, 1960s, and 1970s. Pirous appears to have had little or no knowledge of what these contemporaries were doing with "modern Islamic art" at the time of his studies in the US. But we should not be surprised. Ali (1989: xii) explains that most of the Islamic modernists, if I may call them that, worked in isolation and had difficulty finding a public even in their own societies.

Pirous himself hints that changes were afoot in Indonesia during his absence. Returning to Bandung in 1971, Pirous found he was not alone in exploring Islam and its place in contemporary Indonesian art and culture:

> When I stepped forward with paintings and an art inspired by calligraphy, it wasn't as if it were revealed falling from the sky. People already were becoming aware of Islamic themes around 1970: Taufiq Ismail, Muhammad Diponegoro, and Abdul Hadi in literature. The same in dance. Around 1970, religious schools and *pesantren* began to increase, too, and the government began to discuss marriage laws for the Muslim community. *MTQ* [*Musabaqah Tilawatil Qur'an*, Quranic recitation contests] took place. So, things with a religious aspect, not connected with worship, but with *mu'amalah* – everyday Islamic conduct – began to be felt quite often.

Pirous gives an upbeat picture of public interest in Islam at the time. It is certainly fair to say that Muslims were finding better prospects for public expression and

50

exploration of Islamic values in law, education, family life, ethical conduct, and culture more broadly. Left out of the picture, however, are the stirrings of Islamic conservatism. For example, in late 1970, H. B. Jassin, a pious Muslim and the editor of the literary journal *Sastera*, was brought to court and found guilty of offending Islam for having published a story in which a bored Prophet Muhammad is given permission by a bearded and bespectacled Allah to return to earth to look over the turmoil as Sukarno's authority collapses (Maier 2004). Broader cultural and political opportunities for Muslims in general meant that proponents of strict and conservative Islam found more visibility and clout. Creativity for some Muslims might mean blasphemy for others. The Soeharto regime carefully watched and manipulated the diverse aspirations of the Muslim community, giving rein in some circumstances, holding back in others, and fostering statist Islam through government bodies such as the Indonesian Council of Islamic Scholars (Majelis Ulama Indonesia, or MUI) – founded in 1975.

Although 1970 may have marked a new and very public flowering of Muslim expression in Indonesia, we should remember that Islamic cultural energies were stirring well before Pirous left for his studies in the US. Painter Ahmad Sadali (1924–87) was Pirous's senior colleague at the Bandung Insitute of Technology; he too had trained with Mulder and had gone to the US in 1955. Pirous exhibited with Sadali in 1966 and 1967 and knew him as a devout Muslim who saw painting as a spiritually charged experience. Sadali held a longstanding affiliation with PII (Indonesian Islamic Students), the association that published the 1956 declaration on Islamic arts (see chapter 1), and looked upon art as a way to seek God's blessing. As early as 1957, he professed that abstraction made a very congenial fit with Islamic principles (Holt 1967: 327), and through time he came to see painting as a vehicle of *dzikir* (practices that lead to mindfulness of God). Indeed, he told his students that he saw in *dzikir* "the power of imagination, intuition, and knowledge – the power of the senses." Though never his student in a formal sense, and in many ways his rival, Pirous looked up to Sadali: "He was my 'teacher.' He would begin to paint early in the morning, just after sunrise, and while waiting for dawn he would read the Qur'an. He studied it. He was a very devoted and very intellectual Muslim."

Although Sadali might have been an appealing figure upon whom he could model himself, Pirous was not yet all that drawn to painting as a contemplative experience. I asked Pirous if he enjoyed reflecting on Qur'anic passages when he was a young painter. "Not yet," he replied. "I'll tell you something, though."

Sometime before I left for the States my nephew, Achmad Basah, always came by the house. He was preparing a commentary on the Qur'an. He would ask, "In making something, Uncle, do you feel a power or inspiration in you, or in your desire to create, that has some connection to God and to when God created all? Isn't it possible that in making a work of art someone could recall or reflect on the ethical processes and divine character of God who created all that is good? As though creating could take power and inspiration from the Creator Above." At that time I didn't feel it. I didn't feel it because I painted with passion and abandon, with spontaneity. Not with reflection or contemplation. So I told him I'd keep it in mind. When I went to America I came face to face with it, with that moment. And when I came back, he was the one who was happiest about me finding enlightenment.

A Lifeworld Refigured

As I said earlier in this book, the experiential lifeworlds into which we are thrown are open-ended, uncertain, and fraught with power, possibility, and predicament. I have sometimes thought of Pirous's story of his encounter with Islamic art in New York as a kind of conversion narrative, a story told to oneself and others to give a semblance of fresh purpose, stability, direction, and intelligibility to what is actually a continuing path of improvisation (cf., Butler 2005). I don't at all doubt the unexpectedness or sincerity of Pirous's first glimpse of broader painterly horizons, or the passions and resolve they stirred. It was without calculation. All the same, I have tried to bring into the picture the circumstances that may have coaxed him toward that encounter and moment of self-recognition. Questions from a nephew, the influence of a colleague, and the immersion in new materials and techniques all helped Pirous see things in a new light. I place great weight, however, on the compulsions of New York's art world around 1970. The museum and the galleries set the terms of his prospects, excluding him from most every venue of modern art, and requiring instead that he ground his painterly identity in the primitive, the ethnic, or the local rather than in the personal vision he had so earnestly pursued. I don't believe that Pirous ever really challenged the premises or desires of that art world, but found a way to adjust to them through a postcolonial assertion of cultural distinctiveness.

Pirous's first Qur'anic etching speaks to us, too, but needs to be grasped in light of the stories and circumstances I have discussed above. As a "spiritual note" addressed to the artist himself, *Surat Ichlas* seems a fervent affirmation of religious and aesthetic faith in the wake of questioning himself and his world. At the same time, I liken the painting to the inscription Pirous made in his copy of *Mohammed and Charlemagne* in 1958. Instead of quoting Plato as charter for his ethical aims as a citizen, Pirous quotes the Qur'an as charter for a new sort of ethico-aesthetic practice in painting and printmaking. I see in the etching, too, a reply to the nephew who had seen in painting rich possibilities for spiritual contemplation and understanding. But what does the etching say to those of us who do not read Arabic, and who are thus unable to fathom its religious significance? We perhaps sense a secret, something withheld from us, yet visibly there in aesthetically pleasing form. In that, there may be the will to power, a postcolonial gesture from a Muslim who refuses to be an art world subordinate even as he depends on that art world.

Surat Ichlas and Pirous's stories give us an important glimpse of a Muslim artist changing his mind and finding fresh direction for his work. In short, they are works of ethical reformulation. These stories are in no way diminished if I point out that

Pirous began to tell them often well after his time in New York and always with the purpose of giving an account of his interest in Qur'anic painting. I have combed through exhibit brochures, artist statements, and newspaper clippings published since 1971, and have not come across a public account of his "conversion narrative" before 1985, when it appeared in the catalogue to his first retrospective show in Jakarta. It figures centrally in interviews with art historians Helena Spanjaard and Astri Wright in 1988, and in a few magazine interviews around that time. I become familiar with it in 1994. By this time it is a polished and well-rehearsed story. It no doubt had a life in his conversations with colleagues, students, and collectors some time before 1985. My point is that it took over a decade for the story to take settled form as a set of reflections on how his exploration of Islamic aesthetics began when he saw the West's low regard for Indonesian modern art. The story comes most fully into view only after fifteen years of work that bring him national and international acclaim as pioneer of contemporary Indonesian Islamic art. From this we might draw many lessons. For this book, I mention but one: "Islamic art" was for Pirous not a set of ready-made images, projects, and ideas fully known to him, but a set of problems and principles that he needed to discover and explore – a path of improvisation and ethical self-cultivation that would transform his lifeworld as a Muslim artist-citizen.

3

DIPTYCH – MAKING ART ISLAMIC AND MAKING ISLAMIC ART INDONESIAN

Part 1: Making Art Islamic

... the Qur'an – God forbid I'm misunderstood – the staggering power of such a book arises from the impossibility of its being depicted. (Orhan Pamuk, *My Name is Red*)

Late March 1994. As soon as Ramadhan was over, Pirous threw himself back into his ongoing work with the Istiqlal Festival Foundation (Yayasan Festival Istiqlal). The foundation had its "Bandung branch office" just a mile or so downhill from Serambi Pirous on Jalan Dipati Ukur, in an aging, late colonial-era house with stucco walls and terracotta tile roof. The house once would have served as a home for a well-to-do family, when the mountain city attracted Dutch civil servants, peasants and elites from around West Java, educators, Chinese merchants, and the modernist architects who would design the grand, art deco buildings on Bandung's northern slopes. Pirous and some fellow artists took over the address in 1973 as the studio and commercial gallery for their new design and art group, Decenta. Twenty years later, Decenta had more or less disbanded, leaving Pirous, Achmad Noe'man, and Machmud Buchari to use the space for spearheading the national Istiqlal festivals that took place in 1991 and 1995, festivals that showcased Indonesia's Islamic cultural heritage.

For years, Pirous had used the Decenta studio and gallery to explore questions about Islamic art. It was here and in his home studio that he turned out scores and scores of paintings and prints inspired by Qur'anic verse. By the time I visited Bandung in 1994, Pirous and his colleagues had transformed the warren of studio and gallery spaces into the production headquarters for the *Al-Qur'an Mushaf Istiqlal*, an immense, illuminated "National Independence Qur'an," planned for

54

Figure 3.1 Pirous at work at Decenta preparing the serigraph, *Noah's Deluge*. Bandung, 1976. Photograph courtesy of Yayasan Serambi Pirous.

presentation during the country's fiftieth anniversary celebration of independence in 1995. (A *mushaf* – pronounced *mus'-haf* – is a bound manuscript copy of the Qur'an, usually inscribed by hand.) Although the first Istiqlal Festival (1991) had met with wide popular acclaim, leading Muslim figures and organizations in Indonesia did not always like the mixing of art and Islam. Muhammadiyah, the second largest Islamic organization in Indonesia, with roughly 25 million reform-minded followers, had yet to declare that art was not *haram* (forbidden on religious grounds); it would not do so until 1995. To Pirous's dismay, the *mushaf* project routinely drew critical remarks from Munawir Sjadzali, the Indonesian Minister of Religious Affairs (1983–93). "The Qur'an," roared Sjadzali to the press in 1992, "should not be sacrificed for art." The latest headache for Pirous and the *mushaf* design team were complaints from the Ministry of Religious Affairs and the Indonesian Council of Islamic Scholars over the proposed placement of verse markers. Pirous, Noe'man, and Machmud readied themselves for a trip to Istanbul, Cairo, and Amman to fetch back examples of Qur'ans to show the authorities the flexible and diverse ways for placing recitation markers in Qur'anic texts.

During Pirous's many years, a question mark always seemed to hang over the idea of Islamic art. His father, you may recall, saw art as a pursuit that was

55

Figure 3.2   Pirous, Machmud Buchari, and architect Ahmad Noe'man meeting with the Indonesian Minister of Religious Affairs Munawir Sjadzali (standing at left and wearing official attire), Jakarta, 1992 or 1993. Photograph courtesy of Yayasan Scrambi Pirous.

incompatible with the teachings of Islam. The *ulama*, who by tradition were the figures most vested in the custodial care of the Qur'an, by and large frowned on the mixing of art and religion, too. And not every artist appreciated the religious gestures in Pirous's calligraphic works. "Why do you want to ruin a fine painting with writing and Qur'anic verses?" moaned one of his campus colleagues. That same artist gave me a gruff work-over at a dinner party. When I told him that I was interested in learning about "contemporary Islamic art,""he shot back, "What do you mean by that! Any art made by Muslims? Just religious art?" That was only the beginning of a rather blunt, five-minute primer on art and religion.

Anthropologists – and many artists, to be sure – are fully aware of the moral and conceptual relativity of terms like "religion" and "art" when they are seen from different cultural, ideological, or theological standpoints. Our world is one of contentious cultural plurality. Although most observant Muslims insist on the unity and integrity of their faith – Pirous certainly does – "Islam" itself is a slippery entity, and without a central authority that can speak for its followers. Mohammed Arkoun (1994) and Aziz Al-Azmeh (1993) see Islam largely as a name or term used to join together a vast array of very different societies, histories, and cultures. "There are as many Islams," says Al-Azmeh, "as there are situations that sustain it" (1993: 1). Art historians Sheila S. Blair and Jonathan M. Bloom echo these sentiments in their reflections on what they call the "mirage of Islamic art." They insist that "there never was, nor is, a single Islam, and so any attempt to define the essence of a single Islamic art is doomed to failure" (2003: 153).

Blair and Bloom also tell us something that is crucial to understanding Pirous's venture into Islamic art. They write:

There is no evidence that any artist or patron in the fourteen centuries since the revelation of Islam ever thought of his or her art as "Islamic," and the notion of a distinctly "Islamic" tradition of art and architecture ... is a product of late nineteenth- and twentieth-century Western scholarship, as is the terminology used to identify it. ... In short, Islamic art as it exists in the early twenty-first century is largely a creation of Western culture. (2003: 153, 154)

A Muslim reading that passage might feel suddenly dispossessed of an important part of his or her art heritage. Yet the story of Pirous's moment of self-recognition at the Metropolitan Museum of Art, the moment when he comes to possess (and be possessed by) "Islamic art," accords well with Blair and Bloom's argument. The museums and art histories erected in the West were mirrors in which Pirous saw his own reflection. The passage leaves little room, however, for those Muslims who, precisely like Pirous, have begun their own exploration of Islamic art and culture following a glance at themselves in those mirrors. Recuperating an artistic vision through the rubric of "Islamic art" does not destine today's Muslim artists to an inescapable and derivative identity, but potentially equips them with a way of talking back to and reclaiming authority from the West in a bid to change our globalized art circuits. We should not mistake "Islamic art" as the only aesthetic venture of interest to Muslim artists. Just glancing at the vast accomplishments Muslims have achieved in architecture, film, graphic design, fashion, performance art, painting, pottery, metalwork, or video art, we quickly see that Muslims do not confine themselves so narrowly. But by inhabiting the term "Islamic art," as Pirous had begun to do in 1970, more than a few postcolonial Muslim artists have translated what is arguably a discourse of Western (and largely secular) origin into a compelling aesthetic and ethico-religious language of their own.

First Gestures

As T. K. Sabapathy, one of Southeast Asia's leading art historians, put it to me one day over mugs of steaming Singaporean coffee, "Pirous was no rookie" when he started his exploration of Islamic art. We must imagine an alert and receptive artist, who at the same time was already deeply shaped by modernist ideologies and habits. He was not looking to transgress the modernist legacy, but to assert a visible role in it as an Indonesian painter. Returning home to Bandung in 1971, he remained comfortable with two-dimensional easel art and with painterly abstraction. Nothing that I know about him suggests that he saw new social, cultural, or ideological functions for his painting. What was different was his newfound interest in expressing his Indonesian-ness through images and ideas drawn from Islamic sources in his Sumatran homeland of Aceh.

Interviewed a decade later by student painter Syaiful Adnan, Pirous described that interest as a "contemplation of form" (*kontemplasi bentuk*) aimed at pulling his work back from the influence of the West (Adnan 1981: 82–83). The gesture proved to be one of retrieval and return, of revisiting – in his memory and imagination – the Aceh of his youth in a search for familiar forms and images that he might confidently use for artistic expression of his Indonesian-ness. Although the idea was to apply the fruits of this search to future work, the hunt went back in time, a retrospective prowl through Aceh as a kind of visual archive. Indonesia's diverse cultural tapestry surely offered other prospects, as well. We can understand, however, that Pirous felt, and continues to feel, a special belonging to Aceh and an affinity with its visual culture. All the same, the "return to Aceh" – if I may call it that – is also a "return to the Met," the scene of his inspiring encounter with Islamic art in New York. It was not so much a broad or open-ended search for all that might be called Acehnese, but an alert look through Acehnese visual culture for signs of the Islamic glories he had already seen in New York – Arabic calligraphy in particular, the form of visual art, say Blair and Bloom (2003: 168), that is universally admired by Muslims.

Pirous's initial study of calligraphic themes, *Surat Ichlas*, involved his experimenting with high-viscosity etching techniques. Though his experience with etching proved quite brief (he made only a few etched prints after 1970), it had a lasting impact on his painting. As he applied layers of ink to the plates he had etched with calligraphic verse, he was struck by how much they looked like paintings:

> The inked plates already looked like heavily textured paintings with a very antique feel, ancient and archaic. Don't calligraphic verses come from long ago when Islam began to flower and spread? So I felt a visual relationship between the archaic surface and texture of the plates and the holy verses of the past.

The idea thus dawned on him to re-create the textures and reliefs of the plates on his painted canvasses. His subsequent experiments in heavy relief texture were not just a matter of aesthetic form, but a reaching for content too.

Although he continued to work with oils, by 1972 Pirous had begun exploring acrylic paints and modeling paste, using the latter to build up the surface of a canvas. Acrylic paints at the time were a rather new and expensive manufacture that had really caught on in the US and Europe only after 1960. Acrylics, as Philip Ball (2001: 320–25) has explained, helped artists abandon the "painterliness" and subjective "signature touch" associated with oils. Their colors are very intense, and they dry flat and without brush marks. The fast drying times changed the pace of layering or overpainting but, above all, they changed the way artists worked through paintings. When using slow-drying oils, artists have time to experiment. As they wait for the oils to dry, they may turn to work on other paintings. Fast-drying acrylics lend themselves to carefully planned paintings – they offer less time to experiment – and allow an artist to focus and work quickly and continuously on a single painting.

After Pirous returned from his travels in the Middle East with the *mushaf* planning team, we spent a few evenings in his study talking about the new direction his work took after 1970. "Before, when I was in abstraction, it was spontaneous, very spontaneous," he explained. Pirous's eyes left me and rested on a make-believe canvas just in front of him. He started working his hand back and forth on the imaginary painting, adding the hurried sounds of slapping brushstrokes:

> Chk ... chk ... chk ... plahk ... plahk ... plahk ... plahk ... taking it again, still damp, or waiting until it was dry, playing with it again. All that spontaneity could no longer be put to work as I visually took what was there in printmaking, very saturated and built, integrated between structure, texture, and color.

He never discussed with me the challenges posed by paints as such. Nonetheless, the move from oils to acrylics took place as he relinquished his interest in expressivist abstraction and made painterly exploration of calligraphic form. That story could be told by the works themselves.

Almost all the paintings made between 1971 and 1974 feature what Pirous calls "expressive calligraphy" (*kaligrafi ekspresif*), usually worked up in oils, acrylics, and modeling paste, or sometimes in just acrylic and modeling paste. These canvases display disfigured Arabic letters on what look to be surfaces weathered by time. In some of the paintings, Pirous has put together legible Arabic characters in a random way, with the purpose of thwarting viewers from reading anything beyond the figure of the character. No one can make out any words. In other paintings, Pirous has deformed the letters beyond the point of legibility, yet they still bear some resemblance to Arabic, as in *White Writing* (*Tulisan Putih*; Plate 6). All the paintings bore titles that referred to writing or to inscribed objects – tombstones, manuscripts, pillars, plaques, and tablets – objects that Pirous associated with Aceh's past. With a few exceptions, each of these paintings captures the symmetry and proportionality we associate with texts and textual surfaces. As many of the titles suggest, these works were also studies in color, efforts at exploiting or controlling the intense acrylic palette.

Expressivist habits died hard. Pirous was not interested in verbal meaning or content, but in the expressive potential of calligraphic *form*. He grappled with a wish to make Arabic a pictorial rather than a verbal sign:

> I did not want to be held back by the dynamic of calligraphic writing, or the form of calligraphy because I still reckoned that it inevitably would be read. But I could be free if I just painted characters by themselves. Some were curved, some upright, some to the left, some to the right, with periods, inside of curves that were very expressive. That gave me more freedom, and also gave me a kind of satisfaction in the dynamic of the lines themselves. I didn't feel it necessary to keep it so that the writing could be read. It was very clear that they came from Arabic. There clearly were *ha, ka, la, mim*, and so on. But I didn't feel it necessary to combine them into a sentence. I was building an atmosphere, an atmosphere. I also sensed that atmosphere in the Qur'an, how a sura came into being, how a sura was brought down as *wahyu*, divine revelation. With Arabic writing, we have a specific icon, a specific world, something spiritual, meditative, and contemplative. I took this up with the idea of not being wrapped up

in the word, but rather, of being wrapped up in the *unexpressed* word. I didn't want to say anything, but wanted to create a certain feeling, an expressiveness.

Pirous's remarks on the pictorial power of calligraphy call attention to the compromise between untethered expression and the careful planning that went into the representation of calligraphic form in built-up surfaces. Preparing the surface of a calligraphic painting required much the same planning and time as preparing an etched plate. Modeling paste carried the calligraphic form, not paint per se. Surface texture was crucial to its representation. So too was modeling paste key to making images of inscribed and embossed objects: plaques, tombstones, fragments of plates, and manuscripts. Built up in this way, textured calligraphic forms occupy the front-most visual plane of Pirous's work. They do not appear in the depths of a painting and, indeed, the paintings from this period usually feature shallow expanses of color.

Perfecting the Work, Sacrificing the Self

With these early paintings, Pirous wished to picture something of his cultural and spiritual heritage. Visually, nothing about them was explicitly Islamic, Acehnese, or Indonesian. All the same, gallery-goers at the time recognized them as innovative and unusual works, and the jury for the Jakarta Art Council selected *White Writing* as best painting at the First Indonesian Biennale in 1974. Differences between legible and illegible Arabic may have been lost on most of the Western or non-Muslim viewers who saw the paintings in Pirous's shows in Jakarta in the early 1970s; for them, Arabic is unreadable or hard to fathom. For some of the Muslims who came to these shows, however, the effect of looking upon images of something that was "written" and "Arabic," and yet unreadable, was disturbing.

Pirous remembers that response to the paintings quite well, for it propelled him further away from spontaneity and self-absorption and into greater discipline and ethical concern:

> When I exhibited, people began to talk. "What are you writing? What are you saying?" "Oh, this painting is very close to the treasure of Islam!" "If this is Arabic writing, maybe this is *Sura Al-Fatihah* (QS 1, The Prologue) and this is *Sura Al-Falaq* (QS 113, The Rising Day)." I thought about it a long time. Those comments pushed me into thinking about art and message. In the beginning, the aesthetic in my works of art didn't know compromise with meaning. Through the visual someone could feel meaning within the abstraction. But think how happy people would be, think about their sense of belonging to works of art like this – the aim of which is to approach Islamic concerns – think how much fuller it would be, if they could look and read, "Oh, this statement is about *Sura Al-Ikhlas* (QS 112, Pure Faith)" and so forth.
>
> I said to myself, "If I do *Sura Al-Ikhlas* the way it is bound together in the Qur'an, it will restrict me in a way that will be extremely awkward for my expressive work."

I saw this as a limit that I didn't want. And then suddenly I woke up. Me, what is my life all about? What is a good person? A good person is someone who is useful to others. If I give them something they want, I will be useful. And so I decided to be useful. This is the concept of *khairuqum an-fa'aqum linnas* – a person useful to others.

So I sacrificed myself, putting a limit on my free expression, but I came back to values that I could explore more frequently and more meaningfully in the Qur'an. I planted in the paintings concepts and philosophical values that would make them more enjoyable. *Aesthetic pleasure and ethical pleasure together.*

Pirous's remarks are exceptionally revealing and bear careful reflection. He is describing a moment of insight and purposefulness no less significant than the one he experienced at the Metropolitan Museum of Art five years earlier. From this moment forward, he more or less abandoned "expressive calligraphy" to pursue what we might call a "Qur'anic aesthetic." It would be an ethical pursuit as well. He began to refashion himself, and his art, once more, in a response to the desires, hopes, and expectations of others.

Pirous speaks of sacrificing his expressive freedom in this new pursuit, a sacrifice of the artistic subjectivity he had so carefully cultivated in his early career. The spontaneity and easy, uncontained expressiveness he had found in abstract painting gave way to reflection, planning, discipline, and control. Choosing a Qur'anic sura, and interpreting it visually, demanded careful preparation. This was something more than moving from emotional to spiritual expression, for surely the spirit can know ecstasy, alienation, or tears. As I suggested in the last chapter, making a "visual recitation" of Qur'anic verse in a painting does not turn on an outpouring of inner feeling so much as on a sincere gesture of submission and surrender to God's one-ness and the divine message. Emotion may play a deep and powerful role in painting Qur'anic verse, but at root, say most Muslims, the effort calls for reason and self-control.

It is fascinating that Pirous mentioned *Sura Al-Ikhlas* (QS 112) as he spoke to me of his reluctance to embrace the demands of painting Qur'anic verse: "I said to myself, 'If I do *Sura Al-Ikhlas* the way it is bound together in the Qur'an, it will restrict me in a way that will be extremely awkward for my expressive work.'" That is, paradoxically, the very sura that appeared in his first Qur'anic etching, *Surat Ichlas*, made just after his visit to the Met. I may make too much of it, but I think Pirous's remark suggests how in the early- and mid-1970s he deeply asso-ciated representing Qur'anic verse with the medium and demanding techniques of etching. As in New York, the feel of materials and play of technique enter into the artist's self-questioning and self-fashioning. Oil paints, for Pirous, were a medium for self-expressive freedom, not for discipline and self-surrender. "Chk … chk … chk … plahk … plahk … plahk … plahk." Recall the sound of slapping brushstrokes working with oils. They might be suitable for capturing the felt or imagined *atmosphere* of *wahyu*, of revelation, but not for the representation of Qur'anic verse. Going back through catalogues and my records of Pirous's work, I find but one Qur'anic oil painting, done in 1974 and sold long, long ago to someone in Jakarta. It is the last painting Pirous would ever do in oils: *Life Will Vanish Like the Dry Grass* – a reference to a verse from QS 18, *Al-Kahf* (The Cave) concerning the shifting and ephemeral nature of life. I am sure Pirous had something else in mind, but with the passage of time the painting's title and themes seem like an epitaph for oils. Fast-drying acrylics – so suited to planning a work and subduing painterly subjectivity – would become the medium for his Qur'anic painting.

Legibility: though not difficult in a technical sense, legibility – treating Qur'anic calligraphy as a pictorial *and* verbal sign – posed the challenges of self-sacrifice and self-surrender. To God, of course, in that the Qur'an was revealed – and already written by the divine pen – in Arabic. Yet legibility, too, is an acknowledging and sacrificial gesture of reply to the desires of viewers who would derive pleasure from seeing and recognizing Qur'anic verse in his painting. A private, painterly language of calligraphic expression won't suffice; it cannot acknowledge or be acknowledged by others. If he is to be useful to others, he must paint Qur'anic verse in legible fashion.

The larger challenges of legibility had to do with the sacrality, perfection, and immutability of Qur'anic Arabic, and with bringing self-expression into line with the Qur'anic message. Not just any sort of legibility would do. Visual recitation of Qur'anic verse in a painting should not have a contingent or chance outcome. Rather, it should aspire to the perfection of the verse being quoted. It is supposed to be flawless. For this reason, Pirous has been careful to present Qur'anic verses in their entirety on his canvases; they never appear broken off in mid-verse. A further gesture has been to keep the passages from straying too close to the margins of a work. I asked Pirous about this once, pointing out that the verses on the likenesses of ancient plaques and pillars never appeared weathered, chipped, broken or obliterated by time. "C'mon, Ken," he chided, laughing at my sudden expression of archaeological realism, "These verses are not found objects. I want to keep them whole and perfect." Surprise and improvisation are not wholly absent from his painting, of course, but Pirous was determined that they should never spoil, corrupt, or take away from the divine verse of the Qur'an. He planned – and would allow – no transgressive or blasphemous gestures toward the Qur'an in his paintings. Muslims, after all, are, as Niloofar Haeri (2003) reminds us, "custodians" of the Qur'an and its language. Thus, Pirous's painterly approach toward the Qur'an displayed his own "good conduct" toward material expression of the divine message. That is, he aimed to enhance the beauty and meaning of the divine message through painterly means.

His calligraphic paintings now started to carry titles taken from Qur'anic themes and passages. Explicit references to Qur'anic themes, sura titles, and verses seem to go hand in hand with his commitment to calligraphic legibility. Pirous's embrace of legible Qur'anic verse did not diminish, however, his penchant for symmetry, his interest in color and texture, or his fascination with objects and forms from Acehnese visual culture. Compare, for example, *The Night Journey* (*Perjalanan Malam*), a Qur'anic painting Pirous completed in 1976 (Plate 7), with the "expres-

62

sive calligraphic" work, *White Writing* (Plate 6), made just a few years before. Both images feature a symmetrically placed pair of weathered, upright panels or plaques, segmented much like inscribed tombstones (*nisan*) found in Aceh. Although both works have simple color schemes, *The Night Journey* uses color and form in iconic fashion: the background field of blue suggests the dark of night; and the vertical luminescent "zip" dividing the painting hints at the *me'raj*, the Prophet's legendary and miraculous night journey of ascension to heaven. The effect is to enhance the Qur'anic passages featured in the painting: its eight verses come from QS 17 *Bani Isra'il* ("The Children of Israel," but usually translated as "The Journey by Night"). The initial verse makes reference to the Prophet's journey and ascension; the others admonish the faithful about the ledger of deeds that will record their every gesture of kindness, justice, obedience, arrogance, and evil during their earthly existence.

Around this time, too, Pirous begins to reveal an eye for the geometries and alluring color contrasts of Acehnese ceremonial fabrics, a form traditionally made by women (unlike the inscribed or embossed monuments and plaques, which are made by men). Look at the 1978 work, *And God the Utmost* (*Dan Dia Yang Maha Segala*), reproduced here as Plate 8. Symmetries and triangular forms reminiscent of Acehnese ceremonial fabric designs called *tilampandak*, rendered in white and turquoise and set off by gold leaf, surround a field of blue in which is inscribed the 189th verse of QS 3 *Al-'Imran* ("The Family of Imran"): "God rules over the heavens and the earth, and God has the power over all things." By way of contrast to the Qur'anic verses in *The Night Journey*, the passages illumined here extol God's perfection and all-determining magnificence – a religious gesture known as *tasbih*. *And God the Utmost* also displayed what would become a signature touch in later paintings. Pirous here used gold leaf for the first time to iconically emboss the surface of a canvas. Its eye-catching radiance and color are for Pirous a sign of God's magnificence, and a painterly gesture of visual *tasbih* – praise for the divine. As with this painting, Pirous never embosses Qur'anic calligraphy with gold leaf, except in occasional adornment of the letter known as *alif* (the Arabic equivalent to the Roman "a"), which he associates symbolically with the name Allah. He reserves this material, then, for non-calligraphic gestures in his work – dazzling shafts of light, luminescent horizons, or liquid springs of gold that appear to bubble up through the surface of a canvas.

These two works alert us to a different register of legibility in Pirous's Qur'anic paintings, the legibility of mood. Pirous does not approach a Qur'anic canvas with critical, transgressive, or ironic intent. The work comports visually and adorningly with the Qur'anic verse featured on its surface. In a sense then, color, form, line, and texture "obey" the Qur'anic message. They have an ethical aim. Their structure and dynamism work iconically and in harmony with the verse, enhancing the visual recitation of the passage. We may also read Pirous's working of color, texture, and structure as a sign of the artist's own surrender to God and the holy Qur'an, and so as a display of *akal*, of reason and self-control. He is making himself legible as well.

63

Perfecting Verse in an Imperfect World

Pirous's effort to please and ethically engage his viewers with legible Qur'anic verse ironically led to trouble with religious scholars from time to time. At one of his shows in the 1970s, an Acehnese *ulama* angrily accused Pirous of defacing and playing around with the Qur'an. The Qur'anic calligraphy on one of the paintings had been damaged during installation: a couple of the diacritical marks needed for Arabic letters had been scraped away inadvertently, leaving the pronunciation and meaning of the verse skewed. For this *ulama*, there was no difference between the Qur'an and a painting of Qur'anic verse. Qur'anic calligraphy had to be without flaw. Legibility thus brought Pirous's paintings under special scrutiny, and even raised a new issue: if a calligraphic figure is both a pictorial and verbal sign, what prevents a splash of paint on a Qur'anic painting from being "read" as an Arabic letter or diacritic?

Much of the anxiety and scrutiny heaped on Pirous's work, in my view, stems from the fissured history and consciousness of Arabic in the Indonesian archipelago (George 2009). With the exception of Arab minorities and Muslim religious scholars in the country, Indonesians typically have not been well versed in Arabic save for the utterances and professions required by Islam (for example, the *syahadat*, or witness to faith). Many are able to read Arabic script with the goal of reciting the Qur'an or another text, but mere recitation of the sound values attached to the letters does not assure grasp of a text's meaning. Familiarity with the local or regional languages once commonly written in Arabic script – such as Jawi – has faded. The Roman alphabet came into ascendancy under colonial rule, driving Arabic writing out of the place it held in everyday communication and sequestering it within religious practices. I believe the key effects were two: first, heightened worries and doubts about locally produced Qur'ans or Qur'anic texts; and, second, further enchantment with Arabic as a script of exceptional power and agency. Despite the reach of modernist Islam and improved rates of literacy in Classical (or Qur'anic) Arabic, many of today's Indonesians regard Arabic script with broad and uncontained reverence. As one Indonesian wag commented to me several years ago, "If an Indonesian buys a fish wrapped in a Jordanian newspaper, the fish will get fried, but the paper will be carefully folded and kept on top of the family cabinet as an heirloom."

Pirous has always had to work in light of this popular enchantment with Arabic in which every instance of Arabic writing is construed as sacred, or as the Qur'an itself. Attitudes like this perhaps assure that Pirous's calligraphic paintings will be greeted with some reverence, but they also place his artworks at risk of public scrutiny by self-appointed scripturalists. Pirous commonly has had to fend off religious authorities who see art and aesthetics as a threat to the integrity and purpose of the divine message, like the Minster of Religious Affairs who had complained that the Qur'an should not be sacrificed for art.

Figure 3.3 Ilham Khoiri (left) and A. D. Pirous (right) at Serambi Pirous reviewing the calligraphy on *The Poem of Ma'rifat*. Bandung. February, 2002. Photograph by Kenneth M. George.

I became familiar with some of these anxieties from my time with Pirous and the planners for the second Istiqlal Festival in 1994, but was surprised at how acute and enduring they were seven years later when I arrived in Bandung to help Pirous with his solo retrospective show in 2002. About a month or so before the show, Arabic specialist Ilham Khoiri began to examine all of Pirous's calligraphic paintings for errors in Qur'anic Arabic (see Figure 3.3). Pirous and Ilham found and set about correcting errors in a couple of paintings, but in the frantic two weeks just before the exhibit was to open, Ilham was drawn to other tasks. Then 160 works traveled to Jakarta for hanging in the national gallery, Galeri Nasional. There, on the eve of the exhibit's opening on March 11, Ilham discovered a rash of further errors in Qur'anic calligraphy. Taking up a penknife, brushes, and paints, Pirous altered more than a dozen paintings – some dating back over two decades or more, and virtually all having been exhibited many, many times without complaint.

I was astonished at the degree of worry over the Qur'anic paintings, and must confess that I felt that altering the works was an act of iconoclasm – a mutilation. "But you've shown these before with no problem," I protested. Pirous and Ilham replied that the Indonesian Muslim community includes three groups: "literalists" who insist on standards for correct and precise transcriptive renderings of Qur'anic verse; "moderates" who forgive or do not even perceive errors; and "liberals" who put emphasis on the Qur'anic message, not its recitation or scriptural reproduction. Even though they acknowledged a plurality of views in the *ummat* on the matter of depicting the Qur'an, their practical response was acquiescence and concession to

Figure 3.4 Pirous correcting the Qur'anic calligraphy on *The Verse of the Throne*, Galeri Nasional, Jakarta, March 10, 2002. Photograph by Kenneth M. George.

literalists. Pirous's gesture of self-censorship bothered me for days, for it seemed too much of a concession to an uncompromising and zealous few. In the long run I relaxed and saw in Pirous's response a consistent effort to perfect his Qur'anic paintings in the most thorough way possible. After all, perfecting the painted calligraphy is a way to show good conduct toward the Qur'an.

Part 2: Making Islamic Art Indonesian

Indonesia is *already* 30 years old?
What is the face of Indonesian art these days?
Is nationalism in art narrow? Chauvinist? Hysterical? Sloganeering?
Does art have to be universal?
Isn't modern art a sign of Western domination in the arts?
Which communities have a role in Indonesian art these days?
Are ethnic and national cultures moving toward a uniform world culture?
Does that mean uniformity in art, in feeling, in tradition and custom?

Perhaps there doesn't need to be Indonesian art.
Because Indonesia is too young?
Indonesia is *just* 30 years old?
> Excerpts from a list of questions: "Exhibition of Screenprints 1975,"
> Artists of Decenta, Bandung

Pirous and Decenta

We should not forget the broader art worlds that summoned Pirous as he worked through the possibilities and dilemmas of Islamic art. Throughout the 1970s and much of the 1980s, patronage for the arts in Indonesia came from the Soeharto government, newly unleashed corporate and business interests, and diplomatic circles. Private galleries and public museums scarcely existed. Indonesia's urban elites and emerging middle- and upper-middle classes did not yet offer a steady market for paintings. In these circumstances, sustaining a reputation as a painter required hustle and connections, and a willingness to do more than just paint. If one sought a national or international reputation, exhibiting in Jakarta, the nation's capital, was essential. After his return from the US in 1971, Pirous found sponsorship for his two Jakarta solo shows in 1972 and 1976 from the Chase Manhattan Bank's art program, and burnished his reputation by winning top prizes in the government-run art biennials in 1974 and 1976. Although his faculty position at the Bandung Institute of Technology gave him some visibility and influence in Indonesia's nascent urban art world, his participation with fellow artists at Decenta did far more to secure his reputation and livelihood, and to nurture his artistic pursuit of Indonesian-ness.

Decenta was a professional, commercial, and upscale transformation of the *sanggar* studios of the 1950s (see chapter 1). It thrived on commission work with the government and with businesses, and assisted studio associates in exhibits, some of which were sponsored by or held at Decenta's gallery. It also ran an art shop at Jalan Dipati Ukur 99 that sold prints, ceramics, paintings, fabrics, and household items featuring design elements taken from or inspired by Indonesia's many ethnic groups. Decenta thus played an instrumental role in professionalizing Bandung's artists, in providing artwork and shaping tastes for an elite clientele, and in sustaining discussion and interrogations of Indonesian art, what it meant, and where it was headed. Pirous and the other Decenta artists put together a working collection of traditional, ethnic, and classical art and art documentation from around Indonesia. As Helena Spanjaard (1988) and Astri Wright (1994) have previously noted, the Decenta artists made a mark for themselves nationally by reworking these materials into a modern idiom. Pirous's thinking about his art thus unfolded as he and his associates were producing artwork and designed environments for the homes, offices, meeting halls, and mosques of an elite clientele.

Soeharto's government, as Pirous keenly recalls it, was "allergic" to Islam through the 1970s and 1980s, fearing it as a potentially overwhelming political force that would threaten the regime and its plans for national development – plans that accorded well with the rise of Western and ultimately global neoliberalism. Given the country's immense Muslim community, Soeharto chose to coopt Islamic groups by establishing state-run Islamic organizations (like the Indonesian Council of Islamic Scholars), pressuring Islamic groups to uphold secularist state ideology, and financing programs of mosque-development and religious education. The Islamic Revolution in Iran in 1979 gave the regime special worry, and led it to tightly monitor or subvert Islamic activism. Pirous seldom involved himself with the national or international political agendas of Islamic parties and movements, if at all, so his interest in Islamic arts and culture never posed an acute worry for the regime. If he embraced Islamic art, it was for the benefit of his nation, not in criticism of it. All the same, it seems clear that Soeharto's authoritarian government dampened prospects for artistic expression of global Islamic solidarities.

The Decenta group did well at securing support from the government and foreign embassies for the purpose of taking part in international shows in Europe and elsewhere in Asia. In this way, Pirous was able to keep an eye on international trends, and gain international visibility, particularly as a printmaker. Although Indonesian artists did not take significant part in it, the World of Islam Festival, organized by Western curators and held in London in the spring of 1976, made a huge splash internationally. Wealthy collectors and institutions, especially those from the Middle East (who were awash with oil-dollars), began to pour into auction houses and galleries around the world looking for Islamic art. The Indonesian government gave the Saudi royal family one of Pirous's calligraphic canvases, *Doomsday* (*Al Qiamah*), as an official gift, and Bahrain's Qur'anic Museum (Al Hayat Museum at the Beit Al-Qur'an) purchased his immense, five-meter long, five-panel Qur'anic painting *Prayer* (*Doa*), for its collection. (While working with the museum's representatives, Pirous expressed misgivings over the accuracy of the calligraphy in this Qur'anic painting. Please don't worry," replied the buyers, "We know that Arabic isn't your native language.") Further purchases would continue to come from abroad.

Pirous's reputation as a calligraphic painter took off. It won him and colleagues at Decenta commission work for calligraphic installations at the Istiqlal Mosque in Jakarta (see Figure 3.5); restorations at the Sabilal Muhtadin Mosque in Banjarmasin and the Baiturrahman Mosque in Banda Aceh; and design work for the mosque at President Sukarno's burial complex in Blitar, East Java. He also spearheaded exhibitions of calligraphic painting and prints around the country, a style that was now beginning to catch on with other Indonesian artists. Yet it was commission work in Aceh that gave him special opportunity to explore Islamic visual culture as the visual culture of his homeland. The occasion was the Twelfth National Musabaqah Tilwatil Qur'an (Qur'anic reading competition), or MTQ, held in June 1981 in the city of Banda Aceh. Qur'anic recitation contests – also known as *tilawah* competitions – are religious events. Convened at the national level, they take on the air of

Figure 3.5 Muhammad. Calligraphic installation at Istiqlal Mosque, Jakarta, designed and supervised by Pirous. Photograph by James B. Hoesterey, 2008. Courtesy of the photographer.

spectacle. Pirous's most taxing effort for this event was staging a massive 3×60 meter display of Qur'anic calligraphy – a passage from Sura Al-Ikhlas written in neon lights for ceremonies attended by President Soeharto. The MTQ, however, also included an exhibition of calligraphic paintings, prints, photographs, and carving, and so further introduced Islamic visual culture into what was usually an austerely conceived, if pleasurably conducted, religious event. It was here that Pirous displayed the first of his works that would make explicit reference to Aceh in their titles: *The Wall of Aceh I-III* and *Prayer XII/Homage to Tanöh Abée*, a serigraph (silkscreen print).

The *Wall of Aceh* series consisted of three mixed-media works prepared from panels, etched copper, and acrylics. *The Wall of Aceh I/The Beautiful Names of God* (*Dinding Aceh I/Asma Tuhan*) included six etched plates bearing twenty-three of the ninety-nine beautiful names for God (*Asma Ul Husna*) and borders patterned after Acehnese fabric design (with some alteration of the traditional palette). *The Wall of Aceh II/Recite in the Name of Your God* (*Dinding Aceh II/Bacalah dengan nama Tuhanmu*) featured a large copper plate shaped and etched in the fashion of an Acehnese *nisan*, or tombstone. The etched plate displayed the first fifteen verses of Sura 96 *Al-'Alaq*, generally regarded as the first sura revealed to the Prophet Muhammad, and thus holding special place for Muslims of any background. Two vertical curtain-like panels framed the copper etching. *The Wall of Aceh lII/Humankind* (*Dinding Aceh III/Manusia*) included Sura 114 *An-Nas* ("Humankind") in full, the recitation of which is considered a talisman for warding off evil:

> In the Name of Allah the Compassionate the Caring
> Say, "I take refuge in the Lord of humankind
> Sovereign of humankind
> God of humankind
> From the mischief of the slinking whisperer
> Whispering evil in the hearts of people
> Whether they be jinn or humankind."

Pirous no longer has any documentation on *The Wall of Aceh III*. The series as a whole suggests to me a visual recitation of Qur'anic passages that most famously lead to mindfulness of God (*dzikir*) and give refuge to believers. I like to think of the paintings as amulets intended to give Aceh spiritual protection in the face of adversity.

The serigraph, *Prayer XII/Homage to Tanöh Abée* (*Doa XII/Penghormatan kepada Tanöh Abée*; Plate 9), makes reference to a famous Muslim library and *pesantren*, or boarding school, founded by the revered historical figure Teungku Tanöh Abée. The library is the pride of Aceh and holds hundreds of religious and historical manuscripts dating back to the seventeenth century. The library is also home to a revered, handwritten copy of the Qur'an, said to have been finished in Mecca at the Haram Mosque by the Acehnese scholar Teungku Syech Abdul Wahab. Arabic calligraphy abounds in this silkscreen print: some from the Qur'an; some from fragments of Acehnese and Malay manuscripts; and even some in the form of seals, such as the one in the lower left that bears Pirous's name in Arabic script. The print in its entirety presents a landscape of sorts, with sky, clouds, sunlight, hills and mountains, sea, and earth – visually suggesting how Aceh is "grounded" in Muslim manuscript culture. Above and below are recognizable Qur'anic passages – QS 3 *Ali 'Imran*, verse 29, "And God has power over all things," and QS 5 *Al-Ma'idah*, verse 74: "Why do they not turn to God and ask His forgiveness? God is forgiving and kind." The text fragments forming hills and mountains in the center of the print are in Arabic and in Jawi, that is, in Malay and Acehnese written in Arabic script (the dominant form of writing in Aceh until the twentieth century).

Pirous himself made a trip to this library in preparation for the 1981 MTQ exhibit, and it was this visit that prompted him to make *Prayer XII/Homage to Tanöh Abée*. In contrast to the spirit of the *Wall of Aceh* series, the Qur'anic passage from QS 5: 74 in this serigraph sets a tone of warning or admonition:

> That trip startled me spiritually, because I didn't think there were still any treasure-houses of authentic Islamic manuscripts like that left. That experience led to *Prayer XII/Homage to Tanöh Abée*. The passage from Sura 5 was for all Indonesians. The shock of modernization and development in Indonesia included several kinds of secular deviations and distractions, ones that were increasingly colliding with the faith.

"Development" was code for Soeharto's unaccommodating ideological vision for the nation's growth and prosperity.

But I intended the passage especially for the people of Aceh. Aceh's identity as the "Veranda of Mecca" (*Serambi Mekah*) was being ruined. The life of the *meunasah* – the prayer and meeting hall – was slowly disappearing because of modern urban values. You could feel the direction of society and economy, ala Jakarta, colliding with local tradition and faith. The passage from Sura 5 is a reprimand, an admonition. Through a visual note about the library at Tanöh Abée, I wanted to warn the people of Mecca's Veranda that an erosion of values was taking place.

These works brought into view for the first time explicit visual references to Pirous's Acehnese identity. Patterns and colors drawn from Acehnese fabric traditions are important, as are forms resembling inscribed objects from Aceh's past – tombstones and manuscripts. The use of Jawi, too, is an innovation of immense significance. Qur'anic Arabic is, of course, common to Muslim communities everywhere and so can only make ambiguous reference to Aceh. But Jawi is characteristic of Aceh and other Sumatran or Malay principalities of the past. Put to use as an icon of identity, Jawi evokes the ethical world of *tamuddun*, culture suffused with Islam.

I place special emphasis on Jawi because, with it, Pirous has found a visual means to indigenize or domesticate Islam, to make it Indonesian. As I have explained, Indonesians broadly regard Arabic script as sacred. To put Indonesian or Malay into Arabic script – into Jawi – is to bring Indonesian into the script of divine revelation. Yet Pirous has also used Jawi in his paintings to place Qur'anic verses into local language. One of my favorite displays of Qur'anic verse in Jawi can be seen in a 1985 work, *A Forest of Pens, a Sea of Ink, the Names of God Never Cease Being Written* (*Sehutan Kalam, Selautan Mangsi Tiadalah Asma Allah Habis Tertuliskan*; Plate 10). The central figure in this work is a tablet, or perhaps a page from a *mushaf*. Surrounding the tablet are lines of Arabic letters-in-embryo, rather like ancient Kufic script, but not yet born into legibility. The tablet is divided in two by a vertical gold strip, a gilded *alif* – the Arabic "A" and the gold connoting Allah. The right half of the tablet is inscribed in Qur'anic Arabic with the twenty-seventh verse of QS 31 *Luqman*, which reads: "If all the trees on earth were pens and all the oceans were ink, with many more seas to replenish them, the words of God would never come to an end. He is indeed all-mighty and all-wise." The left half of the tablet rephrases this verse in Indonesian, using Jawi. The interplay of painted texts in works such as this suggests how Islam and Indonesia are bound together in Pirous's imagination.

In the introductory chapter to this book, I acquainted readers with two Qur'anic mixed-media works that Pirous placed in his home, *At the Beginning, the Voice Said "Recite"* (Plate 1) and *For the Sparkling Morning Light* (Plate 2). These works feature unblemished Arabic and Jawi inscribed on stone-like surfaces, and bracketed by vertical panels of color patterned after Acehnese ceremonial curtains (*tabir*). Qur'anic passages, I have pointed out, characteristically occupy the central visual field in Pirous's paintings. The Acehnese ceremonial patterns on the margins of these two works suggest an eye-catching, ritual display of the Qur'anic verse. The

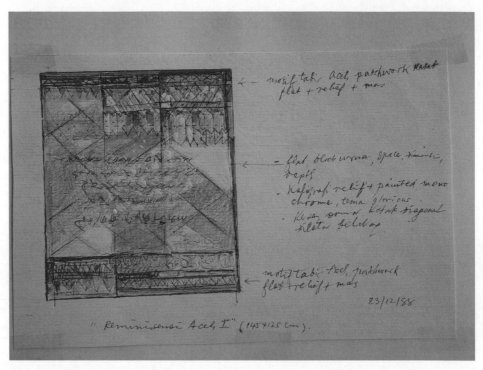

Figure 3.6 Sketch for *Reminiscences of Aceh, I*. December 23, 1988. Note the mix of Indonesian and English. Top right: "Achenese tabir motif, kasab patchwork, flat and relief and gold." Middle right: "Flat black, space, dimension, depth; relief calligraphy and painted in monochrome, glorious theme; trace of the same, diagonal squares in the background." Bottom right: Acehnese tabir motif, patchwork, flat and relief and gold." From sketchbooks kept by A. D. Pirous. Photograph by Kenneth M. George, 2002.

curtain-like panels also could be said to "contain" the Qur'anic verses, rendering the global and universal message of Islam within indigenous, Acehnese aesthetic space. I see reprise of this Acehnese framing in Pirous's sketchbooks from the late 1980s (see Figure 3.6), and in the illuminated pages of the *Al-Qur'an Mushaf Istiqlal* (see below).

In sum, Pirous's effort to make Qur'anic art "Indonesian" relied on a folklorization of Acehnese visual culture. Aceh was for Pirous, by birthright, a visual archive: he borrowed freely, if selectively, from objects and designs that he considered of local manufacture and of collective and anonymous origin – like Jawi, tombstones, fabrics – to supply icons that would adorn and indigenize a global, religious message of divine and transcendent origin. More should be said, however. The iconography in Pirous's work also suggests to me a transcoding of masculine and feminine difference, and a suppression of Aceh's cosmopolitanism and modernity.

Pirous's connection to Acehnese art was of course personal and experiential – it was all around him in his childhood and especially in the figure of his mother

Hamidah. Most of the stories he has told me about Acehnese art leave his father, Mouna Noor Muhammad, out of the picture. "Boss Piroes," it will be remembered, was rather cool toward the arts, finding them at odds with Islam, and perhaps with masculinity. No surprise, then, that as we look through decades of interviews and articles about the painter's views on art, we find that Pirous makes virtually no mention of his father. There is a very telling exception. Speaking with art historian Astri Wright in June of 1988, Pirous described his experience of seeing calligraphic inscriptions in the Islamic art collection at the Met in New York:

> It felt very close, very familiar, very intimate … all those things. When I was still a child in my village in Aceh, all those things were scattered around me, on tombstones, in the mosque, in books, *in my father's Arabic writing.* (Wright 1994: 72, emphasis added)

Pirous says nothing about his mother to Wright, as he would in his conversation with me six years later (see chapter 2). In light of what Pirous has told me over the years, this interview excerpt suggests that Pirous's embrace of a Qur'anic aesthetic is both a return to and a revolt from his father and, by association, to and from the popular religious orthodoxies that shape understandings of art in many Muslim communities. Pirous embraced his father's Qur'anic Arabic and Jawi, but applied them in an unconventional pictorial manner in the largely secular world of modern art.

Another sticking point remains. "Boss Piroes" was not Acehnese by birth, but part Gujarati, part Sumatran. The "foreign-ness" of his father has presented a dilemma in the artist's search for influences, not to mention a problem in the way Pirous thinks about Aceh. The Aceh Pirous has claimed in his art is not the pluralistic and modern Aceh of his youth. It is a "pure" and "traditional" Aceh, uncomplicated by foreign fathers and foreign culture, and recuperated in the figure of his Acehnese mother. The foreign or the fatherly are not jettisoned, but contained by and intermingled with the local and maternal: organizational energies for the visual structure of his work.

Islamic Multiculturalism and the Istiqlal Festivals

As we have seen, Pirous's search for Indonesian-ness through Islamic art was a search for the artistic essences that would help him address and distinguish himself from peers in the global world of modern art. Like it or not, he had to confront the ubiquity of Islamic art. It was not confined to Indonesia or to Aceh.

Pirous, in my experience, has been careful to distinguish Islam, as a set of religious teachings, from Islamic art, as the cultural expression of Islamic thought and experience. Speaking to me thirteen years after the MTQ in Banda Aceh, and almost a decade after his first solo retrospective show in Jakarta (1985), he seemed to have well-rehearsed ideas about how "Islam" and "culture" came together, especially in Aceh:

> It is already a blend, a blending of Islam – the substance of Islam, the teaching of Islam – into law, custom, and the way of life. Cuisine, fashion, everyday domestic life, all of them have been possessed by the substance of Islam, the teaching of Islam. Islamic thought is already built into the local principles that guide Acehnese life.

If Islam was for Pirous a transformational and unifying force, local or national culture was a distinguishing or differentiating one:

> Islam is not Indonesia. Islam isn't Persia, either. Islam is not Turkey. Islam is not Morocco. Islam is Islam itself and can be found everywhere in the world, but with footprints that differ. There is something that is the same, and that is Islam. Islamic art is international, but it is pluralistic and multicultural, too. The factor of "local genius" usually plays a role. When Islam arrived, it gave a certain flavor or aroma to local culture and local art. The teaching that came to Aceh gave rise to something quite different compared to what it spurred in Madura. That's what happened in Indonesia, and in fact, that's what happened everywhere in the world. Persia will be different. So will China. So Islamic art is truly an international art. At the same time, it is pluralistic, and multicultural.

For Pirous, then, Islam is transcendental and universal, while culture is relative, particular, and territorially expressed in the nation or ethnic region. Religious universalism meets cultural particularism.

We can discern in Pirous's account of culture and religion a reprise of issues that were debated during the cultural polemics of Indonesia's early nationalist era (see chapter 1), and that shaped the list of questions that appeared in a 1975 Decenta exhibition brochure (above). Most questions about aesthetic and cultural foundations are political and ideological – questions about solidarity and sovereignty, about ideas that bind and ties that are denied. We have had a glimpse of how making art Islamic and making Islamic art Indonesian were crucial to Pirous's project of self-definition. I now turn briefly to a different, but intimately related challenge for him: fashioning Indonesia's Muslim community into a public that would look upon art as a Muslim concern, and see itself as an art-producing collectivity committed to art as a spiritual and ethical venture.

The opportunity came when President Soeharto began courting the Muslim *ummat* in the late 1980s. The regime showed firm support for Islamic courts and family law; endorsed Islamic banks; sponsored mosque-building and religious education; and helped fund *da'wah* programs. The president himself went on *hajj* – the pilgrimage – for the first time, and took the name Haji Muhammad Soeharto. Pirous and a few colleagues from Bandung met with representatives from several government ministries and hatched plans for the Istiqlal Festival. Inspired by the World of Islam Festival that had been held in London in 1976, Pirous and his associates envisioned a grand festival to be staged in the halls and grounds adjoining

74

Jakarta's Istiqlal Mosque. The plans for the month-long festival came to fruition with lavish patronage from Soeharto, Soeharto's Director General for Tourism, Joop Ave, and corporate leaders eager to expand their influence in government and business circles.

Soeharto shrewdly reworked the discourse of the first Istiqlal Festival from the start. Some months before the festival, Pirous and the other organizers had a personal audience with Soeharto, and proudly showed off their promotional materials. These materials – printed in Indonesian and English versions – announced a "Festival of Islamic Art in Indonesia." Soeharto vetoed the publicity campaign. If the festival was to have his sponsorship, he wanted the name to be changed. Reaching back to the vocabulary of the 1956 manifesto from the Indonesian Islamic Students (see chapter 1), Soeharto declared that the Istiqlal Festival should be known as a "Festival of Indonesian Culture Inspired by Islam" (Pesta Kebudayaan Indonesia yang Bernafaskan Islam). Soeharto wanted the project to display Islam in harness to Indonesian national culture. Nationalist aspirations and sensibilities had to precede and be served by religious ones. Soeharto thus put a check to those interested in the global dimensions of Islam and Islamic culture. At the same time, the festival would serve to publicly acknowledge the role of Islamic faith in the making of the nation.

"Be careful, Pirous, don't get used" warned some friends who feared that the event would be manipulated by politicians and religious hardliners. "That's okay," replied Pirous, "I will use them for my purposes." The first Istiqlal Festival (1991) brought together artists, performers, and religious authorities from around the country. The program included competitions in Qur'anic recitations and traditional calligraphy (*seni khat*); fashion shows; dance performances; an exhibit of contemporary Islamic painting (*seni lukis Islami*); a gallery of traditional and modern mosque architecture; material folk culture (weaving, carving); and religious ceremonies. *Salat* prayers at *lohor* and *maghrib*, at noon and sunset, punctuated festival activities by bringing doors closed until obligatory religious observances were complete. The festival was careful to show how traditional and modern arts could be part of a progress-oriented, national Muslim culture. Further, it underscored the way in which participation in religiously inspired arts could serve as an exercise in piety or *dzikir*; art was shown to be a Muslim concern. By the same token, the festival revealed religious practices and objects as things of beauty and creativity, and worthy of aesthetic reflection. It made Islam "artful." Last, the festival brought across the idea that the arts did not have to be radically sequestered from places or scenes of worship. Indeed, there had been debate and anxiety among some religious authorities about the propriety of running an arts festival so near to a place reserved for prayer and the adoration of God. Pirous and the organizers responded that markets and bazaars had often been erected next to mosques in the Middle East and South Asia; they simply made sure the Istiqlal Mosque proper was free of festival activity, and that all exhibitions and festival crowds were kept from intruding into the sacred space of prayer.

Nothing prepared Pirous or the government and corporate sponsors for the success of the month-long festival. It drew an estimated 6.5 million visitors. Pirous returned to Bandung and organized the design-team for *Al-Qur'an Mushaf Istiqlal*, which was now in the works for presentation at the second Istiqlal Festival in 1995 (see George 1998). Pirous, Noe'man, and Machmud aimed to make an icon of the country's national Muslim *ummat*, viewed as "united and peaceful in its ethnic plurality" (Buchari 1994). Carving Indonesia into forty-two Muslim culture regions, Pirous and his team of graphic artists and computer-assisted-design specialists borrowed freely from the country's folk arts, and came up with border illuminations representing each cultural area. Aceh, for example, was divided into several regions and had designs on eighty-eight pages of the finished text, including the opening and closing sura of the Qur'an, QS 1 "The Prologue" (*Al-Fatihah*), and QS 114 "Humankind" (*An-Nas*) (see Figure 3.7). Within this *mushaf* manuscript, then, we

Figure 3.7 Reproduction of the last page of the *Al-Qur'an Mushaf Istiqlal*. QS 114 An-Nas (Humankind). From Buchari (1994). Courtesy of Yayasan Festival Istiqlal.

see Pirous and his associates trying to reveal the Islamic multiculturalism they feel constitutes Indonesian national culture. We see, too, that the logic of design behind the *mushaf* was the same that long informed Pirous's paintings – selecting a number of patterns from local material culture to serve as icons of ethnic location within the national Muslim community.

I went to Jakarta in September 1995 for the opening week of the second Istiqlal Festival. Arriving a few days before festivities began, I got a room at the same hotel as Pirous, Erna, and a small group of visiting artists from Malaysia. Every morning we would step out into withering heat and find our way by cab through the incessant clog of traffic to the Istiqlal Mosque. The opening approached, with only a day left. Organizers and staff swarmed the mosque's grounds and lower hallways. A very large, very famous, and very sacred *bedug* (a drum used to summon people to prayer – this one from the Sunan Ampel Mosque in Surabaya, East Java) had arrived in a festive procession of trucks and musicians, and was being put in place out front for the gala opening (van Dijk 1998). I watched for a while and then headed into the lower galleries to see the exhibit space.

I recognized many of the curatorial team working with Pirous, Noe'man and Machmud – most of them art students from Bandung – hanging paintings and adjusting display cases and display lights. I had to laugh: for two years I had brought or sent designer suspenders to Pirous from the US to help him out in his fashion contest with Ahmad Noe'man, as they competed to see who between them could more look like Larry King, their television hero. Machmud had joined the contest by mid-1994 and, as I looked around the gallery, Pirous, Noe'man, Machmud, and almost all the male Bandung students were wearing suspenders too. (The few women helping out wore the Indonesian *jilbab*, or headscarf, with jeans or a comfortable skirt). I pulled one of the students, a young painter I knew, away from his work: "What's with the suspenders?" He gave a look around the room and then met my eyes. "Bandungstijl" he deadpanned, making a playful reference in Dutch to the art movement that so influenced the art academy in Bandung earlier in the century with utopian ideas about abstraction, harmony, and color. Fifty years after decolonization, painters from the academy were now known as the *Mazhab Bandung* (Indonesian Arabic for the "Bandung school of thought") for their allegiance to modernism and Islamic aesthetics. And maybe imported suspenders.

The vision for the Istiqlal Festival may have belonged to "Bandung," but it was President Soeharto who presided over the opening ceremonies the next evening beneath a large canopied veranda. Muslim dignitaries from around the world, and from Southeast Asia in particular, were in attendance, as were most of Jakarta's bureaucratic and corporate elites, decked out in batik, *péci*, and *jilbab*. Upon finishing his speech of blessing and welcome, Soeharto sounded the *bedug* to summon all to the festival, and led his entourage and security team into the festival gallery to formally present the *Al-Qur'an Mushaf Istiqlal* to the nation. Festivities lasted well into the night. Pirous, Erna, and I returned to the hotel exhausted, well past twelve or one o'clock.

Doors opened to the public the next morning. The size of the opening-day crowd rivaled those I had seen at Big Ten football games at the University of Michigan. I managed to get inside after noon prayers. The *Al-Qur'an Mushaf Istiqlal* sat in eye-catching display just inside the main entrance to the festival hall. The thousands who crammed into the hall that (and every) day saw not only the *mushaf*, but also a selection of roughly forty contemporary paintings and sculpted works, including a painting by Pirous. I hung around in the swarms of strangers for a time, put a generous and attention-grabbing donation into a collection box set out to assist Muslim victims and survivors of the Bosnian War (1992–95), and headed out into the afternoon heat to my next stop: another 120 contemporary works were on display less than a half-mile down the street and across from Gambir Train Station at the newly established National Gallery (Galeri Nasional). In contrast to the scene up at the Istiqlal Mosque, this site was virtually deserted. Ignored by the crowds, it drew at best a handful of visitors on any afternoon during the week I was in town. I had the place mostly to my video camera and myself.

Largely missed at this overlooked venue was the curators' statement about "contemporary Indonesian art inspired by Islam" (Abdul Hadi et al. 1996). Addressed to many but read by few, the statement acknowledged outside influences on the arts of Islam, and pointed out that ideas borrowed from Western and Asian cultures proved the open-mindedness of Muslim artists. At the same time, those borrowings had to "contain elements in harmony with the basic principles of Islamic teachings." It continued:

> Within the tradition of Islam, art falls inside the framework of service and devotion to God. As such, art is a realization of God's oneness (*tauhid*), and witness and proof to the unity of God. … The art of Islam is also about mindfulness of God (*dzikir*) and spiritual vision (*musyahadah*). … [It] constitutes freedom and independence from all aspects of this material world. … Islam is the very breath of Indonesian culture … and is expressed in the Indonesian aesthetic (Abdul Hadi et al. 1996: 16–17)

Enormous crowds of people attended the second Istiqlal Festival – as many as 11 million visitors by some estimates – but scant few convened there to reflect on Islam and contemporary Indonesian art in any deep or prolonged way. For all the hopes Pirous vested in the festival, and for all the satisfactions he may have derived from it, a broad public for contemporary Islamic art remained fleeting and elusive.

This chapter has looked at some of the circumstances that summoned Pirous to fashion his art work as Indonesian and Islamic. It has not been my goal to portray Pirous's career in excessive detail or in chronological fullness and precision. I have felt, however, an allegiance to showing how his art, his artistic subjectivity, and his views about art have unfolded over time.

Finding recognition on the international stage as an Indonesian artist was a driving ambition for Pirous. Yet he also sought acknowledgment and a reputation as a painter in Indonesia's national art world. These paired and mutually defining ambitions nudged him away from a private and secular expressivist style in search of recognizable signs and emblems of his indigenousness and spirituality. "Expressive calligraphy" gave way to what I have called a "Qur'anic aesthetic," with its highly legible mix of Qur'anic calligraphy, abstraction, and iconography, the last drawn from the gendered "visual archive" of his Acehnese childhood. Fusing Qur'anic calligraphy, the most privileged form of Islamic art, with abstraction – which for a time was the most privileged vehicle of Western modernism – resulted in paintings that revealed a hybrid and decidedly elitist allegiance to the most exalted, if ortho-dox, expressive forms through which one might conjure and distinguish the "spir-itual East" and "secular West." Pirous's work from this time suggests a certain neo-traditionalism, a going back to select and conventional ideas of what counts as "Islamic art" and "Acehnese art," but without scrapping modernist aesthetics. The resulting art is both a critique of modernity, and a way to inhabit or domesticate it.

Legibility, I have suggested, was a way of perfecting his art, lending it both ethical and aesthetic shape. A new sort of subjectivity came into view, and a new sort of intersubjectivity as well. The impulse and self-absorption of modernist expressivism yielded to discipline and self-surrender – to the the Qur'anic message, to the desires of his viewing public in Indonesia – and signaled in his handling of new materials and techniques. With legibility, Pirous imagined a new function for his work – bringing ethical pleasure to viewers. But with that gesture, that new understanding, Pirous brought himself into new relationship with himself. Being useful to others was a path to his very own goodness and pleasure.

4

SPIRITUAL NOTES IN THE SOCIAL WORLD

I don't think of galleries and museums as loud, noisy places. It is true that some hum with the murmurs and whispered chatter of visitors when a big show is on. The mannered and admiring throngs that put themselves on display at openings can surely put up a clamor too. And for years the storms, chants, and digital keening of installation and performance art have sculpted gallery soundscapes. But the white cubes and high-ceilinged halls that house much modern or contemporary painting are often hushed spaces, rather like sanctuaries. We commonly come face to face with paintings in a contemplative quiet that is as much a modern and ideological manufacture as the art itself. Serambi Pirous – "Pirous's Veranda" – was meant as a calm, breezy, and light-filled version of the modernist gallery, a genial and inviting space for admiring Pirous's paintings. It usually is. Then there are the days when the facade of quiet gets a rude slap.

For a few hours one day during my visit in 1994, the gallery was nothing but a din of clattering hammers and rustling sails of plastic. An immense crate had arrived from Bank Muamalat – Indonesia's first "Islamic" bank, established by the Indonesian Council of Ulamas and several government ministries in 1991 as part of an effort to launch a banking industry that would follow the "straight path" of *syari'ah* law. The bank had sponsored an exhibit of calligraphic painting in Jakarta and two of Pirous's works were now being returned from loan. Pirous summoned a team of workers. They fell upon the crate, pried it open, and lifted out the paintings. This was the first and only time I would see *For Nothing Whatsoever is Hidden from God (Tak Ada yang Tersembunyi BagiNya)*. It was the last time Pirous would see it.

80

The painting is a large, abstract work – 125 × 145 centimeters to be exact – and features raised slabs of marble paste, acrylics in panes of gray, cyan, and saturated blue, and not a little gold leaf. A line of Qur'anic verse runs across it, the thirty-eighth verse of Sura 14, the chapter entitled "*Ibrahim*" (Abraham). In this verse, the Prophet Muhammad quotes the prayers of Ibrahim, who says, "O Lord, You have knowledge of what we hide and what we reveal, for nothing on earth or in the skies is hidden from God." Pirous had finished it in late 1993, and had shown it in public just once, at the Jakarta exhibit sponsored by Bank Muamalat. Now it was destined for a new owner. Pirous had personally picked this painting from his private collection for the Indonesian Minister of Religious Affairs, Dr Haji Tarmizi Taher, the figure who succeeded Munawir Sjadzali in overseeing the religious activities of the country's Muslim community.

Whether novice or knowing connoisseur, the Minister of Religious Affairs sure got a deal on *Nothing Whatsoever is Hidden from God*. The bargain was struck earlier that week, when Pirous and Tarmizi together had taken part in a planning session at the Minister's Jakarta home for the second Istiqlal Festival. Tarmizi asked Pirous to pick a painting for him from his own collection, something appropriate for the room where the minister received guests at home. For works measuring roughly a meter square, Pirous usually could command a price of $10–15,000 or more at the time (equivalent to $15,000–21,000 in 2009 US dollars). Very large paintings might carry a price of $30,000. For picking out a painting for the minister, he was paid 12½ million rupiah, about $6,250.

"This is tough," said Pirous, as we watched his team of workers ready the painting for shipping, fixing its frame, rebuilding a shipping crate, and packing it carefully. "If he had picked this out himself, I wouldn't be so worried. But he has asked me to do it. It is a big responsibility." Pirous paused a moment in contemplation. "He is getting a good painting for a good price."

Pirous, I have to say, looked sad. As much as he may have liked the idea of selling a painting to an influential public figure in government and religious circles, I got the impression that he wasn't yet ready to let the piece go. He ran his fingers over the raised calligraphy – a "final touch" – and stepped back a few paces to look the painting over. I wondered whether it was my place to ask if he felt Tarmizi had taken advantage of him, but did not want to press my friend with such a probing question with workers nearby. A few moments later, Pirous reached for a copy of the Qur'an from a cabinet behind him. He leaned back into a chair and opened the Qur'an to Sura 14, verse 38. It did not occur to me that he might want to check the Arabic on the canvas, and I'm not sure that he did. Perhaps he was trying to decide if this was the right sort of Qur'anic passage to send to the Minister of Religious Affairs. I had, instead, a sense that he was brooding, as if weighing the painting's spiritual or emotional pull on him.

Maybe he was so bound up with the picture that letting it go felt like losing a friend. Or, I should say, another friend. Just a few months before, the distinguished painter and critic Kusnadi had paid a visit to Serambi Pirous to look over the artist's private collection, ostensibly to make a set of notes for the Department

81

of Education and Culture. "For informational purposes only," he had explained. The Indonesian government had long been the country's foremost promoter and patron of the arts, effectively dominating the institutional contexts for legitimating and recognizing the work of artists well into the 1990s. The government's institutional support had been a true boon to Pirous for twenty-five years or more. For that very reason, the mere threat of its withdrawal might be enough to haunt him.

On the face of it there was nothing amiss, for Kusnadi, a prominent art writer, had prepared booklets about modern Indonesian art for the Department of Education and Culture. But to Pirous's alarm, an official letter arrived from Jakarta following Kusnadi's visit, asking the artist to donate two works to the "national collection." If one is a citizen, one should of course feel honored at receiving such a request, and therein was the coercion. Kusnadi had identified the two Pirous canvases that the writer felt were suitable for the collection being put together in Jakarta. Pirous was not given the opportunity to choose the paintings he might wish to donate, but was expected to turn over these two canvases for the good of the "national gallery." It was bad enough that these were two paintings to which he was attached and had no desire to give up, but, worse, in 1994 there was no established and curated national gallery or collection. To give two paintings to the so-called "national collection" meant giving up two paintings that would likely find their way into the offices or homes of influential bureaucrats and ministers, or be left to decay in a humid warehouse. "How can I say no?" Pirous protested to me over tea one day. "If I say no, I embarrass Kusnadi, and cause trouble for myself if I want support for an exhibition."

As we have seen, sponsorships and commissions from the Indonesian government have been very important to Pirous, helping him to find acclaim and a livelihood as an artist over the years. That patronage and its sometimes predatory reciprocities remind us that Pirous – like many in the early generation of postcolonial artists in Asia and Africa – have had acute and ambivalent attachments to the nation-state and the idea of national art. The late 1980s, however, saw the beginnings of a boom in art and painting in particular. Although state patronage and censorship continued to throw deep shadows over Indonesia's art world, the energies of neoliberalism and a heated, global market in art started to usher in an era of private galleries and auction houses in Indonesia. Making art, talking about it, and assigning it value no longer relied so deeply on state institutions. Taste and reputation were in tremendous flux.

It was a time of vertigo in the art market. Southeast Asia was flush with capital, and its elites were buying up paintings, both as signs of their cultivation and class status, and as investments. Modern and contemporary "Asian-Pacific art" had caught on, enjoying critical attention in a regional triennial in Australia and a new journal, *ARTAsiaPacific*. Southeby's and Christie's would open auction houses in neighboring Singapore, boosting the traffic in Euro-American art into the region, but also pulling Indonesian painting deeper into international circulation. Prices climbed. A shadow market for fakes and stolen works developed as well (George 1999).

So it was against a backdrop of anxiety, opportunity, sales to an influential clientele, and state patronage for Islamic art and art festivals, that Pirous took me into his company to talk about his life and work as a painter. From the very start of our conversations, Pirous has always called his paintings his "spiritual notes" (*catatan spiritual*). That term has stayed with me through the years. When we speak of taking notes, we commonly imagine putting something into writing for later reference, as when cultural anthropologists write down fieldnotes in the course of ethnographic fieldwork. For Pirous, painting is writing, or at least a kind of writing. After all, both painting and writing share a fundamental materiality; their signifying or semiotic properties presume it, and their social and interpretive lives demand it (Keane 2007). Pirous himself speaks of the "visual language" (*bahasa visual*) in his works, and so suggests some affinities between verbal and visual codes. And, of course, Qur'anic calligraphy brings to his paintings a kind of writing, in the conventional, everyday sense of the term.

As for understanding the ethical dimensions of Pirous's work, the signifying affinities between painting and writing in his work seem to me less revealing than the purposefulness of his spiritual notes. Thinking of paintings as a set of "spiritual notes" is to think of painting as a way to record something for later reflection: an experience, a something said or done, an idea, a quote, or an especially meaningful event. Addressed to himself, the spiritual note invites the painter to review or reflect on the note's substance and the circumstances of its making. Yet the painted spiritual note is addressed to others as well. It invites others to look over the painter's shoulder to reflect on the note's substance, on the note-taker, and the world-under-note. There is an element of time: one comes back to one's painted notes *in and over time*. The spiritual note anticipates further reflection and meditation, as the note-taker returns to be with it. Unless, of course, gift or sale puts it into the hands of someone else. After that, who is to say whether the painting will endure as a spiritual note?

The aim of this chapter is to briefly explore what goes into these "spiritual notes" and what they may have to do with the way Pirous leads his life as an artist. Pirous paints as a way to discipline and improve his sensibilities as both an artist and a Muslim, and to display himself (and those sensibilities) to others. Further still, his personal collection of painted spiritual notes at Serambi Pirous suggests to me an alert – some might say calculating – effort to sustain a particular autobiographical account of himself as an artist, for the paintings in that collection are also the ones that make it into public shows. It is the source of his reputation. As I have hinted already, the art market and the patronage of an authoritarian nation-state have posed challenges to his making and relinquishing his spiritual notes. So we must take into account, too, how Pirous regards the collectors, galleries, investors and religious authorities that express interest or dismay over these notes.

Making Spiritual Notes

God
We are that close
Like fire and heat
I am heat in your fire
God
We are that close
Like cloth and cotton
I am cotton in your cloth
God
We are that close
Like wind and its direction
We are that close
In this time of darkness
I am aglow
in your dimmed lamp

Abdul Hadi W. M., "God, We are That Close"

By the time I began to work closely with Pirous in 1994, he already had well-rehearsed ideas and attitudes about Islamic art. These dovetailed with his longstanding creative regimen of reflection and painting. Not surprisingly, the religious, visual, and philosophical vocabularies surrounding his art work show a kinship with that of other Muslim painters and intellectuals in Southeast Asia, and appear to me broadly in accord (or at least in touch) with the conventions and trends of contemporary Indonesian Islamic thought and practice. In most respects he is an orthodox modernist Muslim, at least when it comes to outward conduct and religious obligations. His thinking about art, meanwhile, shows an affinity for the neo-Sufi spiritualism that was gaining popularity in Indonesia in the 1980s and after (Howell 2001). Very much an artist-scholar, he avidly built a library of books and translations on Islamic art (principally ones in English or Indonesian and published in the 1980s or later), and on Acehnese culture. Pirous's own lectures, addresses, and essays over the years show that his thinking about Islamic art has been enormously influenced by Seyyed Hossein Nasr – with whom he corresponded – and Isma'il Raji al-Faruqi, two scholars of Islamic philosophy, ethics, metaphysics, and art who took much of their training, and produced much of their work, at universities in the US. (Nasr's work draws strongly on Persian Sufism, and al-Faruqi was known for applying Islamic ethics to modern thought. Nasr visited Bandung in 1993 to meet with Pirous and examine work on the *Al-Qur'an Mushaf Istiqlal*, mentioned in chapter 3.). Although he is familiar with traditional and contemporary work produced by Muslim artists in the Middle East, Africa, and South Asia, he seldom mentions them as a source of inspiration or ideas for his painting.

Published interviews with the artist and the reviews of his shows that appear before 1987 make it plain that his regimen of spiritual reflection and painting was by that time well in place. But I find no mention of "spiritual notes" or any use of the sophisticated conceptual vocabulary that shaped our conversations in 1994. For example, the essays for the catalogue that accompanied his solo career retrospective show in Jakarta in 1985 (Buchari and Yuliman 1985) have little to say about the relationship of his work to Islam and Islamic spirituality; they focus instead on biographical detail, the artist's development in terms of theme, style, and technique, and formal characterizations of Pirous's work. (Some paintings are described as *kenangan* – recollections or reminiscences of personal experience.) What might have led him to speak and think about art in a more profoundly Islamic register by 1994? The rise of neo-Sufism and the availability of books on Islamic art are a large part of the answer. All the same, some other factors deserve consideration. In 1987, Pirous's friend and elder colleague, Muslim painter Ahmad Sadali (see chapter 2), passed away. Not long after, in 1988, Pirous and Erna went on the *hajj*. The passing of his friend and the experience of making the pilgrimage did not leave him spiritually untouched. It is about this time, too, that the Soeharto regime began to court the Muslim *ummat* by promoting Islamic concerns. Plans for the Istiqlal Festival were underway by 1990, and Pirous's prominent role in helping define Islamic culture for the project led him to greater depth and sophistication in "thinking with" an Islamic conceptual vocabulary.

For Pirous, Islamic art is *any* art or artwork that is in harmony with the Qur'an, its values and its teachings, and with the idea of *tauhid*, the one-ness of God. Calligraphic painting is only one of its possibilities. Art that takes inspiration from the Qur'an, however, holds a special place for him. As he explained to me one afternoon at Serambi Pirous, painting can be a way of interpreting the Qur'an:

> The Holy Qur'an itself may not be changed, but to understand it, you must be free to interpret it. Each and every person may interpret it and glorify its essence, its message. So, I take a verse and I try to animate it with my personal vision, with my personal understanding. Now, why did I take that verse at that moment? And what is it that I want to say in such a personally meaningful way? If it all comes together and is read by someone else, that's what you call expressiveness, that's what you call spirituality. The meaningfulness might come from something I read, something I saw, something I dreamt about, or something I heard in a story that gets into the back of my head. And if it stirs me as an artist, I will want to put it onto my canvas. When I express it in visual language, that's when I use aesthetic knowledge: composition, color, texture, line, rhythm, everything. I use all of that to make my dream real, so that it can be felt. So that I can tell a story. At last, the painting, its meaning, the Qur'anic verse, all of it becomes clear.

Painting, then, is a way of interpreting and grasping the Qur'an as it illumines and is illumined by meditative vision and personal experience. It is a way of animating and adorning the Qur'anic message.

As we saw in the curators' statement at the second Istiqlal Festival (chapter 3), Pirous and many of his colleagues feel that Islamic art is art that is subordinate to, in accord with, or devoted to the faith, just as Muslims are subordinate to God in their surrender to Him (the term *islam* means "submission to God"). Sincere surrender and submission are key to this frame of understanding; there is no room here for blasphemy, for irony, or for an art that calls the faith into question (the sort of transgressive or critical work that plays such a large and important role in our contemporary and largely secular art worlds). Rather, Islamic art should spring from *batin*, one's inner being, as it is guided by *tariqah* (the spiritual path) and *haqiqah* (divine truth). Making and encountering art are thus creative opportunities for *dzikir*, mindfulness of God. Art should promote spiritual contemplation (*tafakkur*) and inner vision (*musyahadah*), and, like Sadali before him, Pirous sometimes speaks of *dzikir visual*, or "visual *dzikir*" as the chief feature of his paintings.

For some Indonesian Muslims, *dzikir* is a basic, rather than exceptional, part of spiritual life. A friend of mine, Nurmawansyah Rahman, explained to me that *dzikir* for him was an aspect of the daily *salat* prayers that are an obligation for all Muslims:

> *Dzikir* means remembering and drawing oneself close to Allah. Generally speaking, people practice *dzikir* in *salat*-prayers by reciting praises (*tasbih*) to God: Subhanallah (33 times), Alhamdulillah (33 times), and Allahu Akbar (33 times). The Qur'an teaches us to remember Allah wherever we are, and especially in *salat* prayers. *Salat* is an ocean or sea of *dzikir*. *Dzikir* is medicine for cleansing the heart (*tazkiyah*), and with it we may feel calm, peaceful, and content. (personal correspondence 2004)

For other Indonesians, however, *dzikir* is a practice associated with *tasawwuf*, the process of becoming a Sufi. In that context, *dzikir* is part of the effort to interiorize a mystical "being-with" Allah through meditative recitation of the Qur'an or of God's ninety-nine "Beautiful Names" (*Asma Ul Husna*). Different Sufi schools have cultivated distinctive methods of *dzikir*, methods that could include bodily posture, breathing, music, chant, fasting, silence, and amulets. Overall, then, vision has not been an especially prominent avenue for *dzikir* except in the visualization of God's names in calligraphic form, and in the mystical experience of light, the color of which may be correlated to one of the six or seven *lata'if*, or "subtle senses," in Sufi psychology (Ernst 1997: 105–9).

When Pirous speaks about visual *dzikir*, I believe he means to suggest how there is something in experiencing modern art that has brought him, and that might bring others – even in the "white cube" of secular gallery space – to an awareness or experience of the divine. The trick is to persuade Muslim viewers that art does not deflect experience of the divine, but facilitates it. For Pirous, *dzikir* and *tafakkur* are aspects of art that can enrich one's *batin*. Making art in this way may deepen one's inner faith and religious understanding (together, *iman*), and help lead outwardly to *ihsan*, showing one's goodness and responsibility to others in everyday conduct (*mu'amalah*). It is in that sense that Pirous long ago pledged himself to be useful to others through making Islamic art, and Qur'anic art in particular. Giving others aesthetic and ethical pleasure is for him an act of *ihsan*, of goodness.

Not every Muslim thinks of art this way, nor should they be under any compulsion to do so. As I mentioned in the introduction to this book, diversity, debate, and change are the rule in Muslim art worlds, not timeless orthodoxies. In working through these ideas about Islamic art in the way that he has, Pirous has sought to comport himself with a particular line of theological and art historical thought, one that in its encounter with the West has tried to refigure modernity in light of Islamic ethics and spiritualism. Pirous typically puts his art into visual and iconographic comportment with this school of thought too. Abstraction (as an expression of divine being and divine principles) is its chief feature, rather than the imitation or mimetic representation of this world. Although recursive geometries of line and form enjoy popularity, Qur'anic calligraphy customarily and consensually stands as the preeminent form of Islamic art. In fact, Arabic calligraphy is itself abstract. It does not imitate anything in nature, but renders the miracle of language through abstract (if conventionalized) form.

In this framework, visual representation – except by way of abstract renderings of divine speech and divine principles – could be considered a distraction, and worldly. In Islam, God and God's essence are transcendent and elude representation. It should come as no surprise, then, that a major theme in Islamic art discourse is its fluctuating, uneasy, and troubled regard for representational and figurative form: representation looks away from God, or so a believer might argue. Pirous knows that many Muslims look upon human figuration with suspicion or condemnation, even if there is no explicit theological basis for censoring them. (The theological injunctions are against idolatry, not image-making per se.) With minor exception, then, he has avoided human figuration throughout his experimentation in Islamic idioms. Abstraction is his path to picturing Islam.

In this light, we see here one reason why Pirous feels modern abstract art was so congenial to Islamic aesthetics. Yet I would argue that the congeniality between modernist approaches and Pirous's brand of Islamic art went beyond questions of abstract form. Both were preoccupied with interiority and interior experience, albeit in different metaphoric and ideological registers. The Western (and decidedly masculinist) avatar of the abstract modernist strived for the signature expression of an inner self; painting enjoyed a privileged status as the most direct expression of a unique interiority and subjectivity. As Michael Leja (1993) has observed, the abstract modernists of the US (and Jackson Pollock in particular, in Leja's study) were exceptionally drawn toward psychoanalytic and anthropological writings in understanding their own artistic subjectivity, and thought of interiority as space belonging to primitive and unconscious drives, rationalities, and emotions. In contrast, my time with Pirous suggests that the Muslim artist cultivates an interiority predicated on sincerity (*ikhlas*), conscious rationality (*akal*), and pursuit of the divine. *Originality and self-expression are not missing, but are beside the point.* For a Muslim painter like Pirous, one aspires to goodness and the subordination of the self to the divine. Discipline, reflection, submission, and responsibility are paramount, not sovereign selfhood.

We should not be surprised, then, by Pirous's fascination with Qur'anic calligraphy. As Nasr (1987: 19) writes, beautiful calligraphy is a sign of "a disciplined mind and soul." Pirous, I want to note, has not formally studied or sought mastery of the six classical styles of Qur'anic calligraphy (Ar., *aqlam i sitta*), and, in my experience, he almost always bristles at being called a *khattat*, a calligrapher. He thinks of himself as a painter (*pelukis*) who makes contemporary art (*seni rupa kontemporer*), not classical calligraphic art (*seni khat*). He is concerned with a painting or a work of art in its totality, not just with calligraphic form. He takes what he feels to be the universal visual language of modernist abstraction to express his inner reflections on the transcendent magnificence of *tauhid* and the Qur'an's lessons.

Pirous's objection to being called a *khattat* stems in particular from his interest in non-calligraphic expression. Already we have seen how he has explored Acehnese visual culture for forms that he associates with Islam, such as tombstones, manuscripts, fabric designs. He takes inspiration from nature, as well, simplifying and abstracting it in imaginative search of its basic forms, its color, and its light. For Pirous, the miracle of God may be found inscribed in nature. Like the Qur'an, then, he finds nature itself worthy of painterly meditative reflection:

> Actually, in my paintings you can find a penchant for abstract patterns and shapes taken from impressions of nature. Things around me, impressions of water, land, sky, and earth. It's very abstract. ... So paintings like these derive from a meditative process that offers visions of signs and those other things in nature that make me aware, as a Muslim, of the Creator.

We can see explicit meditations on nature, for example, in paintings like *Green Valley* (*Lembah Hijau*; Plate 11) or *The Horizon on the Southern Plain* (*Kaki Langit Dataran Selatan*; Plate 12). Paintings such as these, Pirous would have us understand, are works no less "spiritual" or "Islamic" than Qur'anic calligraphy. In fact, he has remarked to me that non-calligraphic paintings often require more work and forethought that his calligraphic ones:

> Without calligraphy, it takes a lot of work to convey a spiritual mood or idea. You have to figure out how to use color, light, form, and texture to render a spiritual feeling or concept. It is easier with Qur'anic calligraphy. You can express your moods, your philosophy, and ideas in a more direct way, and mesh them with the work.

For these reasons, we should not overlook Pirous's meditations on nature and worldly form as part of his project in making "spiritual notes."

For example, over the many years I have known my friend, he often has remarked on the transient (*fana*) nature of life, about its fragility and impermanence. Not surprisingly, the theme of life's transience and God's infinite, eternal being finds

Figure 4.1 *Ephemeral Mountain: Travel Note VI.* 1989. 145 × 100 cm, marble paste, gold leaf, and acrylic on canvas. Photograph courtesy of Yayasan Serambi Pirous.

expression in his spiritual ruminations on nature. One of his "spiritual notes" from going on the *hajj* in 1988 was inspired by reflections of this kind (Figure 4.1). It is called *Ephemeral Mountain: Travel Note VI (Jabal Fana, Catatan Perjalanan VI)*. For years Pirous kept it in his home, on a wall near the entryway:

> This is a note from the journey between Mecca and Medina, a few hundred miles along a road that splits the desert. On both sides of the road there are rocky deserts and mountains, very sharp and hard, with foreboding colors. This made me think about something the whole trip long: is this landscape eternal or ephemeral? Seeing the strength and ferocity of these stones, it was as if they were eternal. But in fact, that's not so. One day all this will be gone. It is something ephemeral. So this work offers a reflection on the brevity of human life in comparison to infiniteness of eternal life. This is a look back at time. Time. This is a note that I think is extremely spiritual, one that can be expressed without using a single verse from the Qur'an. It can be seen directly in nature. And that has meaning for us in life.

Sky and earth and the horizon on which they meet often provide a backdrop to the Qur'anic passages in Pirous's calligraphic works. As I noted in chapter 3, textured calligraphic forms occupy the front-most visual plane of Pirous's paintings. They do not appear in the depths of a painting. Typically, then, we find the revelatory verse of the Qur'an on textured abstractions of earth or weathered, broken stone, and placed below his representation of earth's horizon. For just one example, look at the painting in Figure 4.2, *Come Back to the Lap of Your Lord with Devotion (Pulanglah ke Haribaan Tuhanmu dengan Ikhlas)*, which presents the last four verses of QS 89 *Al-Fajar* (The Dawn):

Figure 4.2 *Come Back to the Lap of Your Lord with Devotion*. 2000. 70×72 cm, marble paste and acrylic on canvas. Photograph courtesy of Yayasan Serambi Pirous.

> O tranquil soul
> Return to your Lord, well pleased and well pleasing
> Come in among my servants
> And enter into my garden

The Qur'an is thus revealed upon and read against his "earthen" or "geological" representation of time and life's transience. The sky, by way of contrast, is a space of light, color, and depth associated with eternity and the vastness of God's firmament. We do not find Qur'anic verse in the painted space of the sky. (This is not true of his printed etchings or serigraphs. There, Qur'anic verse may appear in the sky, as in Plate 9, *Prayer XII/Homage to Tanöh Abée*.) Some viewers might find such symbolism or iconography clichéd, rather than inspiring. We should keep in mind, however, that the Qur'an itself uses the whole of nature as a metaphor of God's magnificence and dominion. Pirous's iconographic renderings of earth and sky are legible, and in their legibility they may offer viewers – and especially Muslim viewers – the pleasure of recognizing familiar symbolisms.

Calligraphic symbolism appeals to some Muslims, but, in my experience, Pirous has not taken much interest in it, save for his associating the first letter of the Arabic alphabet, *alif* – and the vertical stroke needed to write it – with Allah. But he does have a working philosophy of abstract and iconographic form that relates them to ethical thought and conduct. As he remarked to me in 1994, he thinks of painterly line and space as symbolizing ethical relationships:

> Vertical relationships are with God. Horizontal ones are between people. Diagonal relationships are with our environment. As they say, "*Hablun min Allah, hablun min an-nas.*" *Hablun min Allah* – love for Lord Allah. *Hablun min an-nas* – love for humankind. *Rahmatan li al-'alamin* – compassion and care for nature, and for all of the environment.

We should think of these three relationships, and their "triangular" connection, as ethically charged dimensions of Pirous's spiritual notes. We see them in different ratios in his work, and at play in his harmonization of color, space, and balance. For example, the gilded vertical gestures of *It Pierces the Sky* (*Menembus Langit*) in Plate 13 and *The Night That is More Perfect than 1000 Months* (*Malam yang Lebih Sempurna dari 1000 Bulan*) in Plate 14 make painterly reference to Qur'anic revelation as the principle axis of human relationship to God. (*The Night That is More Perfect than 1000 Months* features all five verses of QS 97, *Al-Qadr*, "The Night of Destiny," and refers to the night of "destiny" or "power" when the Qur'an was first revealed to the Prophet Muhammad.) Even those works that might appear as straightforward mediations on form, such as *Triangle with an Ascending Vertical Gold Line* (*Segitiga dengan Garis Tegak Lurus Emas*) in Plate 15 or *Meditation on a Circle with a Vertical Line* (*Meditasi Lingkaran dengan Garis Vertikal*) in Plate 16 seem to comport with the spiritual geometry with which Pirous describes ethical relationships.

At the same time, we need to refrain from looking for a "triangular" spiritual geometry in each and every painting, as if Pirous pictorially applied his ideas in a rigid or deterministic way. The strong horizontal gestures of *Ephemeral Mountain: Travel Note VI* (Figure 4.1) and *The Horizon on the Southern Plain* (Plate 12), for example, appear unrelated to human sociality; they have much more to do with finding the spiritual grandeur of nature, or the divine written into the world. Pirous has never told me so, but it seems to me most helpful to think of *hablun min an-nas* as an intersubjective and interpretive relationship – a scene of human encounter, I called it in the introduction to this book – forged on the "horizontal" axis between the work of art and the viewer. It is the axis of aesthetic and ethical communication between Pirous and those viewing his art. For that very reason, it would also be the axis, or line of sight, along which Pirous's works become politicized. That is, quite apart from the political gestures a painting may seemingly contain, it is in the painting's public display that a politics truly enters the picture.

91

Pirous's notion of spiritual notes thus applies to both calligraphic and non-calligraphic paintings. As an exercise in *dzikir*, painting does not require Qur'anic reference. But, given that Qur'anic passages define and illumine so many of his "spiritual notes," I should say something about how he selects passages for his work. Very generally, he chooses a passage after periods of reading and personal reflection grounded in a lifetime acquaintance with the Qur'an, and while observing the world around him. Reflection on Qur'anic verse thus leads to an idea for a painting, a set of sketches and notes, and in time, the painted work itself. A glance at Pirous's sketchbooks suggests another process as well, one beginning not in Qur'anic reflection but in an image or a sketch. That is, an image of painting comes into view in his mind's eye or on his sketchpad *prior* to Qur'anic reflection. It is an image that summons a verse, not a verse that summons an image.

Whether he begins with a Qur'anic passage or with an image, Pirous's outlook is one of optimism, and he strives for sincerity and harmony, which he regards as two key principles in Islamic art. For this reason, he more frequently begins with or turns to verses that admonish the faithful to do good, that urge us to be useful, or that praise the magnificence of God and God's creation. Seldom does he select passages to frighten; it goes against his optimism and his search for spiritual and aesthetic harmony. He has, of course, used some of the Qur'an's most famous passages for his art, such as the "Verse of the Throne" (*Ayat Kursi*, which appears in QS 2, *Al-Baqarah* verse 255), considered by most Muslims to be the most glorious verse in the Qur'an. And we shouldn't overlook his tendency to use the short, hymnic suras that are said to be the first revelations to the Prophet Muhammad. These early revelations, Qur'anic expert Michael Sells (1999: 3) points out, include the verses most often memorized, quoted, and recited by Muslims around the world. Thus, we see Pirous rendering as art the very sura upon which so many Muslims have grounded their faith.

I should not leave out Pirous's taste for the mystical moments when the divine and the human are so close, as on the Night of Destiny during the holy month of Ramadhan. Look again at Plate 14, *The Night That is More Perfect than 1000 Months*. It includes all of QS 97, *Al-Qadr*, which makes lyrical reference to the night the Qur'an was revealed to the Prophet:

> In the Name of God the Compassionate the Caring
> We sent it down on the night of destiny.
> And what could be said to you about the night of destiny?
> The night of destiny is better than a thousand months.
> The angels and the spirit come down with permission of their Lord for every task
>   and errand.
> There is peace that night until the rise of dawn.

Michael Sells (1999: 101) says that this sura is at the heart of the *qadr* festival, a Ramadhan event during which a youngster may try to fast for the first time, or the occasion for a nightlong vigil of prayer and meditation by an individual, family, or community. The radiant gold zip in Pirous's painting, set here against a figural backdrop of earth, horizon, and a deep blue night sky, suggests both descent of the divine sprit on that night, and the warm, luminous love and awe a Muslim might feel for God. Exalted as this painting's theme might be, all of Pirous's works that feature Qur'anic calligraphy potentially bring Muslims into intimate relationship with God. Reading Qur'anic verse potentially fills their minds with nothing but revelation and divine grace, and so deflects inner turmoil and burdensome physical sensations. It lets Muslims give themselves over to God. In short, the verses are signs of revelation and miracle that prepare one for remembering and being with God (cf., Graham and Kermani 2006: 125).

It is true that Pirous has avoided some Qur'anic elements. Chief among them are the mysterious syllables that appear at the beginning of several sura: *alif lam mim*. As he insisted in our conversations in 1994:

> I don't use writing like that, because my point of departure is to give meaning. I want to give a message. I want to give a moral. I want to give ethical value. I want to give something beneficial to our daily lives, as a warning to us. The writing *alif-lam-mim*? Nobody knows what the meaning is. I have no interest in using that.

Although it is typical of him to steer away from mysterious, dark, or foreboding passages in the Qur'an, it is also striking how often Pirous is drawn to the same Qur'anic verses over and over. Each verse seems an inexhaustible source for artistic exploration. Similarly, his painter's repertoire of iconographic and compositional gestures may seem finite or limited, but it too permits endless variation and nuance.

None of Pirous's "spiritual notes" should be called finished until he has signed and dated them (by year) and given them titles. Title, date, and signature, of course, are but further ways to make these spiritual notes legible to oneself and others. But we might put it a little differently: title, date, and signature give a painting a social destiny, or at least anticipate one; they tell us something about the others to whom the painting is addressed. Pirous does not sign his paintings in Arabic script, but in Roman. He composes titles in Indonesian and English, writing them on the rear of the canvas in Roman letters, never in Arabic script. As for dating the works, Pirous does not use the Islamic (or Hijri) lunar calendar, but the modern Gregorian (or international civil) calendar. (A few works do include a date in Arabic script as part of the painted image itself.) These paintings thus invoke and dwell in secular time and secular language. I don't think this is a concession on Pirous's part at all. Although the paintings draw inspiration from religious experience, and may even lead to it, they exist largely within the horizons of a secular art world inhabited by artists, curators, gallery-goers, journalists and writers, collectors, and investors. It is true that Pirous's public is (at present) largely Muslim. All the same, he is not summoning them to religion, but to art. The paintings may have religious effects, but Pirous does not give them religious purpose. Not everyone sees it that way, of course.

Displaying and Selling Spiritual Notes

Making his spiritual notes public or putting them up for sale has brought Pirous face-to-face with the contradictory energies and attitudes of those who try to keep "art," "religion," and "commerce" from mingling with one another. Pirous himself has conflicted views and feelings about the ethics in making, displaying, and selling spiritual notes. But let me turn first to the charges from others.

Paintings that featured Qur'anic verse made Pirous vulnerable to two complaints: first, "selling" the Qur'an, and, second, pursuing *da'wah*, that is, campaigning or proselytizing for Islam. In most instances, Pirous might reasonably shrug off the first charge. After all, Indonesia is strewn with stalls that sell Qur'anic materials – decals, books, CDs, DVDs, dashboard and living-room kitsch, Qur'anic text-messaging services, calendars, and the many other accessories consumed in expression of middle-class popular piety. But the charge of "selling" the Qur'an came from his elder friend and rival, Ahmad Sadali, a disapproving remark that stung Pirous and for a time brought strain to the friendship. I do not know the circumstances that led Sadali to make the remark, but what it implied seems plain enough: Pirous was building a reputation on painting Qur'anic verse, as well as commanding handsome prices for his canvases. Calculated personal gain or God's blessing? Sadali seems to have suggested that this was unethical use of the Qur'an.

The more serious and frequent charge came from conservative *ulama*, a few Muslim organizations, and some journalists: that by making calligraphic paintings Pirous was practicing *da'wah*, an activity that properly should be left to religious authorities. As we learned from Pirous in the introduction to this book, Indonesian religious authorities seemed "blind to art" well into the 1990s. For many of them, art was and is a superfluous and distracting activity and does not have a place in understanding or talking about the Qur'an; for others, like the former Minister of Religious Affairs, Munawir Sjadzali, art was a potential threat to the Qur'an. Indeed, for not a few Muslim organizations, art was *haram*, forbidden. One journalist, interviewing the artist for *Tawakal* magazine in 1987 pressed Pirous for clarification on the matter of *da'wah*:

Tawakal: What is it that you want to do when you use verses of the Qur'an as the source for your calligraphy?

Pirous: I want to give further value to the meaning of the verse through a kind of commentary that might lead someone toward a deeper aesthetic appreciation of God's greatness or glory, for example.

Tawakal: Perhaps it is a kind of interpretation (*tafsir*) in the form of a calligraphic painting?

Pirous: Yes, that's true.

Tawakal: As a Muslim, how far would you go in picturing the ties between aesthetics and communication in calligraphic work as a medium of *da'wah*?

Pirous: *Da'wah* is a very broad term. Maybe I am wrong, but I would say *da'wah* is when we communicate with conviction. If you use the term *da'wah* to mean the spreading of religious philosophy and teachings, you probably could not include me. I am trying through the language of beauty to give people something that will stir them to appreciate ethical values. By this I mean those ethical values that have a close connection with the values found in Qur'anic verse.

Tawakal: You are not aware that you are performing *da'wah* in your calligraphic works?

Pirous: I can't really answer that because I don't know. But I'm happy when I hear that someone has been touched by one of my paintings, for instance, when they feel cooled, or taken and caressed, and given an "acting spirit" that will help them become more deeply convinced by what is said in the Hadith or the Qur'an. When someone once came and asked for a painting called *Al-Lail* ("The Night", QS 92), I thought that they would be able to connect with spiritual things through several paths, through reading, through seeing form, and so on. I should tell you, however, that they couldn't read Qur'anic verse. Nonetheless, they felt calm and cool when they gazed at it.

In this exchange we see Pirous sorting through some of the ambiguities that surround his calligraphic work. The interviewer from *Tawakal* seems convinced that the verbal dimensions of Pirous's calligraphic paintings promote Islam. In replying, Pirous calls attention to the pictorial dimensions of his calligraphic paintings, to a "language of beauty" (*bahasa kaindahan*) that speaks of ethical values (*susila*). His paintings don't teach Islamic doctrine, he suggests, and so should not be considered as a vehicle of *da'wah*. But they can stir spiritual feelings of calm and coolness, even among those who cannot read Qur'anic verse, like the visitor who wished to buy *Al-Lail*. Pirous does not call his paintings "sermons" (*khotbah*), even if they do admonish or praise. They are spiritual notes (*catatan spiritual*) intended to give himself and others spiritual enjoyment through aesthetic and ethical reflection.

The complaint from Sadali and the one from religious authorities do not concern painting as such, but instead have to do with bringing a Qur'anic painting into public view. For some Muslim religious authorities, it is the public exhibition of Pirous's Qur'anic paintings that counts as *da'wah*, not their display in the homes of the artist or his collectors. Sadali, meanwhile, found it unseemly that Pirous would carve out a public reputation among his Bandung peers through the painterly display of Qur'anic verse; as his own work showed, Sadali had no objection to drawing inspiration from the Qur'an. The two complaints, then, call into question Pirous's judgment and conduct as a public figure, not as a private artist or believer. Let me return, then, to a matter I raised earlier in this chapter, the question of when and in what circumstances Pirous began to use the term "spiritual notes" to describe his paintings. To the several factors that coaxed him into a more spiritual and Islamic conceptual vocabulary, I believe we should add the criticisms leveled at

Pirous for selling the Qur'an or performing *da'wah*. Declaring his paintings "spiritual notes" downplays their life in public, and instead highlights their personal significance or connection to the artist. It blunts the force of criticisms brought against him. At the same time, the gesture of showing one's personal "spiritual notes" in public comports well with the modernist tradition of putting one's unique subjectivity on painterly display.

The exchange in the *Tawakal* interview also tips us off to how Pirous's spiritual notes come into the possession of others. Pirous tells the interviewer how someone came to him to *ask* for a painting. Although we are not told whether he lets the painting go, we see the artist sizing up the buyer, and getting a sense of the pleasure that the latter finds in gazing at the work. I have not been present for more than a few sales involving Pirous's "spiritual notes." All the same, I want to argue that the exchange of a painting between the artist and collector involves more than a passing commercial transaction, but rather a complex negotiation of social and ethical relationships that might deflect the perils of market activity. The presiding tone of exchange between Pirous and a collector is one of friendship and solicitude. The vast majority of spiritual notes that Pirous has decided to relinquish go into the hands of friends, acquaintances, and collectors with whom the artist has developed friendly relationships. Indeed, Pirous attributes much of his professional success in life to his capacity for friendship. "I have done well as a painter," he once told me as we relaxed at his hillside home, "because I always have liked being with others and making friends."

As I mentioned at the outset of this book, not a few Indonesian collectors and gallery-owners complain that Pirous keeps his best work for himself – a select collection of spiritual notes, as should be clear by now, inspired by the Qur'an or special life experiences. Holding on to all your paintings is, of course, no way to make a living as an artist. Pirous has sold hundreds of paintings, and not just to friends. But reserving the spiritual notes, holding them back from the market, suggests to me a way in which Pirous may be trying to care for the fate of these works and the social relationships around them. In fact, I would say he is very apprehensive about the market for his paintings and the market more generally, as if it posed a certain danger to him and his friends, and to his spiritual notes.

Pirous routinely sells small, non-calligraphic studies, prepared in acrylics and modeling paste and measuring under 50×50 cm. These he usually would price by size. Individual buyers and collectors might come to Serambi Pirous to look them over, but with the rise of private commercial galleries in Jakarta and Yogyakarta in the late 1980s and early 1990s, Pirous has had abundant opportunity to place sets of paintings with gallery owners and agents. He also licenses photographic reproductions of his large calligraphic works to banks and business firms who have plans for company calendars and Lebaran (Idul Fitri) holiday cards. Pirous routinely donates 2 percent of his income from sales and licensing fees to Islamic charities as *zakat*, one of the five duties incumbent on every Muslim to perform, and done to improve the welfare of the poor. Although he knows that collectors will view their purchases as investments, he takes exception to investors who snap up a number

96

of his paintings without regard for the art itself. As just one example, I recall his grumbling back in 2002 upon being told by a Jakarta gallery owner that an investor had bought eleven of his paintings without looking at the works. The investor's art consultant had spotted the paintings, took out his cell phone, contacted the investor, and then took instructions to buy the lot. "The paintings will just sit in a warehouse. He doesn't care about them," muttered Pirous. "I don't like it when people do that. That's not about art, that's just about making profit."

Spiritual Notes and Friendship

Let me turn, then, to the Qur'anic paintings, the "spiritual notes" that typically wind up in the hands of friends or acquaintances who collect art. As a rule, Pirous will sell his Qur'anic paintings only to those who have shown an appreciation for the paintings' aesthetic and spiritual richness. He likes to see these paintings in the hands of people for whom the paintings will be "useful" as spiritual notes, and not just as a clever investment or as an attractive item for interior home design. That does not preclude his selling Qur'anic paintings to non-Muslims, but the greater share of these works by far has gone to Muslim collectors in Indonesia and abroad. I should mention, too, that the vast number of Muslims who collect his Qur'anic work are from Indonesia's privileged urban elites, including those of Indonesian-Chinese descent. Although we should not be blind to the class and religious background of these friends and collectors, I want to put stress on the way Pirous will look to them for shared views about the intrinsic goodness of life and the pleasures that come with religiously inspired art (cf., Ricoeur 1992).

Pirous is quick to make friendships, and I have known him to give prints or small paintings to friends as a gifts. It gladdens him to bring pleasure to others with these meaningful works of art, as he did on the night of his gallery's "soft opening" (chapter 2). These gestures are acts of goodness and a way to show his mutual care and regard for friends; they are an expression of *ihsan*. Friendship and solicitude are also the backdrop to the exchange of his Qur'anic spiritual notes. As cultural anthropologists have shown since the foundation of their discipline over a century ago, idioms of kinship and friendship often surround trade and market relationships, and so may bring a stabilizing ethical dimension to what can be an anxious, fraught, or volatile scene of exchange. What interests me here are the ethical postures and aims in the transaction between the artist and collector when a "spiritual note" is being exchanged.

Following the work of anthropologist Marilyn Strathern, the late Alfred Gell (1998) saw paintings – and art objects more broadly – as material embodiments of distributed personhood and subjectivity, and thus as vehicles for an artist's intentions and agency. In selling paintings, artists are letting something of themselves circulate. A painting featuring Qur'anic calligraphy is a bit more complicated: in all Qur'anic verse, no matter what its manifestation, be it in a painting or in recitation, there is "divine presence," or "distributed divinity," in addition to distributed personhood and subjectivity of the one orally or visually reciting the divine message. God is present in, or through, the painting. (Perhaps this is another reason Sadali frowned upon selling paintings of Qur'anic verse. But, as I have pointed out, all sorts of Qur'anic materials are for sale in Indonesia.)

I have a deep sense that Pirous is extremely careful to entrust a spiritual note into the good care of someone whom he would deem a worthy collector. He wishes the painting to endure as a spiritual note in the life of another, bringing the collector both aesthetic and ethical pleasures. Selling a collector a spiritual note is a gesture of Pirous's confidence in the collector's aesthetic and ethical sensibilities. There is no better way to gain that confidence than through the mutuality of friendship. Although a sale is taking place, we ought to see it as but one further step in the mutual exchanges that make a friendship. For this very reason, we see collectors blandishing Pirous with praise, long soulful talks, invitations to family gatherings and meals, ethnographic interviews, feelings of kinship, and displays of their own everyday piety and *ihsan*. I make their gestures of friendship sound calculating and false. The friendships do not come to a halt with a sale, nor are they insincere. These friends, however, are alert to small signs that Pirous may relinquish a painting, giving in to their coaxing or the coaxings of rival collectors. For Pirous, then, selling a spiritual note also involves sustaining one of the friendships from which he derives mutual goodness and pleasure.

Over the course of ten years I got to know several people who have collected Pirous's work. Let me mention just one couple whose collecting illustrates my points. They were corporate lawyers with a home in Jakarta and one in Bandung. This cheerful couple treasured their friendship with Pirous and Erna – and with other artists as well – and had a truly broad and stunning collection of contemporary Indonesian works displayed throughout their Bandung home, which included an immense vaulted display gallery. They would from time to time come by the artist's home and gallery or take a meal with the Pirouses. Visiting their home, I counted half a dozen of Pirous's paintings, all dating from 1989 or later. Interestingly, they kept most of them away from guests and in the very private and contemplative space of their library and bedroom, not in the downstairs gallery. One of them said how much she liked having Pirous's Qur'anic paintings close to her, how they brought her "peacefulness" and "calm." Her husband, I keenly recall, made several visits to Serambi Pirous, hoping to coax the artist into letting them buy *Pillars of the Sky* (*Pilar Langit*; Plate 17), a calligraphic painting that features QS 17 *Bani Isra'il* 35 and 37, the verses of which go:

> Give full measure when you are measuring,
> and weigh on a balanced scale.
> This is better, and fairer in the end.
> And do not strut about the land with insolence:
> You cannot break the earth open,
> nor match the height of the mountains in stature.

He would linger in front the painting, and would tell me how beautiful it was and how much he was moved by the passage. The couple never did succeed in buying the painting. Pirous was too attached to it.

From time to time, some of these collector-friends ask Pirous to make a painting especially for them – a commissioned work. He typically balks at doing so, but has not always been able to rebuff or resist the pleading of friends. "If there is one thing I don't like it is commissions for my painting," Pirous told me one day as we rode around Bandung running errands. "I *really* don't like to be told what to put in my paintings." I am not surprised, for if we understand Pirous about what goes into his spiritual notes, a commission of that sort would amount to reflection-on-command. Commissioned verse does not allow him to reflect freely on, and be freely moved by, the Qur'an. To the contrary, a commission obliges him to write someone else's spiritual notes, rather than passing his own on to another. It is an affront to his spirituality and autonomous vision. It limits his freedom, and so undermines his capacity for *ihsan*.

Some clients who want to commission work give Pirous leeway about choosing appropriate verse, but even that can pose difficulties. While assisting Pirous for several months with his 2002 retrospective show, I looked on for several days as he hurried to finish a large Qur'anic painting he promised to a client the year before. The painting had weighed on him for a very long time, and was preventing him from putting final touches on works he wanted to show at the retrospective. I remember the morning he was finally done with it. Pirous called me downstairs into his home studio. "Help me lift this, will you? I have to get this out of the studio or I will never get the other paintings done." As we eased the ungainly painting off the work table, around a cabinet, and into another room, I asked how he came up with the verse for the painting. The client, Pirous began to explain, had come to him the year before saying, "Pirous, you are like a father to me. I want a painting with a lesson in it. I will hang it somewhere in my house where it will keep me company when I am old." So Pirous had the burden of selecting a passage from the Qur'an that would speak to the client. We leaned the canvas against a pillar, and then my friend took out an Indonesian edition of the Qur'an to read to me the verses featured in the painting. They were from QS 17, *Bani Isra'il*, verses 35–37, two of which appeared on *"Pillars of the Sky* (above):

> Give full measure when you are measuring,
> and weigh on a balanced scale.
> This is better, and fairer in the end.
> Do not follow that of which you have no knowledge.
> The ear, the eye, and the heart,
> each will be questioned.
> And do not strut about the land with insolence:
> You cannot break the earth open,
> nor match the height of the mountains in stature.

99

The passages were an admonition to the client. "It is a reminder to seek knowledge (*berilmu*), do good deeds (*beramal*), and to be humble (*merunduk*). If he doesn't like it and doesn't want it, that's okay, so what? I will keep it, I like it a lot."

We stepped back and, standing side by side, looked over the painting some more. "So, do you think he'll like it?" I asked after a few moments. Pirous turned to me, shrugging. "You know, you grasp a painting as a whole," he replied, "In a single moment you either like it or you don't. It doesn't need time. But for the verse here, you need time for that, for reflection. That's why I say there is aesthetic pleasure and ethical fulfillment in my paintings." Another moment passed. "So, Ken, what do you want to call it?" I laughed, not imagining an artist would outsource the task of coming up with a title for a painting. "Give me an hour. Meet you back here at breakfast."

Pirous was already at the dining table as I came down from my room. Bu Anti, the Pirouses' cheerful and indefatigable cook, had set out platters heaped with fried rice, leftover *rendang* (tender cubes of beef simmered in coconut milk and spices), tiny roasted fish, stewed vegetables and soy cake, and some green beans. I ran my choice of title by Pirous as I dug into the tempting bowls of food: "How about 'The Treasure that Comes from Humility'?" Pirous had a different one in mind: "Toward a Life of Knowledge, Good Deeds, and Humility." We swapped our thoughts about the painting for a while and by the time he poured himself some tea and I had peeled open a mangosteen, Pirous had decided on the title he would pitch to the client: *The Treasure of Life in Knowledge, Good Deeds, and Humility* (*Khazanah Kehidupan Melalui Berilmu, Beramal, dan Kerendahan Hati*).

From time to time, Pirous will put up a Qur'anic calligraphic painting for auction in fundraising events organized in support of earthquake or tsunami relief. But, by and large, pricing his Qur'anic paintings for the open market makes Pirous uneasy. The rapid climb in art prices in Indonesia (and for that matter all over Southeast Asia) in the early 1990s caused him, and other senior painters, to complain about the differences between a work's market value and its artistic merit (George 1999). Prices continued spiraling upward over the next decade. By 2002, a few in Indonesia's art circles complained to me that Pirous seriously underpriced his "best work." Selling his spiritual notes to collector-friends has been one way that Pirous has shielded himself from market turmoil and sought an ethics of pricing. But Pirous is not naive. He knows that he cannot control the prices his work will command in auction houses or in private sales between collectors.

What Pirous understandably tries to control, however, is his reputation, not just as a painter, but as a contemporary and spiritually oriented Muslim Indonesian artist. Reputation, of course, gets made in transactions between collectors, galleries, and auction houses. Quite crucially, however, Pirous has done the most to pursue a painterly identity in sponsored, non-commercial shows in national and international venues. As I already have emphasized, Pirous has relied through the years on government sponsorships, subsidies, and stipends to take part in national shows, but also to formally *represent* Indonesia in international venues, or to accept invitations from exhibition organizers abroad. Domestically, government sponsorship has kept his work in the public eye in officially supervised civic venues – art schools, institutes, public galleries, art councils, festivals, conferences, publications, and MTQ celebrations. Endorsements from the Indonesian government also allowed him to accept foundation and intergovernmental invitations (especially from ASEAN – the Association of Southeast Asian Nations) to take part in shows in Australia, Bahrain, Denmark, Germany, Japan, Jordan, Malaysia, the Netherlands, the Philippines, Singapore, Taiwan, the United Kingdom, and in the United States, where a few of his works traveled as part of the Modern Indonesian Art Exhibition between 1990 and 1992 (Fischer 1990). Numerous, but perhaps somewhat less significant to his reputation, are the shows held in cities such as Jakarta, Bandung, Surabaya, Solo, and Yogyakarta, and sponsored by corporations, banks, private galleries, or the Rotary Club.

Works from the artist's personal collection of "spiritual notes" at Serambi Pirous are central to the display of his identity as a contemporary Indonesian artist in these venues. The spiritual notes (which are accompanied by artist statements and commentaries from those curating the shows) reveal him in these venues as a reflective artist-believer whose aesthetic and religious sensibilities are emblematic of Indonesia's modernity and art historical significance. I cannot vouch for the "ethical pleasure" viewers may experience in looking at his work, especially in the international shows. That experience would seem to be confined to Muslim gallery-goers who can read and recognize the Qur'anic verse in his paintings (and, as I pointed out in chapter 3, many Indonesian Muslims do not always have a ready command of Arabic).

Frankly, most of the international shows are secular in thrust and would not draw significant numbers of Muslim viewers; the exceptions are the exhibitions in Bahrain, Jordan, Malaysia, and Singapore. Indeed, *national* or *Asian* modernities and modernisms are the principal themes in the international shows, and typically obscure Pirous's contribution to Asian or global trends in Islamic art and visual culture. Room is made for appreciating the spirituality in Pirous's work, but show organizers typically frame that spirituality as an indigenous sign of "Asian-ness" and not as an artistic – and quite cosmopolitan – intervention in Islamic thought and Muslim community life. The intense interest in the local, the national, and the indigenous in these international exhibitions – including his Acehnese heritage – dampens appreciation of Pirous's work as an Islamic critique of modernity or as a rejoinder to the Arab-centrism that has veiled the face of Southeast Asia's Muslim cultures from public and art historical view.

Being featured in international exhibitions, of course, has burnished Pirous's reputation within Indonesia as a major figure in the country's national visual culture. Yet it is in domestic venues that his spiritual notes convey to gallery-goers the kind of ethical accountability that goes with being a citizen-believer. Although he might wish to be "useful" to Muslims and others within international art arenas, his strongest ethical and empathetic bonds have been with Muslim Indonesians. As I worked with him in 1994, I could not overlook, too, his abiding ethical and emotional bond with the Indonesian nation-state, a bond that may have been prefigured by the aphorism he placed in his paperback copy of *Mohammed and Charlemagne* in 1958 (chapter 1). Responding to its political and aesthetic summons, he had placed his art in service of the nation, and that ideological commitment drew him inescapably into serving the political goals of the Soeharto regime as it pursued programs of national "development" or courted the country's Muslim communities. There have been times, especially in the context of the Istiqlal Festivals, when Pirous has sounded like a publicist for the state and its policy toward Islam and the arts. All the same, Pirous has never been *wholly* or *merely* an agent of the Indonesian nation-state or its government. Further still, he has been able to take advantage of the state and its patronage in arranging his solo retrospective shows in Jakarta in 1985 and 2002, the first at Taman Ismail Marzuki, the latter at the National Gallery. Although they were endorsed by public officials and councils, the planning, labor, publicity, and funding for the shows fell largely to Pirous. Without putting too fine a point on it, these were self-organized shows in state-administered spaces. Readers might raise eyebrows at the audacity of an artist who rents space at national venues in order to display his work and celebrate his accomplishments. But with Indonesia's lack of public funding, professional curators, trained museum administrators, and experienced art critics, there seem few other paths for an artist to reach a national art public, if one can be said to exist.

Writing about Pirous's retrospective show in 1985, artist G. Sidharta Soegijo called attention to something other than the artist's audaciousness. "His exhibit," said Sidharta, "highlights the responsibility and obligation an artist has toward society. With this exhibition, it is as if the artist has opened the whole of his experience to society. In its turn, society can assess how far Pirous has struggled with his art and how far his toils have produced works that affirm his artistic presence" (Soegijo 1985). Sidharta was one of Pirous's associates at Decenta and a faculty colleague at the Bandung Institute of Technology, and we can be sure his assessment would have been favorable. Of interest to me in his remarks is the suggestion that an artist has an ethical responsibility to his community, and that this responsibility might be met through "opening the whole of his [or her] experience" to gallery-goers. In light of Sidharta's remark, we have further reason to understand the display of personal "spiritual notes" as more than an act of self-valorization. They may also invite contemplation and conversation, and, in the instance of Pirous's Qur'anic works, might nurture among Muslims a collective sensibility and appreciation for art as a vehicle of *dzikir* and *ihsan*, and so fully compatible with the teachings of Islam.

Spiritual Notes in a Political Arena

Just as I was leaving Bandung in June of 1994, Soeharto's government abruptly shut down *Tempo*, *Editor*, and *DeTik*, three major magazines that had grown increasingly critical of the regime. A government spokesman said that their articles "had not

102

reflected the life of a free and responsible press" (*New York Times*, June 23, 1994), regime-speak for its displeasure with critical or investigative journalism. Pirous and everyone else I knew were left shaking their heads in dismay over this repressive move.

I came through Bandung nearly a year later, and had the chance to go with Pirous to Jakarta to spend some time at the Contemporary Art of the Non-Aligned Countries exhibit, housed in the complex that soon would become Galeri Nasional, the country's new National Gallery. Soeharto and Indonesia had become Chairman and Host, respectively, of the Non-Aligned Movement (or NAM), which was convening on the fortieth anniversary of its first meeting at the famous Asian-African Conference in Bandung in 1955. Soeharto and the Department of Education and Culture arranged and funded the international exhibition, and had brought Pirous aboard, among many others, as part of the curatorial board and the national oversight committee. The show aimed explicitly at interrogating the directions of art in the world "South" and its relationship to the art world of the Euro-American "North." Representative artists from over forty countries took part, and roughly half those countries were predominantly Muslim nations. Pirous pointed out a couple of Indonesian installation works that he said were critical of the Soeharto government, but in no case were they explicitly or unambiguously so. A more derisive if marginalized show simultaneously took place at the Jakarta Arts Institute, "Non Go-Blok Exhibition Art" – the title making a pun on the Non-Aligned Bloc (or "*blok*") with "*goblok*", meaning "stupid."

A further companion exhibition also was running concurrently at Jakarta's Taman Ismail Marzuki, this one on Contemporary Indonesian Art. Pirous had two calligraphic paintings on show in this exhibit, both with verses extolling God. Writing later in the year for *ARTAsiaPacific*, Asian art historian John Clark was unsparing in his critical appraisal of Pirous's work and of the shows more generally:

> Notwithstanding his magnificent organizational efforts in support of the NAM exhibition and seminar, Pirous's art now presents the problem of a pioneer of an earlier generation whose former quality has since been eclipsed by a tendency to lapse decoratively into large color panels with calligraphic inscriptions from the Qur'an, the grandeur of whose religious inspiration is not matched by the formal superficialities of their decorative site. ... [All] in modern life [is] not so easily graspable from an Islamic perspective by redeployment of calligraphy or decoration. ... To judge from the works on show in "Contemporary Indonesian Art," contemporary Indonesian art now consists almost entirely of more or less agreeable decorative dreamings for the rich. No doubt an Indonesian wag might dismiss it as "Golkar art" [i.e., art for Soeharto's regime and political party] but this would be perhaps to overestimate the position of the governing elite's taste in producing such work. (Clark 1995)

So much for art in an authoritarian country. I believe Clark saw in Pirous's work, and the work of many other Indonesian artists, a failure of political and aesthetic nerve. It is hard for me to see Pirous take a critical punch of this kind, but Clark was responding to the conservative, acquiescent, and bourgeois strains of Indonesian art under authoritarian political rule, never mind the less than sympathetic views of the country's Muslim religious authorities toward art.

Jim Supangkat (nd) and T. K. Sabapathy (nd) later took Clark to task for wishful and "excessively political" misreadings of certain works at the NAM show, misreadings that emphasized criticism of the Soeharto regime and overlooked more plausible or nuanced political and cultural gestures within the works in question. With respect to Pirous's work, Clark missed how his "decorative dreamings for the rich" might have broad appeal to an emerging Muslim art public. Arguably, popular appeal may not be a reliable or critically useful index of political and aesthetic worth. Yet the appeal of Pirous's paintings, as I have tried to show in this book, rests significantly in the ethical function of the work, not just in their sensuous pull on the eye. If through 1994 they had been politically mute with respect to state rule, they nonetheless broke new expressive ground in the country's Muslim community.

It is surely necessary to recognize – as does Paul Ricoeur (1992: 194–202) – how ethics extends to living together in a community predicated on justice and equality among its members. Following Hannah Arendt (1958), Ricoeur speaks not just of the bond of common mores. He points, as well, to how power-in-common stems from the human condition of plurality and acting in concert. These, say Ricoeur, precede relations of domination and are not reducible to the state. Here, then, I come back to Sidharta's remark about the responsibility of the artist to society. The artist may and should be free to speak out regarding relations of domination and state rule, but before all else, an artist might lead us to reflect on the necessity and fragility of wanting to live and act together in pursuing goodness and pleasure. It is this dimension of Pirous's work that I think escapes Clark's critical sensibilities.

Soeharto's abuse of power did not go unheeded by Pirous or others. I returned to Jakarta just a few months later that year, for the late September opening of the second Istiqlal Festival. Showcased on one of the gallery walls beneath the Istiqlal Mosque was a new painting by Pirous (Plate 18). It was an immense calligraphic work in acrylic, gold leaf, and modeling paste, two and half meters long and almost two meters high. Two vertical gold lips that split the work in two touched one another beneath a large red "seal" inscribed with Pirous's name in Arabic. The title of the painting was *An Admonition to the Leader: Concerning the Transient Palace and the Beginning and End of Life* (*Amanat kepada Sang Pemimpin: Tentang Mahligai Kefanaan, Tentang Awal Akhir Kehayatan*). The Qur'anic passage was from QS 3 *Al 'Imran*, verses 26–27. The verses read:

> Say "O Lord of all dominions
> You give power to whomever You will
> and You take it away from whomever You will;
> You exalt whom You please and humble whom You will.

104

> All goodness is Yours.
> You have the power over all things.
> You merge night into day, and day into night
> raise the living from the dead,
> and the dead from the living,
> and give to whomsoever You please,
> and in measure without number."

Pirous had at last made a spiritual note in explicit address to Soeharto and his regime. It stayed within the bounds of civility and caused no ruckus. I doubt it even crossed the threshold of the President's attention. But it is hard for me to see it merely as "decorative dreaming for the rich."

In this chapter, I have tried to give readers a glimpse of what Pirous sees in his "spiritual notes" and what place they have in his social world. A fascination with spiritualism and spirituality has long played a part in the history of modernist art and literature. Thus, Pirous's talk about paintings as "spiritual notes" very much continues a modernist interest in mixing one's subjectivity and inner experience with the sublime. In fact, his work and thought seem to me an obvious effort at aligning aesthetic modernism with Islam. This mingling of conceptual vocabularies is as strategic as it is heartfelt. With his spiritual notes, Pirous is able to demonstrate how making art might help Muslims pursue their ethical and religious goals; he is making art "safe" for the observant Muslim. More than that, he is acquainting Indonesian Muslims – and Muslims elsewhere – with the emblems of upper- and middle-class life; he is cultivating a religiously acceptable taste for fine art. Less clear are the effects of his project for a transnational art world dominated by Euro-American interests and institutions. On the one hand, the making of spiritual notes ought to be quite familiar to that art world, even if painting has lost some of its luster and caché since the 1970s. On the other hand, an Islamic vocabulary may serve to make those spiritual notes unrecognizable, indigestible, or even threatening to the predominantly secular interests of the transnational art scene. Islamic spirituality may not yet be the most welcome or warmly anticipated expression of non-Western indigeneity for those who prize transgression, protest, and critique.

As I have tried to show in this chapter, the exchange or sharing of spiritual notes may be intended to strengthen the bonds between friends and citizens. Within Indonesian Muslim circles, they are a gesture of *ihsan* and *mu'amalah*, of goodness and good conduct. They are a testament to Islamic sociability. They speak to the idea of community, the *ummat*. How they speak within the political space of the nation-state is another matter. I have never doubted the sincerity of Pirous's attachment to Indonesia. His spiritual notes do seem like a civic and even communal project, aimed as they are to appeal to Indonesia's huge Muslim community. All the same, describing paintings as "spiritual notes" is a good way for artists to protect themselves from state censorship. The painter becomes the main referee of meaning, and can readily disavow any of the critical messages political authorities might see in the work. The remaining danger, as we have seen in this and earlier chapters, is the capacity of Islamic religious authorities to challenge the propriety of making spiritual art by equating it with *da'wah*. Yet even on that score attitudes have been changing. In part because of the success of the Istiqlal Festivals and MTQ exhibitions, many Muslim authorities in Indonesia no longer think of art as intrinsically set against the interests of religion. In fact, some organizations, like Muhammadiyah, have begun to look to art as a welcome medium for *da'wah*.

5

ANGUISH, BETRAYAL, UNCERTAINTY, AND FAITH

In the Name of God the Compassionate the
    Caring
Time and age are witness
The human is always at a loss
Except those who keep the faith
    who do good deeds and seek justice
    who counsel one another to truth
    and who urge one another to bear with forti-
        tude and patience
    the trials that befall them

QS 103 *Al-'Asr* (*The Epoch*)

I gratefully remember a letter from Pirous, written in longhand, and sent to me many years ago before email and text-messaging became our main way of keeping in touch. Consoling me over a personal setback, and trying ease my worry and confusion, Pirous wrote, "No one knows what plans God has for us. There will be a purpose for you in the troubles you are facing." I have always known my friend to be a thoughtful Muslim, and I was not surprised he would offer me words of faith as a compass for dealing with difficulties. One does not have to go the path of Islam to find a steadying lesson in Pirous's remark: We live with uncertainties, and it is up to us to figure out how to keep our resolve and goodness when confronting them. No more so than in times of danger and treachery, when both our sense of self and our relationships with others are called into question.

This fifth and final chapter tells the story of some circumstances that led Pirous to call his art, his allegiances, and his capacity to understand into question. This was a time when Qur'anic verse briefly disappeared from his paintings. Complaints from *ulama* weren't the problem, and neither was the market. His reputation and the demand for his Qur'anic paintings were as strong as ever. The problem was far

107

broader and far more shattering. The spectres of corruption, lawlessness, and state violence had finally caught up with him, forcing him to acknowledge at last how deeply he and his art had been swallowed up in a malignant atmosphere of Soeharto's authoritarianism. Pirous, I think, was for a time thrown off balance by feelings of anger and betrayal. To regain his ethical footing, he had to work out once more what it might mean to make art that was Acehnese, Indonesian, and Islamic.

Sky Split Asunder and Tombs Burst Open

Pirous pushed into 1997 with tireless ambition. Group exhibitions in Germany and Jordan had gone well for him and he accepted an invitation to take part in a show in Denmark on modern Indonesian art. More prestigious still, the Rockefeller Foundation had recruited Pirous to take part in the global curatorial team that would put together an exhibition for the 47th Venice Biennale, *Memories and Modernities: Recent Works from the Islamic World*. Back home, he was a prominent advocate and one of the founding figures for the Museum Bayt Al-Qur'an ("House of the Qur'an Museum") in Jakarta, which was planned as a permanent, government-sponsored showcase for Indonesian Qur'anic art. And the boom in Southeast Asian art kept booming.

The political climate in Indonesia, however, turned darker. Soeharto had ruled the country for thirty-one years and showed no signs of giving up the reins of power. The government took brutal measures to choke its opponents in the pro-democracy movement and to stifle public protest. As part of this effort, authorities for the administration recruited ultraconservative Muslims in organizing a "regimist Islam," resistant to democratic reform (Hefner 2000). In equally sinister fashion, the government had a hand in manipulating simmering ethnic and sectarian tensions around the country, and incessantly warned of "communist" and "separatist" threats to the nation. Painting its critics as communists was an old and deadly trick of the regime, dating back to the anti-leftist bloodbath of 1965 and 1966 that brought Soeharto to power. The nation-state's fear of regional separatism had precedents in Indonesian political history, too (see chapter 1). But those fears had grown increasingly acute over two indigenous independence movements that had gained strength and international support.

One was the East Timorese independence movement, which was aimed at restoring the sovereignty denied to East Timor under its annexation by Indonesia in 1975. The other was the Movement for a Free Aceh (or GAM, for Gerakan Aceh Merdeka). Launched in 1976, GAM drew its energies from popular regional resentment over the central government's policies on economy, political representation, and Islamic law – policies that many Acehnese saw as a guise for Javanese colonialism. Like East Timor, Aceh was under military occupation. The Soeharto government had succeeded in putting into place a governing cadre of Acehnese politicians who owed allegiance to Jakarta, but when GAM showed renewed spark and popular support in the late 1980s, Indonesia unleashed a deadly program of counterinsurgency and military terror in the province. In short, much of what the government did during the mid-1990s aimed at deeper surveillance, intimidation, and militarization of the public sphere. Soeharto's Indonesia was a republic of fear and reprisal.

I made a quick visit to see Pirous and Erna for a few days in October of that year, just as the Southeast Asian financial crisis reached Indonesia and began to send its currency, the *rupiah*, into a tailspin. Stopping in at Serambi Pirous, I did not see any new works suggesting acute doubt or anger over regime politics. *An Admonition to the Leader*, shown at the second Istiqlal Festival in 1995 (and described in chapter 4), was the sharpest criticism Pirous could summon. That painting had encouraged me to think that contemporary Islamic art might have oppositional potential. At the very least, Islamic art could give Muslim artists like Pirous some room for maneuver in a time of authoritarian rule. After all, how might the regime censor Islamic art without appearing to censor Islam itself? Only the *ulama* were able to do that, such as those who criticized Pirous for making paintings with flawed Qur'anic verse. Thus political protest conceivably could be cloaked in the dress of religious expression. Could such veiled protest be effective? Maybe. But the truth is that painting and other visual arts just did not count for much in Indonesia, even if they were in the public eye. Indonesia's art world was, and continues to be, a limited one, centered on upper-class consumers and cultural elites. Authorities for the regime seldom policed the art world with the same scrutiny they gave to festivals, films, television, literary works, and theatrical productions. For this reason, even if painters and other artists exercised their considerable political latitude in their work, it largely went unnoticed.

Pirous was hardly a Muslim ultraconservative. Sincere and observant, perhaps, but not *fanatik* as many Indonesians of a younger generation might describe the zealous and narrow-minded religious hardliners. That October, I was surprised to find that Sufi poetry from Sumatra, films about sacred sites around the world, and CD recordings of Korean Buddhist chants and Diné (Navajo) rain prayers had captured his curiosity. The atmosphere of religious orthodoxy that I had associated with the household in 1994 no longer seemed so enveloping. Always earnest and curious, Pirous seemed in no way deafened to the religiosity of others. It was a time of expanding hope for Pirous, Erna, and their family; everyone was in motion. Their daughter, Mida, who worked in graphic design, had married product designer Dudy Wiyancoko the year before and now lived in Japan while Dudy pursued studies there; they were expecting their first baby in December, and Erna was anxious to join them. Their younger daughter, Rihan, had resumed advanced course work in graphic design at the Bandung Institute of Technology, and was making plans to go off to the Netherlands for an internship. Iwan, meanwhile, was preparing for ethnographic fieldwork in Kalimantan (Indonesian Borneo), having finished an undergraduate degree in social anthropology at the University of Indonesia in Jakarta just a few months earlier.

If good fortune had visited the household, so had sorcery. Pirous and Erna had discovered some suspicious things around their house: a package of red clay wrapped in sandpaper and planted by a rear door, and bits of broken windshield strewn beneath their bed. A local seer told them they were under magical assault from someone who envied them. "We think we know who did it," Pirous confided to me late one night as he, Erna, and I lingered at the dining table swapping stories and family news. "Someone here in Bandung who has been jealous of my success." I ventured a name, and they nodded. The Soeharto regime was surely a menace too, but Pirous did not have much to say about it or the situation in Aceh. I asked about East Timor and mentioned how José Ramos-Horta, the 1996 Nobel Peace Prize winner and international representative for the East Timorese cause, had accepted an invitation from me and others on a peace studies committee to visit my home university that coming November. As with Aceh and other matters, Pirous ardently believed in the unity of Indonesia, and argued that East Timor properly belonged to the nation and had even prospered as one of its provinces. I can't say I was surprised, for I knew that a few years before, Pirous had carefully incorporated East Timorese ornamental motifs into the *Al-Qur'an Mushaf Istiqlal*, playing down the fact that East Timor was a predominantly Catholic territory (Muslims make up about 1 percent of the population there), and that most East Timorese might not welcome pictorial inclusion of their local culture in Indonesia's "national Qur'an."

Though he and Erna were ebullient over the birth of their first grandchild near the end of the year, they could not escape the panic and unrest beginning to sweep across the country as 1998 began. The *rupiah* had collapsed. Some took to the streets in riots over the rising cost of food and fuel, while others stockpiled supplies of rice or put their money into goods or more stable currencies. Calls for political and economic reform, and widespread criticism over government corruption and human rights abuses jolted the regime. Riots and looting shook the city of Medan in April. Then, on May 12, 1998, security forces shot and killed four unarmed students taking part in a peaceful demonstration at Jakarta's Trisakti University. Nine more students were killed elsewhere in the city. Massive riots followed over the next three days, during which state security agents, special forces, and paramilitaries provoked mobs against the ethnic Chinese community in an attempt to deflect popular rage onto a racialized scapegoat. Thousands of urban poor died in the riots – both Chinese-Indonesians and others – and a vast number of homes, offices, banks, shopping malls, and businesses burned. Seething over the violence, the public turned on the regime. Soeharto's allies in the military deserted him and he resigned on May 21, 1998. The era of *Reformasi*, political reform, had begun.

The violence and political upheaval of May 1998 left Pirous feeling betrayed, confused, and angry. While his Bandung colleague, Sunaryo, went into public mourning by binding and shrouding his personal collection of paintings and sculptures in black cloth, Pirous went through reversals and splits in his work. His paintings lost their spiritual optimism and composure. Looking at his new work during a visit in August 1998, I saw signs of anguish and troubled subjectivity. I came across a small, untitled canvas at Serambi Pirous, pushed away in corner behind a stack of other work. I have no photo of the painting, but I remember my conflicted feelings of fascination and revulsion as I looked it over, its surface blackened and

110

seemingly burnt, with a lurid and rounded red "wound" of modeling paste and paint at its heart, something between a rose and a festering abscess. It upset Pirous to look at it and he asked me to put it away. He has never put it on public display. It has remained a buried work, a "note" kept out of sight.

Two Qur'anic paintings grabbed my attention, both entitled *Alif Lam Mim* – the mysterious, three-syllable sequence that opens several sura. Neither the Qur'an nor its scholars offer sure guidance on the meaning of these three syllables, and Pirous had avoided the *alif-lam-mim* sequence for years, thinking of it as an icon of mysticism and ambiguity (see chapter 4). In May of 1998, however, the syllables' very ambiguity made them a perfect figure for the political uncertainty and trauma around him. When I asked him why the change of heart, he held me with his eyes, and replied, "Only God knows the meaning of those letters. Only God knows where my country is headed."

Look at the detail from *Alif Lam Mim/Only God is All-Knowing* (*Alif Lam Mim/ Hanya Tuhan Yang Maha Tahu*; Plate 19). The burning crimson letters, *alif-lam-mim*, appear in high relief above the dark depths of the painting, as if wiped clean of any obscuring soot. Two dates are embossed in the dark and dim gray-green recesses of the painting. They are written in Arabic: to the right, the year 1998; to the left, the year 1418, which in the Islamic Hijra calendar came to a close in the last days of April 1998. The painting leads me to think that the chaos and violence of April and May 1998 momentarily overwhelmed Pirous's ability to find an ethical compass in a Qur'anic passage with which he might exhort others. I see in the painting a crisis or collapse of legibility, a cry of "I can no longer read!" Inscrutability and uncertainty, the inability to read our circumstances, do not imply the absence of signs (that is, nothing to read), but are conditions brought about when violence disturbs the production and interpretation of signs, often with the purpose of replacing the social foundations for that activity. There were signs everywhere in the turmoil of May 1998, but Pirous could not read what was going on with them. The tumult and his inability to read his nation upended his reading of the Qur'an. Nothing in the nation seemed rational or familiar, and he was rattled. Unlike the Qur'anic passages in his other calligraphic paintings – passages that offer ethical guidance and meaning – *alif-lam-mim* seems both a representation of and a retreat from his anguished circumstances. I say that *alif-lam-mim* represents his anguished circumstances because these syllables give material expression of the inscrutable and uncertain tumult of May 1998. I say that the syllables are a retreat because, with them, Pirous trades away a political understanding of the social and political upheaval around him for the transcendent, omniscient, but unrevealed perspective that is God's.

The fall of Soeharto in May 1998 was followed soon after by public disclosure of state-sponsored atrocities in Aceh: hundreds and hundreds of innocents had been killed by Indonesian counterinsurgency forces and dumped in mass graves. Pirous seethed. For someone of such creativity, good will, and national pride, this tragedy was very hard to bear. The government had temporarily suspended military operations in Aceh that August, and Pirous took the opportunity to speak out.

111

Delivering a public talk on art and oppression at a ceremony in memory of one of the regime's leading critics, the late H. R. Dharsono, Pirous gave voice to his anguish and anger:

> With every day it is increasingly clear that the dead did no wrong, did not get a proper burial, and were killed without reason. And now it is in the open. This didn't happen just in Aceh, but throughout Indonesia. It happened everywhere.

Devoted to the nation, but betrayed by the violence and lies of its government, Pirous's response was to put his rage and torn feelings into painting.

Just a few hours before that public talk, Pirous showed me the first of the paintings he would make concerning the atrocities in Aceh. It is called, *Once There Was a Holy War in Aceh: Homage to the Intrepid Hero Teuku Oemar, 1854–1899* (*Suatu Waktu Ada Prang Sabil di Aceh: Penghormatan Kepada Pahlawan yang Gagah Berani Teuku Oemar, 1854–1899*). Look at Plate 20. There, as the visual focus of this lurid painting, is the ghostly figure of Teuku Oemar, a martyr from the Dutch–Acehnese War (1873–1914), wielding a sword. Splatters, blotches, and streaks of red paint on the figure's face, hat, coat, sarong, and sword suggest blood. Torn pages and manuscript fragments of the *Hikayat Prang Sabil* (the banned *Chronicle of the Holy War*, mentioned in chapter 1) surround the zombie, animated and brought back from the dead in the painter's imagination. There are raised red Arabic characters to either side of Teuku Oemar's head and shoulders. They are not Qur'anic Arabic, but Acehnese, and they quote the "Oath of the Holy War" (*Sumpah Prang Sabil*). The Oath reads: "Rather than die in the home of your wife, better to be slain by the infidel's weapon. Rather than die on a pillow, better to be sprawled as a martyr in the front lines" (*Nibak matée dirumöh inong, bah le keunong senjata kaphée. Nibak matée diateuh tilam, bah le lam shaf prang syahid meugulée*). Pirous recited the oath in Acehnese, and very visibly shuddered when he finished repeating it to me in Indonesian.

The painting floored me. In all the time we were acquainted, I had never known Pirous to paint a human figure. Although I knew he had firm doubts about Islam's purported taboo on portraying human or living figures, he himself had avoided human figuration in his work for nearly thirty years. In fact, human figures had more or less disappeared from his paintings not long after the anti-communist massacres of 1965 and 1966 (chapter 1), before his exploration of Islamic aesthetics. When I pressed him about his willingness to include figurative elements in his painting he explained:

> In an atmosphere like this, themes in art tell stories of turmoil. Because of that, figurative forms that are realistic rather than abstract have become important. They are a very common language for telling stories. For me the problem of Aceh is beyond the human. It is about human destruction. Using passages from the Qur'an is too complicated. I look at the army, and I look at the people in GAM [the Free Aceh Movement]. They can't think, they can only see. Because of that, a picture is worth a thousand words.

112

In replying to me, Pirous described his painting as a story and suggested that realism and figuration are basic to its language and interpretability. We might ask questions about why realism and figuration work better at telling a story about violence than abstraction or Qur'anic verse. But, more problematic still, to whom is this painting addressed? Why would GAM or the Indonesian army, or the leaders of either side, stop to look at a painting?

The painting offers a visual allegory of resistance. It makes reference to the violence in Aceh in the 1990s through images associated with the Acehnese anti-colonial *jihad* of the late nineteenth and early twentieth centuries. The painting summons the ghost of Teuku Oemar, who for years led the guerilla campaign against the Dutch. Teuku Oemar is not just an Acehnese hero, however, but an Indonesian national hero as well, whose name and accomplishments are enshrined in schoolbooks, museums, and street names all across the country. All the same, we need to recall that he did not fight the Dutch under the banner of Indonesian nationalism. It was only later, after Indonesian independence in 1945, that his tenacious resistance against the Dutch for *local* freedoms became an emblem of the broader struggle for *national* freedom. Pirous, I would say, has raised and reclaimed Teuku Oemar from the dead as the honored figure of Acehnese resistance to all colonialism, be it Dutch or Indonesian colonialism. There is also some projection going on. Like Pirous, Teuku Oemar was born in Meulaboh. Like Teuku Oemar, Pirous is both Acehnese and Indonesian.

Icons of his mother's Aceh are absent in this work. No cheerful geometric patterns; no allusions to bright fabrics. Instead, we see textual icons from a culture of violence that Pirous has long left out of his art work. Though legible, the Oath of the Holy War and the fragments of the *Hikayat Prang Sabil* would mystify most Indonesians. They are written in Arabic script, and so many might think the fragments came from the Qur'an. The fragments are unreadable to those who do not know Acehnese. Even Pirous has difficulty reading the fragments and does not fully understand them. He knows them to be from the *Hikayat Prang Sabil* because he photocopied them from books and manuscript reproductions. Unlike the Qur'anic passages often found in his paintings, the *hikayat* passages here are cut and placed on the work's surface in a way that would thwart a "grammatical" reading of the *hikayat* narrative. There is no order to their placement.

There is another absence: missing, too, is Pirous's signature work in Qur'anic calligraphy. Recall that Pirous said it was "too complicated" to use Qur'anic verse in this painting. Calligraphy remains, but in place of Qur'anic verse, we have the Acehnese Oath of the Holy War. The exhortative verse of the Qur'an is regarded as truth by Muslims, and would call upon the reader to submit to Allah. In *Once There Was a Holy War in Aceh*, by contrast, the Oath of the Holy War is about justice for the Acehnese. It calls upon those who recite it to sacrifice themselves for the resistance. Perhaps one reason it is "too complicated" to use Qur'anic verse in the painting is that doing so would politicize the Qur'an on the matter of justice for the Acehnese. Even so, the mere use of Arabic script in the painting runs the risk of leading some viewers into thinking it features Qur'anic verse.

113

Once There Was a Holy War in Aceh was only the first painting in what Pirous would call his "Aceh Series." Several of them feature pages or fragments of the *Hikayat Prang Sabil*; Qur'anic verse is nowhere to be seen, and, in fact, it has no place in these paintings. The works are not exercises in *dzikir*. They spring from anguish over human injustice, and are fueled by readings of the *Hikayat Prang Sabil* rather than calmed by reflections on the Qur'an. *Hikayat* poetry is no substitute for Qur'anic verse, but they do share one feature. Their proper expression is in oral recitation, where breath comes into the picture. In recitation, *hikayat* poetry and Qur'anic verse become embodied, and made one with the breath and tongue. Recitation of the Qur'an makes one mindful of God. Recitation of the *Hikayat Prang Sabil* or the Oath of the Holy War inflames the heart, and potentially leads one to violence and martyrdom. They are dangerous words. Just uttering the Oath caused Pirous to shudder, as if momentarily possessed.

We may understand, then, another of Pirous's Acehnese paintings, *The Shackling of the Book of the Holy War, II* (*Pemasungan Kitab Prang Sabil, II*; Plate 21). The Indonesian word *pemasungan* comes from the verb, *pasung*, meaning to shackle, restrain, pillory, leash, suppress, or ban. In this mixed-media work, Pirous has literally tied and sealed an image showing the *Hikayat* as though it were compiled in book form. (Note the gilded vertical spine of the book and recollect the symbolic importance of vertical gestures and gold leaf in other paintings by the artist.) The Dutch had banned the *Hikayat Prang Sabil* in colonial Aceh, prohibiting people from reciting it or making copies of it, because it incited people to martyr themselves in anti-colonial *jihad*. Pirous is pictorially shackling and banning it here, containing its danger. But it is bound with light cord, a simple knot, and a red seal – all easily removed with minimal effort. The slightest provocation could unleash the text.

It is hard to think of *Once There Was a Holy War in Aceh* and *The Shackling of the Book of the Holy War, II* as "spiritual notes," as I have described them in chapter 4. Yet, as I listened to Pirous talk about the paintings, I sensed his compassion and ethical concern for others:

> In the end, I am an ordinary human being, a human being who feels hurt, who feels resentment, who feels pride, who has feelings of getting sliced up. When the massacres in Aceh became clear, I felt stabbed, extremely angry, and deeply insulted as a human being. Not just because I am from Aceh, but as someone who could be treated that way. I felt angry. It is unjust.
>
> In a situation like that, what could I do? I thought about warning people, "Don't do it, it is wrong!" Why is it wrong? Study history! Something like this already happened in our history. By studying history we can do something better than what is being done now. It is a moral obligation. Because I can't go there and bring 3,000 of the dead back to life.
>
> The war between Aceh and the Netherlands never really came to an end. Why? Violence. Rebellion. Shooting. Killing. They appear again, this time over there. Stamped out, it all springs up here. Why? The violence and war didn't stop, because it had turned into a religious war, a *jihad*. You can't put that out with violence. The

114

people of Aceh rededicated themselves to the struggle by reciting the literature of the holy war. To the point they fought the Dutch for religious reasons.

But what happened today isn't a religious problem. It's a political one, a problem of authority, exploitation, economics, and injustice. In facing that, the Acehnese are reading the poetry of war again, and their spirit is burning. The ones they kill this time aren't the Dutch, but the Indonesian Army. Who is the Indonesian Army? Our own people! What's their religion? Islam! The same religion!

The regional military operations were started by the army. They killed hundreds and more. We don't know their names and we don't know where they are buried. More violence won't solve the problem in Aceh. I made these paintings to warn us all, beginning with the government down to those who have an interest in making Aceh a cause. Please remember, please find a right way to solve the problem. Diplomacy is the right way to do it. Not with force. Not with violence.

As Pirous describes them, the Aceh paintings are addressed to those locked in civil conflict. Although this struggle pits Muslim against Muslim, Islam is not at the root of the trouble. It is perhaps for that reason that Pirous finds it "too complicated" to turn to Qur'anic verse. For this artist, it seems, the culture of escalating violence in Aceh cannot or should not be rendered "Islamic." That violence is the very antithesis of the peace and harmony Pirous has sought in his faith. Yet he seems unable to turn to the Qur'an to find some way of healing the wound that is splitting his nation apart.

It is hard to fully know what to make of the paintings in terms of self-address or subjectivity more generally. They certainly make visible Pirous's torn and troubled national self, and remind us that individuals do not have a singular and univocal political self, but a shifting and always vulnerable one, formed through conflicting narratives and images of affiliation, allegiance, and betrayal. Pirous had spent decades conflating the nation and his faith with his nostalgic Acehneseness, only to see asymmetries of power and violence call that vision of things into question. The who and what of subjectivity are precarious and improvised standpoints, and always vulnerable to the circumstances into which we are thrown. The two paintings I have discussed are angry ones. Yet, amid the flash and shadow of the artist's anger, I see clues to something else.

In all of the Qur'anic spiritual notes known to me, Pirous has always crafted the calligraphy in his own hand. It is through touch that he makes painterly recitation of Qur'anic verse. The recitative touch of his hand and eye align him with God's transcendent message and being. The calligraphy is whole or unblemished. The Acehnese paintings featuring *hikayat* verse are quite different. The passages are not in Pirous's hand but are photocopied from notebook manuscripts and published volumes, then transferred directly to the canvas surface. There they may be cut or torn, and stained with paint and binder. They are blemished and sometimes broken verses. Pirous has trouble reading the passages. He does not give these *hikayat* verses recitative touch, but places them unread in the painting so as to make them ambient visual objects.

115

There is an exception: the Oath of the Holy War, featured in *Once There Was a Holy War in Aceh*, and in another 1998 painting, called simply *The Oath of the Holy War*. These are the only paintings from the "Aceh Series" with raised calligraphy made in the artist's hand. Like the Qur'anic passages in his earlier spiritual notes, Pirous gives the Oath recitative touch – he has shaped and painted the Acehnese-Arabic script himself – and in this way has put his unique subjectivity on display. Again, both the Qur'an and the Oath are meant to be recited, to be embodied, and thus made one with breath and tongue. Doing so with the Qur'an allows a Muslim to cultivate his or her ethical sensibilities and become mindful of God. Doing so with the Oath allows Acehnese Muslims to cultivate a dangerous, but no less ethical capacity for thought and feeling. It makes them hunger for justice. The Oath is addressed to Acehnese men, summoning them from the comfort of their wives' homes (see chapter 1) for *jihadist* cause. It is a couplet, in parallel verse.

Return again to Plate 20 and look at the calligraphy of the Oath and the likeness of Teuku Oemar's ghost. The Oath appears to either side of Teuku Oemar, whose image occupies the central vertical axis of the painting, a place usually reserved in the artist's spiritual notes for expressing relationships with God. The figure of Teuku Oemar – the avatar of Pirous's own identity – occupies a recitative space of inhalation, of "breathing in." As Pirous recited the Oath to me, he read (from right to left) the first line of the couplet, beginning with the phrase in red Arabic script in the upper right:

Nibak matée dirumöh inong

uttering its syllables, and taking an audible breath at the image of Teuku Omar. He continued with the phrase in the upper left:

bah le keunong senjata kaphée.

He took a breath and returned to the second line of the couplet in the red script on the lower right:

Nibak matée diateuh tilam,

and came again to the figure of Teuku Oemar. He drew in a breath, and finished with the Oath's closing phrase on the lower left:

bah le lam shaf prang syahid meugulée

Thus the image of Teuku Oemar is a kind of caesura, a place of punctuation where Pirous pauses to take an audible breath into his own body between each phrase of the Oath. A space where he breathes life into an oath and a ghost.

Just as we may see the color turquoise (*pirus*) as an icon of the artist's identity, so too, then, may we see the touch of his painterly hand as an index of Pirous's

116

becoming a subject through, and being made subject to, oral and calligraphic recitation of an inspiring sublime text – be it the Qur'an or the Oath of the Holy War. Calligraphic touch is the intimate and material trace of his breath and his being as he recites words that inspire him.

Remind Them: All You Can Do is Be a Reminder

The two paintings called *Alif Lam Mim* were the only Qur'anic paintings that Pirous made in 1998, and, as I have said, they were quite different from the spiritual notes he had made previously. Through much of 1999 I wondered what direction Pirous would take in his work. Back home in the US, I had published a couple of articles on Pirous and the politics of art, and had another one in the works. But the political situation in Indonesia was changing so rapidly, the essays seemed out of date before they went to print.

Soeharto's fall, widespread violence and uncertainty, and atrocities in Aceh had dramatically upended what it would mean for an Indonesian Muslim like Pirous to fear, to remember, to hope, or to paint. The collapse of authoritarian rule had not made life simpler or easier. The last months of 1998 saw an especially frightening display of mass violence that began with the mysterious murder of dozens of Muslim teachers and leaders in East Java. Some suspected that the murders were the work of military and government factions who wished to destabilize the country. But vast numbers of lower- and middle-class Javanese feared the deaths were the work of supernatural assassins, called *ninja* (after figures in Japanese movies), who were said to dress in black, wield magical powers, and transform themselves into animals. The panic led to vigilantism and mob violence as people sought out *ninjas*. Roughly a hundred people were fingered by clairvoyants or interrogated by self-appointed *ninja* patrols. They were then chased, beaten, burned, tortured, garroted, or stabbed to death. Broadcast accounts, media-disseminated images, and wildfire rumors fed this dangerous frenzy of reprisal against outsiders, the mentally ill, and the innocent. Within weeks, *ninja* suspects began to be hunted down outside of East Java. The bonds of Indonesian citizenship were beginning to fray.

Pirous wrote me in late September 1999, telling me of another student demonstration that had ended in bloodshed at the hands of armed troops. "My government has become demon-possessed," he grieved, "Seven shot dead. ... It is shameful." Just a week before the death of the students, he had donated a Qur'anic painting to a charity fund-raiser in Jakarta, *Measure and Weigh Truthfully, and Uphold Justice/Al-Isra' 17, Verse 35* (*Takar dan Timbanglah yang Benar dan Tegakkan Keadilian/Al-Isra' 17 Ayat 35*), featuring a familiar verse which would appear in several of his paintings in the post-Soeharto years. Someone bought it for about $10,000 and immediately gave it to another auction-goer, Abdurrahman Wahid, who would be chosen as Indonesia's president one month later. It looked like Pirous was back to his spiritual notes once again.

117

A few weeks later, Erna called to tell me that Pirous had suffered a serious heart attack and was being cared for in a Bandung hospital. So began a long convalescence, with orders to stop working, and painting, until doctors gave him the OK. He made some sketches while still in the hospital, and after returning home he began avidly collecting videodiscs, DVDs, and VCDs (video compact discs) and holding screenings for students and friends from the Bandung Institute of Technology. My own personal circumstances kept me from visiting Indonesia for well over a year – switching jobs, moving around the country, caring for ailing parents, and getting married, to mention just a few mid-life highlights. Pirous and I swapped short letters and emails through this time. Not long after my mother passed away, Pirous telephoned with news and a favor to ask. He was going ahead with plans for a career retrospective show in Jakarta in 2002; would I help write the book for the exhibit?

So in March 2001, I headed back to Indonesia to catch up on his painting, this time with my wife, Kirin. We met the Pirouses at a hotel in Jakarta, where the whole family had put up for a couple of nights. Like Pirous, Kirin comes from a Gujarati family on her father's side, and both of them are spellbinding storytellers. They hit it off in minutes, regaling each other with tales of family ancestors, their favorite curries, and South Asian art. To Kirin's glee, the whole family was soon telling stories about me, in ethnographic turnabout. All the time I was studying Pirous and his art, his family was studying me. There were cascades of laughter throughout the week as everyone took turns imitating my mannerisms (hands through hair), detailing trademark quirks (passport and pen in shirt pocket … prompting me to check), parsing my backcountry Indonesian (learned in the mountains of Sulawesi but maybe a little odd for urban art galleries), or relating some memorable moments over the years: the spicy shrimp dish I cooked for the Pirouses and declared ready to eat by looking at my watch rather than tasting it; the many times I kept Pirous from eating the Kentucky Fried Chicken he so longed to taste during his trip around the US in 1985; or (Mida's favorite, and brilliantly acted out) the time I so lost patience with a stubborn airline employee who demanded fees for my suddenly "overweight" bags that I threw a wad of *rupiah* notes at him along with a sarcastic, "Yes, here, please take my money, charge me extra!" Kirin even had a dream one night that Pirous was a saint, like one of the charismatic Hindu holy men she had met as a young girl. In the dream, she was annoyed with me because I hadn't told her that Pirous was a saint, but then berated herself because she should have known Pirous's deep spiritual power from the sparkling, playful intensity of his eyes. Pirous laughed merrily when we told him about the dream the next day.

We took the high mountain road back to Bandung at dusk, winding our way past tea plantations and small towns. I pointed out some *ketok magic* ("magic knocks") auto repair shops to Kirin, which used *ilmu*, or magical power, to do body work on cars. Customers were not allowed to enter the shops, but had to leave their damaged cars outside. The craftsmen would bring the cars inside where, it is said, they would use powerful incantations and the miraculous, supernatural heat of their thumbs and hands to bring the auto bodies back into perfect shape. Nightfall had brought a steady rain and the windshield wipers eventually lulled Kirin and Erna to sleep. Pirous sat up front with Ujang at the wheel, his longtime driver and the go-to handyman whom the family had nicknamed "MacGyver" – after the US television series – for his resourcefulness in fixing most any everyday problem. Enveloped in dark, the engine's hum, and the whispered splash of the wet road, Pirous and I talked quietly.

I asked about his health and his heart attack, and it led him to say there are four things in life we cannot foretell: the direction we will travel; the riches that will come our way; who we will meet; and the moment of our death. He was already in a pensive mood, then, when talk veered to collectors who had asked him for paintings, or had commissioned him to make one. My mind ran back seven years to 1994, and *Nothing Whatsoever is Hidden from God*, the painting bought by the Minister of Religious Affairs.

"Pirous, have you seen Tarmizi Taher, what is he up to?"

Pirous replied with a terse, almost sullen, "I don't know." With a little pressing from me, Pirous explained there had been scandals over mismanagement in the Department of Religious Affairs, *hajj* funds had gone missing, and Tarmizi was alleged to have put some of them to wrongful use (as were his several successors). True or not, the rumors and allegations profoundly bothered my friend, leaving him worried that *hajj* funds had been used to buy his painting. "The worst scandals of the Soeharto years were in the Ministry of Religious Affairs and the Department of Education and Culture. That's why Indonesia is in such a crisis today," continued Pirous bitterly. "My painting? He *took* my painting from me!"

Others might have a very different view about what counted as the worst scandals of the Soeharto years. But those views should not diminish our sympathy for Pirous's feelings of betrayal by government figures – some of them his friends – in the fields of art, culture, or religion, fields to which he had devoted himself so earnestly. After all, for Pirous, art and religion are endeavors to which one should turn for ethical guidance, despite the fact that art and religion are also activities with which one can make a living, or a killing. I commiserated with Pirous about the painting he had let go, and ruefully pointed out that the painting's title and Qur'anic verse would be a reminder to the former Minister of Religious Affairs that no deed is hidden from God. As for the betrayal of the goodness he sought in friendship with Tarmizi in picking out the painting and giving it away at a fair if modest price, I could only imagine that Pirous suffered a profound sting. Being useful to others in a time of authoritarianism, corruption, and cronyism often means getting used.

Later in the week I asked Pirous to reflect on the political changes around him and their impact on his art. He had this to say:

This era of reform is truly a time for people to look back at what once seemed absolute, and to ask questions about it. It is very free and open now. In painting, it is clear that people were trapped in a system, shackled, in the Soeharto years. Shackled in the sense that there were no large issues or disturbances, nothing that flared up. Everything was very peaceful, everything was very orderly, everything was safe and quiet. To the point

119

the flame of human life disappeared, even though that flame is so very necessary to stirring creativity in the arts. It was as if everything was guaranteed, everything was safe, everything was "no problem." To the point that art became very barren, very sterile, very – what do you call it – happily singing praises to a world that was peaceful, beautiful, and good. It was paradise for painting that was formalist, and modern art that was abstract and beautiful.

I couldn't call it remorse, but it seemed as if Pirous was calling his whole painterly venture into question, especially his commitment to abstraction. He had more to say, however:

> If you look closely at my work, all the issues, all the problems that were around then – even if I was involved or concerned with them – were sublimated into religious belief. Into what is said in the Qur'an. With those passages, I wanted to say something, to give a quote or to make an allusion to the lessons of the Qur'an itself. About authority with no limits, about arrogance, about feeling that everything is eternal even though everything is fleeting.

Here he seems to be describing the Qur'an and his faith as a refuge and ruse for dealing with Indonesian politics. If Pirous harbored critical political views during the Soeharto years, they were decidedly muted, measured, and oblique – channeled through the language of the Qur'an, tempered with his optimism and his spiritual life as a Muslim, and carefully phrased so as not to lose the favor of government patrons. He never used Islamic art as a bullhorn for political reform. Spiritual notes speak quietly.

Although Pirous had resumed his Qur'anic calligraphic work, the paintings that jumped out at me at Serambi Pirous were filled with human figures. Two of the paintings showed a parade of heads, their ashen faces in stunned grimaces or unsettling smiles: *The Heads I: They No Longer Know What to Think* (*Kepala-Kepala I: Mereka Sudah Tak Tahu Berpikir Apa*) and *The Heads II: They No Longer Know What to Dream* (*Kepala-Kepala II: Mereka Sudah Tak Tahu Bermimpi Apa*) – the titles a commentary on the shock and confusion in Indonesian society during the traumas of 1998–99. Other paintings brought back the faces and corpses of the Acehnese dead as anonymous ghosts. *They Who are Buried without Names* (*Mereka yang Terkubur tanpa Nama*) is the one that haunts me the most (Plate 22). It is a large painting made from acrylics, marble paste, and colored sands. It shows what appears to be a mass grave, with bodies, limbs, and faces in a careless heap. It asks us to imagine victims stripped of their social and human being – we don't know their names and no one was there to care for them in their moment of death. The last rites given to deceased Muslims – the tender washing and wrapping of the dead, placing them to rest in graves, the comforting prayers and condolences from and to family members (*Inna lillahi wa inna ilahi raji'un*, "We all belong to God, and to God we will all return") – were denied to them. The language of the painting's Indonesian title is pained. Verb prefixes tell the story: The buried were ***terkubur*** – covered over by some impersonal, unfeeling, and un-named force, a force

120

without goodness – not *di-kubur*, sorrowfully and respectfully placed in God's care by one's fellows. The painting asks us to ache and to look in anguish at the work of state violence. Its wordless ethical aim is to point at the dead, to acknowledge them and thus retrieve them as fellow human beings. It is a gesture of goodness toward those who were killed in anonymity, and an appeal to the goodness of those who look at the painting. It is an admonition as well, part disclosure and part rebuke. As Pirous had put it in his speech two years before, "This didn't happen just in Aceh, but throughout Indonesia. It happened everywhere."

Another new painting at Serambi Pirous seemed like a talisman aimed at warding off the evil and violence of the state power. This was a Qur'anic painting, *The Truth*

Figure 5.1 *The Truth that Struggles Against the Darkness/QS 113 Al Falaq.* 2000. 105 × 95 cm, marble paste, gold leaf, acrylic on canvas. Photograph courtesy of Yayasan Serambi Pirous.

that Struggles Against the Darkness/QS 113 Al Falaq (*Kebenaran yang Memerangi Kegalapan/QS 113 Al Falaq*), which appears in Figure 5.1. The title of the QS 113, *Al Falaq*, means "daybreak" or "rising day" and so connotes the return of light. In the painting we see some of the painter's familiar iconographies at work: an inscribed tablet; a dark terrestrial space; a horizon returning to color; and morning twilight filling the sky. The painting reads:

> In the Name of God the Compassionate the Caring
> Say, "I take refuge in the Lord of the daybreak
> From the evil of what he created
> From the evil of the dark as it spreads
> From the evil of the sorcerers who cast their spells on knots
> From the evil of the envier when he envies."

Often recited elsewhere to ward off the "evil eye" (Sells 1999: 139), the Qur'anic verses here strike me as an amulet against the menacing spectre of Indonesian authoritarianism and the malevolent spell of political intrigue and ambition.

The Retrospective, 2002

I returned to Indonesia the following January, during a very bad monsoon season. The rich and the lucky had evacuated to higher ground as much of Jakarta's sprawling urban footprint disappeared under swollen, devastating floodwaters. The overwhelming portion of the city's 15 million inhabitants were left stranded for weeks, trying to fend off hunger and illness until power, transportation, and hope were restored. The flood became a metaphor for Indonesia's political and economic misfortunes and for the government's impotence.

Pirous's retrospective show was scheduled for a March opening in the capital at Galeri Nasional. The flooding posed real problems in keeping the needed advance work on track. Pirous and Erna oversaw the project from their home in Bandung, and had recruited two Bandung graduates – Mamannoor and Ilham Khoiri – to serve as curatorial partners who would work with the director and staff at Galeri Nasional. The newly wed Rihan and her husband, graphic designer Eka Sofyan Rizal, were based in Jakarta and pledged the help of their new company, dialogue+design. Mida and Dudy ran planning operations and coordination out of Serambi Pirous, half of which had been converted into a home for the young couple and their son. Iwan took charge of a film crew that was to make a thirty-minute video featuring Pirous reflecting on his work; he and the crew shuttled back and forth between Jakarta and Bandung. I helped out with publications and offered counsel when asked.

Pirous, Dudy, and I nicknamed the group "The Dream Team." It was very much a family enterprise, and spoke volumes about how Pirous viewed the practical challenges of staging a major show in a country with a very scant government budget for the arts and few trained professionals in art administration. Iwan was still single and the family goaded him good-naturedly about finding an art writer or art critic to join the team. "This is too much!" I exclaimed in a burst of mock protest one evening at a family dinner. "Do you have to be working in the arts to get a Pirous family ID? Pirous, you and Erna are painters, your two lovely daughters are graphic designers, your one son-in-law is a product designer, the other is a graphic designer – that makes three graphic designers – and now you want Iwan – my only hope for anthropology in this family – to recruit an art critic! What's going on?" My teasing aside, it was the loyalty of family, friends, and colleagues that helped propel this show into the public eye. In other contexts, and with other people, this sort of arrangement could take a sinister turn toward what Indonesians call "KKN," shorthand for *Korupsi, Kolusi, dan Népotisme* – corruption, collusion, and nepotism. In a country longing for a democratic and smoothly functioning system of just and lawful institutions, personal networks of family and friends provide the lines of trust and expertise that allow people to get things done. The ethics of friendship and kinship prevail when public institutions and society at large are unable to sustain a commitment to goodness and lawfulness for all.

Through the many weeks leading up to the show I wondered how Pirous would choose to represent his work. How Indonesian? How Acehnese? How Islamic? Just what would he do with his painting of Teuku Oemar, let alone his anguish for the homeland he had left nearly fifty years before? As James Siegel has remarked, "there was until recently no contradiction between being Acehnese and being Indonesian" (Siegel 2000: 366). But the riots and killings of May 1998 and the atrocities in Aceh had changed that. Being both Acehnese *and* Indonesian was now a source of pain for Pirous, not a source of easy pride. Affiliations or solidarities so basic to his lifeworld had left the artist vulnerable to the larger political tragedies around him.

I have always thought of Pirous as someone who has located himself rather squarely in the space of Indonesian nationalism. Indeed, it was as an Indonesian artist-citizen that this Acehnese Muslim had found a part on the world stage, politically and aesthetically. Overwhelmed by the violent tragedies in his nation, his paintings seemed to move in different directions. *Alif Lam Mim/Only God is All Knowing* (Plate 19) looks away from the collapse and transformation of Indonesian society in May 1998; it is a shielding of the eyes and a turning toward God. *They Who Are Buried Without Names* (Plate 22) looks in fury and anguish at the brutality of the nation-state; it is worldly and places us within the suffering and wounds of the Acehnese. How well these paintings might reach and touch a broader public is, of course, open to question. Paintings don't often count for much in contemporary society. National and international media and online news far outweigh paintings in terms of impact. In fact, Pirous's painterly explorations of violence and grief came in response to the troubling and spectacular images that he had seen on television, in magazines, and in newspapers; he witnessed violence largely through the media, never in clouds of teargas or amid the flies swarming over the dead. Indeed, his feel for being Indonesian and Acehnese and Muslim no longer relies just on the facts of birth and a lifetime of face-to-face relationships, but also upon mass-mediated forms of national, ethnic, and religious identity.

Pirous decided that his "Aceh Series" would occupy the walls in the gallery's front corridor. Teuku Oemar would stare in challenge at gallery-goers as they came into the show (see Figure 5.2). The gesture seemed bolder and more brooding than those he usually made at exhibits. When I asked whether doing so might bring him some trouble, he shot back "I don't care." Yet it was a new Qur'anic painting that had come to interest me most with respect to the politics of Pirous's show.

Figure 5.2 *Once There Was a Holy War in Aceh* facing outward toward the portico at Galeri Nasional, Jakarta, during Pirous's second retrospective show, March 2002. The Basmallah, painted by Pirous, hangs above the entry. Photograph by Kenneth M. George, 2002.

124

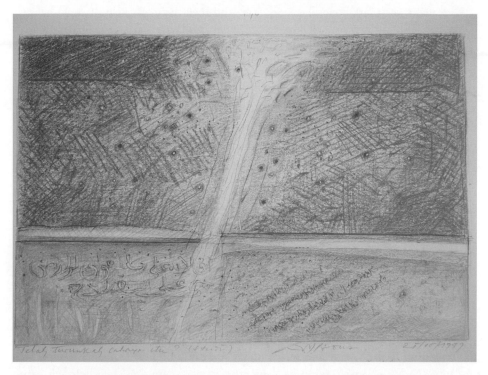

Figure 5.3 Sketch for *Has That Light Already Shone Down from Above?* October 25, 1999. From sketchbooks kept by A. D. Pirous. Photograph by Kenneth M. George, 2002.

This was a dramatic magenta canvas divided by a diagonal column of brilliant light. Pirous first sketched it on May 25, 1998, during the turmoil surrounding Soeharto's fall, and then once more in October 1999 during his hospitalization for a heart attack (see Figure 5.3). The intervening months were precisely those when Qur'anic verse disappeared from his paintings and images of the *Hikayat Prang Sabil* came into being. The sketches sprang from his reflections on QS 13, *Ar-Ra'd* (*Thunder*), one of the Qur'anic sura that begin with a mysterious sequence of syllables: *alif-lam-mim-ra*. The second half of verse 11 in this sura reads:

> God does not change the state of a people until they change themselves.
> When God intends misfortune for a people
> no one can avert it
> and no savior will they have apart from Him.

He gave the sketch the title *Has That Light Already Shone Down from Above?* (*Telah Turunkah Cahaya Itu?*). As Pirous told me one afternoon as he sorted and signed some paintings for his retrospective show:

125

I created a very dark atmosphere. So dark. And then there was light. It could have come up from below or it might have come down from above. That was my question. What will this *Reformasi* bring us? What will it bring to our nation? Has that light already shone down from above? Is this the Just Ruler, the Muslim leader who, tradition says, will bring us justice?

Two years went by. Many changes took place, and, as he recuperated in the hospital, Pirous redrew his sketch, adding another passage, to be taken from QS 2 *Al-Baqarah*, verse 153:

> O you who believe
> seek courage in fortitude and prayer
> for God is with those who are patient and persevere

"If we have passion and patience," Pirous told me, "Allah will be with us."

The sketch eventually made its way into paint and onto canvas in early 2002, and was hanging – without a title – in the painter's home that January, when I arrived to help with the retrospective show (see Plate 23). The steeply pitched diagonal that splits the painting in two perhaps alludes to the flash of lightning that sometimes comes with thunder; as it says in QS 13 verse 12: "It is He who makes the lightning flash for fear and hope!" That same visual gesture formally separates the two Qur'anic verses. In some ways, the verses seem a bit at odds with one another. The verse from *Ar-Ra'd*, to the right on the painting, urges a people (as a community, not as individuals) to take action so as to care for themselves and earn God's favor. The verse to the left, from *Al-Baqarah*, counsels patience: God is with those who endure and persevere.

Pirous was a bit of a wag about this painting with me, in that he refrained from clearing up its ambiguous politics. I frankly saw the painting as a potential incitement to Acehnese separatist sentiment – "take matters into your own hands and persevere" – and told him so. "Well, you see what you want to see," he replied. Smiling. The painting reminded me of the inscription Pirous placed in his copy of *Mohammed and Charlemagne* forty-four years earlier. Both the painting and the quote from Plato put forward the idea that a people's outward state is a product of their spiritual character and interior virtue. I remembered, too, how Pirous once told me he wanted to make Qur'anic paintings legible "for the sake of my people," a remark that prompted me to ask, "Who are your people?" I looked at the painting in front of us and asked him once more: "So, who are your people?" Without a moment's pause or a blink of the eye he replied just as he did before, "Why, the Indonesian people!" With that, he sat down and gave the painting the title it would carry into his retrospective show, *A People's Fate is in Their Own Hands* (*Nasib Suatu Kaum Terletak di Tangannya Sendiri*). He was back on his Qur'anic footing.

Pirous opened his retrospective show on the evening of March 11, his seventieth birthday. About 500 guests or more gathered in front of Galeri Nasional to listen

Figure 5.4 In his own hand(s). Pirous labeling and signing *A People's Fate is in Their Own Hands*. Serambi Pirous, Bandung, February 26, 2002. Photograph by Kenneth M. George, 2002.

to introductory remarks from several distinguished public figures, as well as words of thanks and welcome from the painter. Poets Taufiq Ismail and Abdul Hadi set the mood for the show by reading works inspired by Hamzah Fansuri, the sixteenth-century Acehnese writer and Sufi philosopher whose work urged Muslims to seek union with God through *dzikir*. Passing between curtains of pure white upon which Pirous had painted the *Basmallah* ("In the Name of God the Compassionate the Caring"), the guests, some reporters, and a couple of television crews flocked into the gallery. The place was teeming with guests, and at moments it seemed more like a night market than an art gallery. Some women wore *jilbab* and scarves over their hair in formal attire, but, for the most part, the crowd was looking *tréndi* (trendy) – batik, smart-looking silk jackets and shirts with mandarin collars, knock-off Armani suits and other designer men's wear, crisp jeans, and a few eye-catching black skirts and dresses.

The show stayed open for three weeks. Most of the crowd came on opening night, and total attendance for the three-week run reached about 2,500. A back room was set up as a sales office, and collectors could put bids on items in a secondary collection of paintings or sound out the artist about his willingness to part with a major

127

work. Pirous sold sixteen small paintings that brought in roughly $80,000, and that sum paid for the entire show.

I did not learn of anyone who left the gallery alarmed or offended by the paintings of the Acehnese dead and *hikayat* verses. Qur'anic paintings were kept clear of the "Aceh Series." One reason for this was to keep Qur'anic calligraphic paintings focally grouped and thematically sequestered from other kinds of work. Though never expressed openly, there appeared to me, too, an uneasiness about displaying Qur'anic verse near images of the dead. Last, the question of placing paintings also had to do with anxieties over the juxtaposition of a sacred language – Qur'anic Arabic – with the everyday one of Acehnese. Not that many gallery-goers could distinguish between them, cloaked as they were in Arabic script, but Pirous and others were keenly aware that *ulama* or literalist experts on the Qur'an might come by and complain. No one should confuse an anti-colonial *jihadist* poem for divine revelation, or vice versa. For these reasons, then, gallery-goers would see *A People's Fate is in Their Own Hands* on one of the many walls reserved for Pirous's Qur'anic "spiritual notes." Placed in that way, its ambiguously addressed political rhetoric seemed less likely to stir sentiments around or for Acehnese separatism.

After decades of using Acehnese iconography as a painterly sign of his indigeneity, Pirous tried something new. Clustered together on adjoining walls in the "Aceh" corridor just a few meters from his images of Acehnese ghosts and oaths, were four calligraphic paintings of what Pirous liked to call *sastra Aceh*, "Acehnese literature." These four paintings were a new kind of spiritual note for Pirous. All four were meditative poems that drew on Sufi traditions, and all were rendered in Arabic script. Unlike the impassioned verses of the *Hikayat Prang Sabil*, these poems were *dzikir*-like meditations intended to put the heart at peace. With them, Pirous pictured Aceh as a place of Islamic spirituality, a gesture intended to remind viewers that Acehnese culture was more than a culture of violence. Yet Pirous also told me that with these four paintings he wanted to show that Aceh was part of broader world, a global Muslim civilization – a remark that reminded me of his experience at the Metropolitan Museum of Art in New York City over thirty years before.

One painting was called *God, We are That Close* (*Tuhan, Kita Begitu Dekat*), its verse taken from a poem by the painter's friend, Abdul Hadi W. M. (see the epigraph in chapter 4). It speaks of one's inner union with God. Another painting took its verses from a work by the Sufi poet Hamzah Fansuri (see above), *Our Faith is a Perahu as We Cross the Seas of Life* (*Tamsil Perahu, Mengarungi Kehidupan*). The third work, *The Poem of Ma'rifat* (*Syair Ma'rifat*), drew from the seventeenth-century Acehnese writer and religious teacher, Syech Abdul Rauf Singkel, who, in Sufi fashion and after long residence and study in Mecca and Medina, preached *ma'rifat* – mystical inner knowledge of God – as the path for ethical self-knowledge. It was the fourth work that perhaps connected Aceh most strongly to the major global currents of Islamic culture (see Figure 5.5). The painting featured a passage from an epitaph on a medieval Acehnese tomb located in the former harbor kingdom of Pasai. The epitaph itself was taken from the writings of the famed thirteenth-century Persian poet and storyteller, Syech Mushlihuddin Sa'adi. The

128

Figure 5.5 *Through the Days of Our Lives, There is Nothing That Can Give Us Help, Save for the Doing of Good Deeds*. 2002. 145 × 160 cm, marble paste and acrylic on canvas. Photograph courtesy of Yayasan Serambi Pirous.

epitaph warns us of arrogance, reminds us of life's transience, and urges us toward *ihsan* and *mu'amalah*, goodness and good conduct. Pirous called it, *Through the Days of Our Lives, There is Nothing That Can Give Us Help, Save for the Doing of Good Deeds* (*Hari-hari Manusia, Tiada yang Dapat Memberi Pertolongan Kepadanya, Kecuali Amal yang Shaleh*).

Retrospectives, like other forms of historical and autobiographical reflection, not only tell us something about the past, but they tell us something, too, about the moment of looking back in time. Retrospectives address communities in the present, and Pirous's show was no exception. The show was a chance for Pirous to disclose himself to fellow Indonesians (onlookers from elsewhere notwithstanding), and to offer an account of how he had lived and worked as an artist in their midst for nearly fifty years. It was not a "final reckoning" – which for a Muslim would fall to God – but a reflexive and fleeting account aimed at finding ethical alignment with this community. There are always contingencies and sacrifices, and a play of truth and cover-up in retrospective accounts. The capacity to reflect upon ourselves, as Judith Butler (2005) reminds us, comes with trade-aways and costs; we cannot give full account of ourselves. It has long been Pirous's ethical aim – perhaps not always fully realized – to do good through his art by reminding people that there is refuge in God. Although he may have staged it with other purposes in mind, I like to think of Pirous's retrospective as a show of his "recovery" – and perhaps Indonesia's – from the predations and betrayals of authoritarian rule and violence, from errant hopes and judgments, and from incapacitating doubts.

Pirous and the Dream Team stayed at the opening well past midnight to bask in the company of lingering guests, and then we scattered to our hotel rooms or homes for some much needed rest. It was nearly mid-afternoon before we got back to Galeri Nasional the next day to size up what needed to be done for the next few weeks both in Jakarta and Bandung. After our meeting, I busied myself with some photos around the gallery's portico and grounds as Pirous chatted with some well-wishers who had come by. I was sitting out front, browsing through my notes from the night before, when Pirous stepped out and ambled down the gallery steps. He had on his Adidas cap, a tattersall shirt, and a pair of his trademark suspenders – his casual Larry King look.

"So, Ken, what do you think? Was this a good start to the show?"

"*Dah-syat!*" I replied, using a Dream Team code word and in-joke. "Awesome!"

A few appreciative reviews appeared in newspapers over the next few weeks, and one of the television networks arranged to produce a segment about Pirous for one of its biography shows. Pirous would have liked larger attendance. I know a good many of those who came through the gallery before the show closed down were college students and young artists from around Jakarta. The small overall number of visitors, however, spoke to some of the facets of Indonesia's art world more generally: a scarcity of public art institutions and public art funding; the marginalization of public discourse about visual art relative to the attention devoted to literature, drama, and film; limited art philanthropy; and the eclipse of the "modernist generation" by younger contemporary and postmodern artists. As for prominent Muslim organizations, outside of their intellectual elites, art is not very high on their agenda for personal or societal religious growth and reform.

Pirous gave Kirin and me one of his "spiritual notes" for me to take back home after the show closed, and Erna gave us one of her splendid works as well. Pirous had made his painting as his optimism about his world returned in 2000, and had shown it in Tapei at the Fifteenth Asian International Art Exhibition. Called *Meditation Toward the Enlightened Spirit, I* (*Meditasi Menuju Pencerahan Jiwa, I*), and shown in Plate 24, the painting is perhaps one of his most simple and spare expressions in visual *dzikir*. A square of gold leaf steadies the eye within the calm geometries and depths of the canvas. I was, of course, touched by Pirous's generosity – it is a marvelous canvas and I would have had trouble parting with it had I painted it. But I was touched, too, by Pirous's judgment and care in picking out this work as a gift to us. The painting does not require us to comprehend Qur'anic Arabic, nor does it remind us of the Acehnese dead. Pirous would not compel us to acknowledge the truth of his faith, nor ask us to dwell in his anguish and grief. The painting is an undemanding friend. Kirin and I are both drawn to its serenity, and are always struck by how the painting takes on different moods with shifts in light. It has been a good companion, a reminder of the practical wisdom and pleasurable surprises to be found in art, in stories, and in friendship.

CONCLUSION:
A RETROSPECTIVE

Just before returning home from Indonesia in 2002, I gave a seminar in Jakarta on problems in contemporary Indonesian Islamic art, and of course drew on my collaborative work with Pirous. The role of Qur'anic calligraphy in Pirous's paintings was of special interest to me and I did my best to offer an inviting anthropological approach to what I felt were key issues, issues that I have mentioned in this book. But a challenge from one skeptical scholar at the seminar still stands out in my memory. "You have told us much about Pirous's Qur'anic painting," he thundered, "but I want to know just one thing. Do *you* tremble when you look upon the verses of the Qur'an in his work? Do you feel *awe*?"

These pointed, unsettling words called into question my understanding and participation in the aesthetic and ethical world of Islamic art. For a long time I thought his challenge might have to do with my status as a non-Muslim, a matter about which I felt considerable self-consciousness. But, as exasperated as he might have been, this skeptic did not dismiss me out of hand. As my friend Charles Hallisey has pointed out to me, this challenge may have been about connoisseurship, about how well I could discern the power of Pirous's art irrespective of my religious identity or outlook. I could think, but did I truly see? I have yet to tremble as I look at the Qur'anic verses in Pirous's paintings, and I have yet to feel spiritual awe when doing so. For many Muslims, however, merely looking upon the beautiful name of Allah when written, painted, or etched in calligraphic form is to be close with God and to know God's incomparable magnificence (see Plate 25). How well do I see? Perhaps not so very well yet. Thanks to Pirous and the worlds he has opened up to me, I hope I am getting better at glimpsing other perspectives. For this brief concluding chapter, I would like to look back through this book to

132

remind readers of how I came to see its issues as I did. Then I will offer some conclusions regarding the book's general theme and Pirous's lifeworld in particular.

Lifeworlds and Long-Term Ethnographic Fieldwork

A hallmark of cultural anthropology has been its blend of firsthand ethnographic fieldwork with the comparative, cross-cultural analysis of ideas, concepts, and forms of life in all their historical richness and contingency (cf., Asad 2003: 16–17). Ethnographic fieldwork is not just a method, but a reflexive and experiential project, aimed at learning something about society, culture, and power through "being with" others and "being in" their lifeworld. It raises questions of ontology – that is, questions about being – and for this reason involves ethical concerns as well. I came to know something about how Pirous has pictured Islam and brought it into his art by spending time talking with him and watching him contend with the political, historical, and cultural circumstances into which he has been thrown, and through which he must make his way. Two aspects of this ethnographic work need explicit mention. First, I have put Pirous's reflections on how he has acted and been acted upon in the world at center stage. I have regarded him as a self-conscious actor and have privileged certain points of human encounter: his paintings, our conversations and interviews, and various art events. Second, this has been a long-term project. Had I written this book in 1996, after only a brief and politically circumscribed period of time with Pirous, it would have been a much different one. Not all fieldwork can or should be long term, but let me sketch some of the value I have found in it for the trajectory of this project.

A key virtue of long-term fieldwork is that it can give us a glimpse of change. Questions of art and religion notwithstanding, this book has shown someone, and someone's lifeworld, going through changes. We get to see time at work. Without the decade and more I have spent with Pirous, I could not have witnessed or shown how he has had his hopes fulfilled or thwarted, how he has suffered and recovered from betrayals and setbacks, or how his picture of Islam and Islamic art has mellowed over the years. As my story has shown, the tides and storms of Indonesian politics brought Pirous both opportunities and threats. The collapse of the Soeharto regime, in particular, gave Pirous the freedom to acknowledge the expressive straitjacket authoritarian rule had long put on him and to call into question the powers that had perverted the just and hope-filled civic venture he knew as the Indonesian nation. Throughout, I have tried to capture how Pirous has used the vocabulary of Islamic faith and ethics to interpret and negotiate these changes.

Long-term fieldwork has also made it possible for me to capture or understand the richness and slipperiness of human reflexivity, contingent as it is on time and circumstance. Open-ended life-history interviews with Pirous played a big part in my study during 1994 and 1995, even as I spent time at Serambi Pirous or sat in on Festival Istiqlal planning sessions. With them, I invited Pirous to reflect on his youth, his early career as a painter, and the first twenty-five years of his exploration in Islamic art and aesthetics. As much as I have relied on interview narratives and exchanges in this project, I am careful not to always go so smoothly with their grain. I have needed to understand these conversations in light of art works and transnational art discourses, broader social and political movements, and, above all, the unforeseen life circumstances that through time might have led Pirous to revise or abrogate earlier accounts of himself. Visits to Bandung in 1997, 1998, 2001, and 2002 provided fresh opportunities for reflection – both retrospective and prospective. Fieldwork for Pirous's 2002 retrospective show was especially valuable in this respect, for the show aimed at a pictorial and autobiographical portrait of Pirous's work.

There are always ethical aims to any conversation, even ethnographic interviews. Notwithstanding real differences in power and knowledge, a kind of mutual recognition and esteem is implicit in and cultivated by conversation, a mingling of care and ethical feeling (cf., Ricoeur 1992: 193–94). Long-term fieldwork has given this dimension of our collaboration fuller richness and freer rein. Time deepened our confidence and familiarity with one another. Political anthropologist Fadjar Thufail and his wife Atka Savitri, who together helped me transcribe my recorded conversations with Pirous, mentioned to me how the tone of the interview conversations recorded in 2001 differed from those done in 1994. Profound political changes had taken place, it is true. Yet, as Fadjar put it, "You can hear it. Pirous speaks with you as someone who knows his life and his work. He is more open. You're not a stranger or a naïf."

Lifeworlds and Fieldwork with Paintings

In this book, I have treated my friend's paintings as companionable objects, that is, as things (actually, image-things) with which Pirous or any one of us might dwell. Dwelling with them meant recognizing them, and even developing a kind of ethical feeling toward them, most especially because they are the fruit of Pirous's reflexivity and artistic skill. They are "spiritual notes" about his lifeworld. Muslims dwelling with Pirous's Qur'anic paintings might feel a reverential and awe-filled regard for them; as I am not yet a Muslim, my feeling for them was less acutely spiritual. I was drawn to them as points of encounter.

Asking Pirous to reflect on the paintings, or to account for them in some respect, was my way of reaching for a sense of common encounter with them. I don't think what Pirous had to say about the paintings, or what he "intended to say with them," in any way exhausts conversation about the works or further interpretation of them. As I have argued elsewhere (George 1997), paintings accrue complex – and sometimes unforeseen – social and interpretive histories as they circulate through different cultural, historical, and ideological precincts. For this book, I followed pointers from art historian Michael Baxandall. "The maker of a picture," writes Baxandall, "is [someone] addressing a problem for which [the] product is a finished and concrete solution. To understand it we try to reconstruct both the specific problem it was designed to solve and the specific circumstances [to] which [it was addressed]" (1985: 14–15). Baxandall subsequently invites us to take into account the purposefulness and intentionality behind a painting (41–42). By this, he means not the state of mind or psychological state of the painter, but "the forward-leaning look of things" and "the relation between an object and its circumstances." Accounts of intentionality are as theoretically crucial for anthropologists as they are ethnographically illuminating (cf., Ortner 2006: 134–36), and so I have tried to capture "patterns of intention" in and around the paintings and in Pirous's lifeworld more generally.

I have tried to show, too, a regard for the materiality of the paintings themselves. Art historian Thomas Crow (1999: 5) suggests that paintings may sometimes be able to prefigure their own analysis. That is, paintings may already display gestures crucial to making the works intelligible. I cannot say how well I have succeeded in recognizing these gestures – I am at best a fledgling art historian. But, having paid attention to the materiality of the works, I was able to understand a transformational turn to acrylic paint in the 1970s and the use of modeling paste for an Acehnese oath in the late 1990s as gestures that revealed something vital about painterly subjectivity and the historical circumstances in which the works first appeared.

Treating Pirous's paintings as spiritual notes and companionable objects has inclined me to downplay their status as commodities that circulate in global and Indonesian art markets, or that hang in galleries and museums as emblems of Indonesian or Islamic aesthetic sensibilities. I have focused on Pirous's personal collection of paintings at home and at Serambi Pirous, a collection of work he has carefully kept off market so as to reserve it for personal reflection and for emblematic display in national and international exhibitions. Then, too, I have tried to suggest, if only in anecdotal fashion, how Pirous's paintings have entered into the lifeworlds of others and into the "lifeworld" of a broader Indonesian public.

Picturing Islam – As Lived Religion

My long collaborative project with Pirous has led me to picture Islam rather differently from those who see this religion as an all-encompassing force or tradition that rigidly dictates the worldview, subjectivity, and life choices of its followers. Sharing in this artist's lifeworld and understanding his stories and paintings as reflexive points of encounter, I have come to think of Islam, or, more properly, Islamic life, as a pragmatic ethical and spiritual improvisation. Being Muslim does not rest on unreflective acquiescence to the Qur'an, the *hadith*, *syari'ah* law, and religious

135

authorities. I have learned that being Muslim means seeing one's way through one's political, cultural, and historical circumstances with reference not just to the Qur'an or *hadith*, but also to the ideas, debates, aspirations, dispositions, and images that have found expression in a community of believers. Like Mohammed Arkoun (1994) and Aziz Al-Azmeh (1993), then, I see in Islam a vast spectrum of practical Islams lived out in the push and pull of powerful cultural, ideological, and institutional forces. Islam is not a "ready-made." It is a lived religion: lived, re-imagined, and remade through the intermingling of believers' lifeworlds with all their predicaments, contradictions, and contingencies. It is an applied religion: called upon to serve a wide range of seemingly non-religious purposes and projects, contemporary art being just one of them. Indeed, religion has played a crucial role in the nationalist political imagination throughout colonial and postcolonial Asia (see, for example, Chatterjee 1993; Esposito 1987; Hefner and Horvatich 1997; Nandy 1998; Tambiah 1992; van der Veer 1994; van der Veer and Lehman 1999).

Instead of describing an ideal version of Islam that accords with the views of Muslim theologians and jurists, I have sought the "practical Islam" that informs Muslim lifeworlds. As Pirous has shown us, Islam is not a rigid tradition that is antithetical to modern subjectivity, but a supple ethical path for living in the world, for understanding how to be. Indeed, we have seen him adopt and adapt his faith in pursuit of modernist, nationalist, and cosmopolitan projects and identities. Pirous's reflexive disposition – we could call it his conscience – drew increasingly and unmistakably from an Islamic vocabulary, as he refashioned himself as a cosmopolitan artist and Indonesian citizen after enduring the shock of self-recognition and displacement at the Metropolitan Museum of Art. Religious sentiments and sensibilities began to inspire and shape his art, not just pictorially or thematically – as in his exploration of calligraphies – but functionally as well, as he brought his work more deeply and "usefully" into accord with his ethical bonds and responsibilities toward others and toward God. In this way, Pirous came to find a "companionable conscience" in his "spiritual notes." Although his paintings and prints would find display and acclaim beyond Indonesia's borders, Pirous sought recognition primarily from Indonesian Muslims. Thus, Islam and Islamic art were for Pirous not just about religious principles and select aesthetic conventions and attitudes, but about an imagined – though very real – community of citizen-believers connected through ethical, spiritual, and political bonds.

Overall, then, this book has aimed at restoring the idea of studying people and lifeworlds as a way of studying religion, and studying Islam in particular (cf., Smith 1976). I am not arguing that we should think of Islam as the sum of all individualized, practical Islams, past and present. Studying Muslim lifeworlds, I would claim, brings us closer to understanding Muslim subjectivity, to grasping how Islam might offer ways of cultivating a sense of being a who and a what in relation to others and to God. Rather than begin with an ideal version of subjectivity or aspiring personhood, such as we may find in the Islamic notion of perfect human being, *al-insan al-kamil*, I prefer to start in worldly encounter. The specificities discovered by dwelling in Muslim lifeworlds, and in reflexive ethnographic collaboration with Muslims, would seem to me more revealing and more promising for understanding religious subjectivity than conceding subject-shaping powers to philosophical or theological discourse alone.

I offer my ethnographic portrait of Pirous and his art, in part, as a contribution to a growing conversation among scholars about the relationship of Muslim subjectivity and agency to questions of modernity, secularism, and the politics of the public sphere. Other anthropologists already have done pioneering work on many of the questions raised in this book (e.g., Asad 1986, 2003; Ewing 1997; Fischer and Abedi 1990; Mahmood 2005), and have set agendas for an emerging cohort of specialists interested in the topic (e.g., Hoesterey 2009, Silverstein 2008). Indeed, Charles Hirschkind's study of "ethical soundscapes" in Egypt (2006) has special resonance with this book, for its nuanced analysis of the ethico-political dispositions involved in listening to cassette sermons suggests important ways of connecting aesthetics to ethical conduct. I have been careful, however, not to confuse an ethics of reception for the ethics of making art. As Ebrahim Moosa brilliantly demonstrates in his study of the medieval Muslim intellectual Abu Hamid al-Ghazali (2005), questions of religious subjectivity and reflexivity may be explored and resolved through the writing of narrative and poetry. Pirous's story, too, shows us how religious subjectivity is experienced, expressed, and interpreted, but through a different art form – painting.

Following her years of study with a Hindu holy man and his group of devotees in Nasik, India, Kirin Narayan (1989) argued that stories make up the very fabric of religion. She vividly showed how telling and listening to stories – especially allegorical and parable-like folktales – help people relate religious teachings and precepts to living ethically in everyday life. Like stories, painting and the other visual arts, too, have a place in the fabric of religion and religious life. Like stories, pictures are points of reflexive human encounter and mutual recognition, even as they vary from religion to religion. As Pirous has shown us, painting can be a resource of goodness, aimed at self-cultivation and yet done on behalf of others.

Picturing Pirous – Islam and the Postcolonial Artist-Citizen in Indonesia

We should remember that Islam did not lead Pirous to become an artist. As Indonesia came onto the world stage, questions of nationalism and international art modernism were foremost in his mind, deeply coloring his thinking, and giving him motivating frameworks for much of his work. In time, those forces led him to look to Islam afresh and see in it powerful aesthetic and ethical possibilities. As a way of giving Pirous's story broader weight and comparative significance, let me suggest how this turn to Islam helped him negotiate some of the political and cultural currents around him. In essence, the vocabulary of Islam and Islamic art gave Pirous a language with which to translate ideologies and interests across and within national and international spheres, and to chart out the communities to whom he addressed his paintings. Doing so also came with some problems.

For over 200 years, nationalism, nationhood, and the nation-state have been key to placing collectivities and individuals "in the world" – for making them recognizable to each other and for drawing them into the currents of modernity (Anderson 1991; Calhoun 1997; Chatterjee 1986, 1993; Hutchinson and Smith 1994; Willford and George 2005). The nation-state became the central legitimizing authority for the modern citizen, not only promoting nationalist loyalties and aspirations, but creating, on the one hand, an ambience of "cultural intimacy" (Herzfeld 1997: 2) wherein citizens would use the cover of national culture for personal ends, and, on the other hand, an essential desire or need to be recognized by the nation-state (Siegel 1997: 7).

Postcolonial artists throughout Asia took up the summons of nationalism (Clark 1998: 239–59; Kapur 1996), producing work aimed at representing their national past, present, and future. Being "national" thus made the early postcolonial artists recognizable on domestic and international art circuits; it afforded them legitimacy and visibility. It might have been enough to make them "fully" modern, too. But not quite. To be a modern Indonesian artist (or a modern artist of any postcolonial nationality) "one had first to feel the currents of world communication" (Siegel 1997: 93). Indigenous native traditions were not a starting point for a modern national identity. Rather, competing international modernisms (e.g., socialist realism, abstract expressionism) provided "modern" and "universal" visual languages for expression of the national, and so a mirror in which postcolonial artists could see themselves reflected.

Pirous, we have seen, had deep national sentiments from the time he took up making propaganda posters for the Indonesian Revolution. He gained an early glimpse of "world currents" during his formal training in Bandung, and found recognition through sales to foreign diplomats. In the closing years of the Sukarno era, he and his colleagues at Bandung were in practical and ideological disfavor, and could find no national recognition, no national public; that changed when Soeharto took over the reins of state power and began remaking the nation. Pirous became a rising star on the national scene. His abstract canvases caught the eye of Western art collectors in Jakarta's diplomatic circles, who arranged for him to go to New York, one of the hubs of the international art world. As with so many postcolonial intellectuals, writers, and artists from Asia, Africa, the Middle East, and the Americas, Pirous's journey outside of his national homeland to a global metropolis delivered a profound shock of self-recognition. Feeling marginalized by the cosmopolitan international scene as a modernist mimic who lacked national authenticity, Pirous took inspiration and refuge in the Islamic visual culture of his Acehnese homeland. From that imagined "archive," he conjured a repertoire of ethnoreligious images that he could offer as both indigenous and global, and so potentially worthy of recognition in international art venues.

I do not need to rehearse the drama of Pirous's turn to a Qur'anic aesthetic in the mid-1970s. I would like to frame this turn once more, however, by explicitly suggesting that it was but part of a drama of postcolonial translation and multiculturalism (cf., Bhabha 1994; Chakrabarty 2000; Merrill 2009; Siegel 1997; Young 2001). If nationalism and aesthetic modernism were "languages" for making his painterly subjectivity visible, he found in Islam yet another. In some ways, translating between these "languages" allowed Pirous to substitute Acehnese iconography for national or cosmopolitan or Qur'anic iconographies. Yet the more important function, I think, was to find room to maneuver, the flexibility to declare difference or equivalence between iconographies or styles, or to playfully and elusively code-switch. Thus he could congenially situate his work within the arenas of multicultural nationalism, multicultural Islam, and the global art world's increasingly multicultural cosmopolitanism. Languages are not neutral codes, of course; they are deeply inflected by history and power. Because they are used to address and to find recognition from others – to say "I" and "you" – they have ethical entailments. Pirous's paintings, we could say, were as "multilingual" as they were multicultural: they addressed and sought recognition from multiple audiences and communities, but with no firm way of knowing how the addresses were heard or overheard. The Qur'anic legibility so reassuring and useful to an Indonesian Muslim, so redolent of the transcendental and the sublime, might be pictorially incomprehensible or uncomfortable to an Indonesian who professed a different faith, or to viewers who professed no faith at all.

We should not forget that it was the nation-state that kept Pirous in the Indonesian public eye, and that brokered his presence in international shows; nor should we forget that the international art world expected "Indonesian" gestures from him in his painting, even if Qur'anic materials resonated with international audiences as a sign of the cosmopolitan. As with other postcolonial artists around the world, his work circulated largely in his own country (García-Canclini 1998). Thus, Pirous primarily addressed his work to Indonesian Muslim viewers, and felt toward them a deep ethical responsibility. The habits of translation and address that allowed him to picture solidarities between Acehnese, Indonesian, and Muslim collectivities nonetheless posed a trap: the political and cultural faultlines within any group cannot be wished away, and will often return to disturb those who would cover them up with layers of paint or, more cruelly, with the force of authoritarian rule. Thus, the collapse of the Soeharto regime and the revelations of state-sanctioned atrocities in Aceh delivered a punishing blow to Pirous's artistic vision of the common good and for a time pushed him into a painterly language of anguished figuration and realism.

What began with a project of postcolonial translation between Asian and Euro-American modernisms (an East–West dialogue), soon posed questions about the place of "culture" in Indonesian Islamic life. Like the medieval Muslim poet and intellectual Ghazali (Moosa 2005), Pirous showed a true open-mindedness about diverse ideas and arts, especially those of the non-Muslim West; he was ready to embrace them and use them to enrich Islamic thought and spirituality. Like the modern Muslim thinker, Isma'il Raji al-Faruqi (see chapter 4), he was eager to translate Western arts and ideas into an Islamic vocabulary, so as to transform them and bring them into line with the principles of Islam. Indeed, Pirous's very notion of culture springs from ideas expressed by Johann Gottfried Herder and others in the European Romantic movements of the eighteenth and nineteenth centuries. Coaxing that idea of culture into an Islamic framework, he promoted his work and the work of others as *seni budaya yang bernafaskan Islam*, "cultural arts that breathe [i.e., that are inspired by] Islam."

From 1970 onwards, the Islamic reawakening in Indonesia unleashed a groundswell of interest in outward everyday conduct and piety; "inner" forms of spiritual experience (Howell 2001); Qur'anic education and recitation (Gade 2004); *da'wah* activities; and the implementation of Islamic values across a broad range of social and economic activities for both men and women (Brenner 2005; Hefner 1999, 2000; Jones 2007; Smith-Hefner 2007). Part of this groundswell also had to do with widespread apprehensiveness about the political constraints of authoritarian rule: Islamic schools and mosques were seen as relatively safe arenas for debating public issues. Even when the Soeharto government encouraged a regimist version of Islam in the 1990s, Muslim circles were often the place for critical public discourse.

Against this backdrop, Pirous pushed forward with a select – and potentially contestable – set of ideas about Islamic art and culture, wishing above all to have the national Muslim community view itself as an art-producing community. He was always careful to seek recognition and legitimacy from the nation-state for this effort, exhibiting his paintings in national MTQ events or in other government-sponsored venues. Often he promoted Islamic art as an emblem of national or subnational regional culture, as he did in the Istiqlal Festivals. He thus made Islamic art safe, or at least palatable, for the nation. Although largely directed inward toward the nation, the very idea of Indonesian Islamic culture implied that the world of Islam was culturally plural, that an Indonesian version of Islamic culture could be distinguished from a Saudi or Egyptian one.

Advocating for Islamic culture in this way brought Pirous into potential rivalry and conflict with Muslim religious authorities, for whom art and culture were new and unfamiliar fields of knowledge. The notion of culture as "Islamic" had few antecedents in Islamic theology and jurisprudence, and, as I have explained in earlier chapters, not a few clerics thought that Islam prohibited the arts. Further still, some *ulama* considered multiculturalism a threat to the unity of Islam. Pirous represented a new kind of authority, one who was quickly becoming an arbiter on what made culture "Islamic" and "ethical." Dale Eickelman and James Piscatori (1996) have observed similar or related rivalries in contemporary Muslim communities throughout Asia, Africa, and the Middle East. For Eickelman and Piscatori, these rivalries speak to the fragmentation of religious authority in today's Islamic communities. But Muhammad Qasim Zaman (2006) may be closer to the mark when he describes such rivalries as part of a proliferation of religious authority in those societies.

It has taken me years to fully appreciate what Pirous told me that afternoon in March 1994, as we worked together to get things ready for his gallery opening: "This isn't *da'wah*. I'm not campaigning for religion. I am making art. What you see here,

140

all these paintings, these are my spiritual notes." By insisting that his Qur'anic paintings were personal spiritual notes, Pirous was taking cover from the censoriousness and pleasureless orthodoxies of hardline clerics. The Muslim religious authorities sitting on the Indonesian Council of Islamic Scholars (Majelis Ulama Indonesia, MUI), it is true, have never been uniform in theological or jural outlook. Yet new and unfamiliar matters of art and culture made them uneasy, and so Pirous could hardly count on their support for his vision of things. As we have seen, he was not inclined to test them; indeed, he did all that he could to reassure them that he had no intentions of encroaching on their turf.

The *ulama* held authority over matters of *da'wah*, but one's *batin*, one's inner spirituality was not their business. Like Ghazali, centuries before him (Moosa 2005: 266–80), Pirous brought the power of art to bear on the ethical contours of his lifeworld and subjectivity. My friend had hopes, too, for a broader societal project, and through his paintings wished to offer a gallery-going public a "useful" glimpse of beauty, spiritual fulfillment, and goodness. That, it seems to me, is the mark of an ethical person as well. After all, ethics are not simply about the self, but open out to others. As Paul Ricoeur puts it, ethics are about "aiming for the 'good life' with and for others *in just institutions*" (1992: 172, emphasis mine).

Think, then, about the difficulties thrown onto the path of Pirous's hopes. Just institutions? Under authoritarian rule? Freedom and civic liberty were badly shackled during the Soeharto years, and ethics, as a public venture, cannot thrive without them (cf., Foucault 1997: 284). Authoritarian rule also undermined the foundations for a liberal public sphere where ideas can be debated. Indonesian artists, curators, and gallery-goers might attend a government-sponsored art show or festival as a viewing audience, but how could they come together as a free-thinking art public that could speak for its interests, justify its artistic projects, and set the value of its work (cf. Crow 1985)? No compulsion in matters of faith, avers the Qur'an. But compulsion and constraint surely characterized matters of art during the Soeharto years. For artists to raise an ethics from an interpersonal level to a societal one was an exceptionally problematic and risky undertaking. The kinds of political criticism and expression congruent with the ethical life had to remain oblique in the face of authoritarian threat.

Under those conditions, how could an artist make an influential mark beyond a tightly drawn circle of intellectuals and elite collectors? I have not had enough time with Pirous's collectors to know how they dwell with his paintings or how useful those works may be for them. As for the transnational art world, it is far more welcoming to Indonesian artists than it was in 1970. But, in that time, painting has lost a good deal of prestige as a critical or expressive form, while digital, video, mixed media, performance, and installation art have come to the fore. Explicitly religious work sits uneasily in major contemporary venues, sometimes refused outright or dismissed as reactionary mysticism lacking transgressive or transformative power (Elkins 2004). More than ever before, the Indonesian art world enjoys a vibrant traffic with global institutions, global capital, and global art discourses. No surprise, then, that one very experienced observer could write by the heyday of

Reformasi art that "contemporary Indonesian art is no longer dominated by decorative canvases infused with the spiritual clichés which so easily grace the settings of elite lifestyles" (Wright 2000).

Though political vitality has returned to Indonesian art, I am not ready to write off Pirous's spiritual notes as the decorative clichés of a bygone era. As I hope this book has shown, his spiritual notes may augur a radical but feasible future for Indonesia's Muslim community: open-minded, curious, reflective, and just; fearless about the pleasures and power of art; and reassured of God's company in Qur'anic revelation. Paintings like his, of course, could be turned toward other ends – used to mark the limits of the common good by Islamist cultural police, or to enchant elite collectors in the privacy of their homes. But, again, the works I have discussed in this book are the paintings Pirous did not want to let go, the ones he has kept both to meet his need for habitual self-reflection, as well as his need for recognition from others. They hang quietly at his home and gallery, some beside a door, others on a vaulted wall, each a painted threshold or veranda where we might pause for a pleasurable glimpse into a lifeworld where goodness continues to matter.

AFTERWORD: CHOOSING A FRAME

Theoretical and Disciplinary Frames

Ethnographies take their framing, in part, from the theoretical and disciplinary elaborations at their edges. Anthropologists often use the introductory chapters of a book to explore the details of larger theoretical discussions that inform the work as whole, and gorge their endnotes with richly nuanced asides and extensive comparative, historical, or bibliographic notes. I chose to keep the explicit theoretical and disciplinary thrust of this book rather spare so that the implicit richness of the ethnographic narrative in *Picturing Islam* might address a broad range of cross-disciplinary discussions. I wanted this book to be broadly useful and felt that a sharply etched theoretical or disciplinary framing would limit its appeal. That said, it might be of interest to some readers if I offer a just a few remarks about the implications of this book for the study of art and for the anthropology of subjectivity and ethics.

For a long time I considered situating this book at the intersection of art history and the anthropology of art (e.g., Marcus and Myers 1995; Westermann 2005). Art historians have begun to use ethnographic approaches in the study of national art histories (e.g., Taylor 2004) and diasporic arts (e.g., Drewal 2008), and anthropologists are increasingly writing about the cultural politics of contemporary art (e.g., Fabian 1996; Myers 2002; Roberts and Roberts 2003; Winegar 2006; Zitzewitz 2008) or about the history of colonial and early modern arts (e.g., Mathur 2007; Pinney and Peterson 2003). Out of such work we may find fresh ways to think about the visual construction of secular institutions, histories, and fields of power. I see opportunity, too, to use such studies to rethink art history and the anthropology

143

of art in light of globalization and indigenous art histories (cf., Belting 2003; Elkins 2007).

In *Picturing Islam*, I have taken an actor-and-object approach, not unlike what art historian Thomas Crow calls a "life and work model" (1999: 2), but supplemented with extensive reflections from the actor-artist (who is not the only actor on the scene, of course). The focus of my "ethnographic art history" – if I may coin a term – has been on Pirous and his art work, and considerably less on the many figures, forces, and institutions that drive Indonesia's art world and its art discourses. My choice in doing so comes with some trade-offs. For one, the broad workings of an "art world" – the focal concern of sociological approaches associated with Howard Becker (1982), Pierre Bourdieu (1993), and Janet Wolff (1993) – recede into the background. Another potential problem is to overly privilege the figure of the artist. The dangers in doing so are two: treating a painter as if s/he knowingly is in control of aesthetic self-expression; and giving in to the demands of a global marketplace in art that wants names and painterly reputations. The first overlooks the social, cultural, and unconscious forces at work in creating both art and a self; the latter is to cave in to the ideological forces of global capitalism. A third and related trade-off is to leave unquestioned the modernist ideologies that link a painting to a painter's subjectivity and identity.

These issues notwithstanding, I believe my approach to ethnographic art history, which draws from Baxandall (1985) as well as Crow, takes us into the ideological motivations for making art without losing sight of the practical dilemmas of negotiating the social world in which art projects and art transactions take place. We have seen Pirous as he tried to domesticate and inhabit the modernist legacy within the larger contours of national and international cultural spheres. For purposes of international recognition, he chose to pursue Islamic art as a sign of his indigeneity and national belonging. The key entailments were four: taking possession of and innovating upon a largely Western art historical discourse about Islamic art; working out rival ideologies of word and image as they apply to Qur'anic calligraphy (see Mitchell 1986); seeking legitimacy for his art from fellow Muslims and from religious authorities; and refashioning his artistic subjectivity with respect to ethical relationships and practical technique. Pirous did not work out these questions in the abstract, nor did he always tackle them in an explicitly reflexive way (although that was often the case). Rather, he addressed them through very specific works, projects, and discursive frames. In this light, his notion of "spiritual notes" relates not only to inner subjective experience, but exposes his vulnerability to and dependence upon the push and pull of political, religious, and art ideologies, in all of their contingency and contradictions.

This brings me to the contribution *Picturing Islam* may make to the anthropology of subjectivity and ethics. Questions of subjectivity are central to fields beside anthropology, such as literary criticism, psychology, gender studies, postcolonial and subaltern studies, and visual cultural studies, to name just a few. Although anthropologists draw ideas and approaches from these other fields, their interest in subjectivity tends to coalesce around one of two poles. Some put emphasis on the lived experience and reflexivity of actors (e.g., Biehl, Good, and Kleinman 2007; Good, Delvecchio Good, Hyde, and Pinto 2008), while others situate that reflexivity with respect to the reproduction and transformation of powerful, sub-ject-shaping, social and cultural formations (e.g., Ortner 2006). For the former, "subjectivity is the means to shaping sensibility" (Biehl et al. 2007: 14) and denotes "the most intimate forms of everyday experience" (Good et al. 2008: 2–3); for the latter, it has more to do with the projects that reveal the complex and practical workings of cultural and historical consciousness (Ortner 1995: 183–87; 2006: 110–11, 127–28). These approaches should not suggest that anthropologists fall in theoretically opposed camps; actors and reflexivity are central to both. Yet the different sets of emphases potentially result in different ethnographic directions and protocols.

On the face of it, *Picturing Islam* appears to tilt toward an emphasis on experi-ence and sensibilities. Recourse to ideas about lifeworlds and lived religion would seem to imply this, as would views that link painting with experience, interiority, and expressiveness. Yet I have been careful to write about pictures and not just a painter, about unforeseen social or cultural destinies and not just self-reflexive accounts of subjecthood and subjection, about broad social and political projects and not just the meanings an artist might attribute to a work. I have tried to show how reflexive shifts in self-fashioning depended not just on religious or aesthetic ideologies, but also upon an encounter with materials such as oils and acrylics. Equally, I have suggested how painterly projects were at once aesthetic, political, and religious in gesture and construction; through them, we see how the shifting effort to picture Islam was also a way for Pirous and others to picture a shifting nation-state and shifting self. When major changes sweep the compound ideologi-cal order of the everyday, it is not just subjects that are thrown off balance, but pictures and picturing as well. For these reasons, I place *Picturing Islam* rather closer to the second approach, where we might capture "the multiplicity of projects in which social beings are always engaged, and the multiplicity of ways in which those projects feed on as well as collide with one another" (Ortner 1995: 191).

My treatment of ethics in this book stems from my reading of work by Judith Butler (2005), Michel Foucault (1997, 2005), and Paul Ricoeur (1992), and is but a first step toward a deeper exploration of issues. Their work does not exhaust the spectrum of writings that can contribute to the anthropology of ethics, but they helpfully put forward some key questions. As with the exploration of subjectivity, the study of ethics may skew toward the self and self-fashioning, or toward respon-sibility and the well-being of others, without producing opposed theoretical camps. Of interest to me are the ways these three authors concern themselves with very different social conditions for the ethical life: violence (Butler), freedom (Foucault), and justice (Ricoeur) – concerns that have been as basic to Pirous's life as they are to ours. At the same time, these authors look to language and narrative as the site of ethical practice and knowledge. *Picturing Islam* thus raises a question without answering it: Will we see ethics differently if we look to pictures as the fulcrum of ethical relationships?

145

Ethnographic Frames: A Postscript, 2002–2009

Ethnographies give us but a glimpse of the unfolding of time and human relationships. Ethnographies come to an end. Time and human relationships do not.

Pirous and some of the others in his family read through this book as I worked on the manuscript. In this way we have had the opportunity to continue a long conversation, and to ready it so that others might join in. Some readers may feel that my presentation has been too subjective, and perhaps too constrained by my friendship with Pirous. Kirin has reminded me, however, about something that happened to our friend, anthropologist Sidney Mintz. In 1960, Mintz published *Worker in the Cane*, an anthropological life history of a Puerto Rican friend, sugarcane laborer "Taso" Zayas. As Mintz relates in "The Sensation of Moving, While Standing Still" (1989), early reviewers of the book questioned his objectivity and thought the emotional ties of friendship imperiled chances for a sober, analytic understanding of social life. Twenty years after the book came out, a new generation of readers argued that Mintz had not been friendly enough with Taso and had only deepened the inequality between them by writing as he did. Mintz goes on to tease out some wonderful disciplinary observations about life histories from these contrasting views. I wrote *Picturing Islam* not only for cultural anthropologists, but for readers in religious studies and art history too. I am curious about what these readers from different disciplines will have to say about the mingling of friendship and research.

I have brought my story about Pirous, and how he has made his art and his lifeworld Islamic, to a close with his 2002 retrospective show. Since that time, his son Iwan has married architect Mira Siregar. Two more grandchildren have been born. Pirous and Erna also have built a new house and studio high on a breezy mountain slope overlooking Bandung. After five years of uncertainty immediately following the collapse of authoritarian rule, Indonesia has been making gains with democratic electoral politics, and the political atmosphere remains more open than it was during the Soeharto years.

Islamic themes and sensibilities are today at the hub of cultural expression in Indonesia. Books, magazines, films, television, music, fashion, self-actualization programs, text-messaging, interior design, and accessories for the car and home all reflect the steady interest in religious expression and comportment. As Islam leaves a more pronounced stamp on popular culture in Indonesia, various fields of cultural production have come increasingly under the watch of religious authorities and vigilante organizations, a development that leaves me apprehensive about the future for open expression. Although they have not found electoral success, Muslim ultraconservatives have made inroads into everyday culture, society, and media. Their growing influence has evoked civic efforts from liberal Muslims, who wish to keep narrow religious orthodoxies from prevailing in public life. Indonesia's art world has been a target for the ultraconservative campaign. The hardline Islamic Defenders Front (Front Pembela Islam, FPI), among other vigilante groups, has been successful in disrupting or closing art events through opportunistic, arbitrary, and self-serving shows of power carried out in the name of God. In the wake of one such incident, Indonesian curator Jim Supangkat (2005) remarked that FPI's icono-clastic protests "lie beyond the platform of art" and should not be used to accuse Islam of opposing freedom of expression or of opposing art, a view I know Pirous shares.

Last, my story has not mentioned the unforeseeable tragedy that struck Aceh on December 26, 2004. The tsunami that rolled out of the Indian Ocean that day took the lives of over 160,000 Acehnese. Seventy of them were Pirous's relatives, and Meulaboh, the hometown of his youth, was swept from the face of the earth. He was devastated. Kirin and I went to visit Pirous and Erna in March 2005, and I repeated the condolences I had sent in late December. In his sorrow, Pirous had not been able to bring himself to paint, but he took us to a show of his work in Jakarta that he had organized to raise relief funds. The show was called "Jabal Fana", a reference to the "ephemeral mountain" (Jabal Fana) near Mecca that for Pirous signified mortality and transience, and that had made it into one of his paintings after he returned from the *hajj* in 1988 (see Figure 4.1). Although he has resumed painting, and traveled to Aceh to help with efforts to rebuild the province, he has never gone back to his hometown to look upon the devastation there; he does not want any knowledge of the calamity to wash away the memories of his youth. In that refusal to look at what could only be a source of pain, I think he has wisely cared for himself once more.

REFERENCES

Abdul Hadi W. M. 1995. "*Tuhan Kita Begitu Dekat*" ("God, We are That Close"). In *Takbir Para Penyair (Recitations/Interpretations from the Poets)*. Hamid Jabar, Leon Agusta, Sitok Srengenge, eds. p. 35. Jakarta: Festival Istiqlal Foundation.

Abdul Hadi W. M., Mamannoor, Popo Iskandar, Wiyoso Yudoseputro, and Yustiono. 1996. "Curators' Statement." In *Seni Rupa Kontemporer Istiqlal (Istiqlal Contemporary Art)*. Herry Dim, ed. pp. 16–19. Jakarta: Festival Istiqlal Foundation.

Adnan, Syaiful. 1981. "*Studi tentang Aspek Bentuk Kaligrafi Arab dalam Lukisan A. D. Pirous*" ("A Study on Aspects of Arabic Calligraphy in the Paintings of A. D. Pirous"). Unpublished undergraduate thesis, Department of Painting, Sekolah Tinggi Seni Rupa Indonesia (Art Academy), Yogyakarta, Indonesia.

Al-Azmeh, Aziz. 1993. *Islams and Modernities*. New York: Verso.

Ali, Abdullah Yusuf, trans. 2005. *The Holy Qur'an: Text, Translation and Commentary*. Elmhurst, NY: Tahrike Tarsile Qur'an, Inc.

Ali, Ahmed, trans. 1994. *Al-Qur'an: A Contemporary Translation*. Revised edn. Princeton: Princeton University Press.

Ali, Wijdan, ed. 1989. *Contemporary Art from the Islamic World*. London: Scorpion Publishing Ltd.

Ali, Wijdan. 1997. *Modern Islamic Art: Development and Continuity*. Gainesville, FL: University Press of Florida.

Anderson, Benedict. 1991. *Imagined Communities: Reflections on the Origin and Spread of Nationalism*. New York: Verso.

Anderson, Benedict. 1998. *The Spectre of Comparisons: Nationalism, Southeast Asia and the World*. New York: Verso.

Arendt, Hannah. 1958. *The Human Condition*. Chicago: University of Chicago Press.

Arkoun, Mohammed. 1994. *Rethinking Islam: Common Questions, Uncommon Answers*. Robert D. Lee, ed. and trans. Boulder, CO: Westview Press.

Asad, Talal. 1986. *The Idea of an Anthropology of Islam*. Occasional Paper Series. Washington, DC: Georgetown University Center for Contemporary Arab Studies.

Asad, Talal. 2003. *Formations of the Secular: Christianity, Islam, Modernity*. Stanford: Stanford University Press.

Ball, Philip. 2001. *Bright Earth: Art and the Invention of Color.* Chicago: University of Chicago Press.

Baxandall, Michael. 1985. *Patterns of Intention: On the Historical Explanation of Pictures.* New Haven: Yale University Press.

Becker, Howard. 1982. *Art Worlds.* Berkeley: University of California Press.

Belting, Hans. 2003. *Art History after Modernism.* Chicago: University of Chicago Press.

Bhabha, Homi. 1994. *The Location of Culture.* New York: Routledge.

Biehl, João, Byron Good, and Arthur Kleinman. 2007. "Introduction: Rethinking Subjectivity." In *Subjectivity: Ethnographic Explorations.* João Biehl, Byron. Good, and Arthur Kleinman, eds. pp. 1–23. Berkeley: University of California Press.

Blair, Sheila S. and Jonathan M. Bloom. 2003. "The Mirage of Islamic Art: Reflections on the Study of an Unwieldy Field." *Art Bulletin* 85(1): 152–84.

Bourdieu, Pierre. 1993. *The Field of Cultural Production: Essays on Art and Literature.* Randal Johnson, ed. New York: Columbia University Press.

Brenner, Suzanne. 2005. "Islam and Gender Politics in Late New Order Indonesia." In *Spirited Politics: Religion and Public Life in Contemporary Southeast Asia.* Andrew C. Willford and Kenneth M. George, eds., pp. 93–118. Ithaca, NY: Southeast Asian Publications Series, Southeast Asia Program, Cornell University.

Buchari, Machmud. 1994. *Al-Qur'an Mushaf Istiqlal.* Jakarta: Festival Istiqlal Foundation.

Buchari, Machmud and Sanento Yuliman. 1985. *A. D. Pirous: Painting, Etching, and Serigraphy – A Retrospective Exhibition.* Bandung: Decenta Gallery.

Butler, Judith. 2005. *Giving an Account of Oneself.* New York: Fordham University Press.

Calhoun, Craig. 1997. *Nationalism.* Minneapolis: University of Minnesota Press.

Chakrabarty, Dipesh. 2000. *Provincializing Europe: Postcolonial Thought and Historical Difference.* Princeton: Princeton University Press.

Chatterjee, Partha. 1986. *Nationalist Thought and the Colonial World: A Derivative Discourse?* Minneapolis: University of Minnesota Press.

Chatterjee, Partha. 1993. *The Nation and Its Fragments: Colonial and Postcolonial Histories.* Princeton: Princeton University Press.

Clark, John. 1995. "Art Goes Non-Aligned." *ARTAsia/Pacific* 2(3): 28–31.

Clark, John. 1998. *Modern Asian Art.* Honolulu: University of Hawai'i Press.

Crow, Thomas E. 1985. *Painters and Public Life in Eighteenth Century Paris.* New Haven: Yale University Press.

Crow, Thomas E. 1999. *The Intelligence of Art.* Chapel Hill: University of North Carolina Press.

Dadi, Iftikhar. 2006. "Rethinking Calligraphic Modernism." In *Discrepant Abstraction.* Kobena Mercer, ed. pp. 94–115. Cambridge: The Institute of International Visual Arts and MIT Press.

Drewal, John Henry, ed. 2008. *Mami Wata: Arts for Water Spirits in Africa and Its Diaspora.* Los Angeles: UCLA Fowler Museum of Cultural History.

Eickelman, Dale F. and James Piscatori. 1996. *Muslim Politics.* Princeton: Princeton University Press.

Elkins, James. 2004. *On the Strange Place of Religion in Contemporary Art.* New York: Routledge.

Elkins, James, ed. 2007. *Is Art History Global?* New York: Routledge.

Ernst, Carl. 1997. *The Shambhala Guide to Sufism.* Boston: Shambhala Publications.

Esposito, John, ed. 1987. *Islam in Asia: Religion, Politics, and Society.* Oxford: Oxford University Press.

Ewing, Katherine Pratt. 1997. *Arguing Sainthood: Modernity, Psychoanalysis, and Islam*. Durham: Duke University Press.

Fabian, Johannes. 1996. *Remembering the Present: Painting and Popular History in Zaire*. Berkeley: University of California Press.

Fischer, Michael M. J. and Mehdi Abedi. 1990. *Debating Muslims: Cultural Dialogues in Postmodernity and Tradition*. Madison: University of Wisconsin Press.

Fischer, Joseph. 1990. *Modern Indonesian Art: Three Generations of Tradition and Change, 1945–1990*. Jakarta and New York: Panitia Pameran KIAS (1990–91) and Festival of Indonesia, 1990.

Flood, Finnbarr Barry. 2002. "Between Cult and Culture: Bamiyan, Islamic Iconoclasm, and the Museum." *Art Bulletin* 84(4): 641–59.

Foucault, Michel. 1997. *Ethics: Subjectivity and Truth*. Paul Rabinow, ed. Robert Hurley et al., trans. New York: The New Press.

Foucault, Michel. 2005. *The Hermeneutics of the Subject: Lectures at the Collège de France, 1981–1982*. Frédéric Gros, ed. Graham Burchell, trans. New York: Picador.

Gade, Anna. 2004. *Perfection Makes Practice: Learning, Emotion, and the Recited Qur'an in Indonesia*. Honolulu: University of Hawai'i Press.

García-Canclini, Néstor. 1998. "Remaking Passports: Visual Thought in the Debate on Multiculturalism." In *The Art of Art History: A Critical Anthology*. Donald Preziosi, ed., pp. 498–506. Oxford: Oxford University Press.

Gell, Alfred. 1998. *Art and Agency: An Anthropological Theory*. Oxford: Oxford University Press.

George, Kenneth M. 1996. *Showing Signs of Violence: The Cultural Politics of a Twentieth-Century Headhunting Ritual*. Berkeley: University of California Press.

George, Kenneth M. 1997. "Some Things that Have Happened to 'The Sun After September 1965': Politics and the Interpretation of an Indonesian Painting." *Comparative Studies in Society and History* 39(4): 603–34.

George, Kenneth M. 1998. "Designs on Indonesia's Muslim Communities." *Journal of Asian Studies* 57(3): 693–713.

George, Kenneth M. 1999. "Signature Work: Bandung, 1994." *Ethnos* 64(2): 212–31.

George, Kenneth M. 2009. "Ethics, Iconoclasm, and Qur'anic Art in Indonesia." *Cultural Anthropology* 24(4): 589–621.

Good, Byron J., Mary-Jo DelVecchio Good, Sandra Teresa Hyde and Sarah Pinto. 2008. "Postcolonial Disorders: Reflections on Subjectivity in the Contemporary World." In *Postcolonial Disorders*. Mary-Jo DelVecchio Good, Sandra Teresa Hyde, Sarah Pinto, and Byron J. Good, eds., pp. 1–42. Berkeley: University of California Press.

Grabar, Oleg. 1983. "Symbols and Signs in Islamic Architecture." In *Architecture and Community: Building in the Islamic World Today*. Renata Holod, ed., pp. 25–32 Millerton, NY: Aperture.

Graham, William and Navid Kermani. 2006. "Recitation and Aesthetic Reception." In *The Cambridge Companion to the Qur'an*. Jane D. McAuliffe, ed., pp. 115–41. Cambridge: Cambridge University Press.

Haeri, Niloofar. 2003. *Sacred Language, Ordinary People: Dilemmas of Culture and Politics in Egypt*. New York: Palgrave.

Haleem, M. A. S. Abdel. 2004. *The Qur'an: A New Translation*. Oxford: Oxford University Press.

Hefner, Robert W. 1999. "Islam and Nation in the Post-Suharto Era." In *The Politics of Post-Suharto Indonesia*. Adam Schwarz and Jonathan Paris, eds., pp. 40–72. Washington, DC: Council of Foreign Relations.

Hefner, Robert W. 2000. *Civil Islam: Muslims and Democratization in Indonesia*. Princeton: Princeton University Press.

Hefner, Robert W. and Patricia Horvatich, eds. 1997. *Islam in an Era of Nation States: Politics and Religious Renewal in Muslim Southeast Asia*. Honolulu: University of Hawai'i Press.

Herzfeld, Michael. 1997. *Cultural Intimacy: Social Poetics in the Nation-State*. New York: Routledge.

Hirschkind, Charles. 2006. *The Ethical Soundscape: Cassette Sermons and Islamic Counterpublics*. New York: Columbia University Press.

Hoesterey, James B. 2009. "Sufis and Self-Help Gurus: Islamic Psychology, Religious Authority, and Muslim Subjectivity in Contemporary Indonesia." PhD Dissertation, Department of Anthropology, University of Wisconsin-Madison. Ann Arbor: University Microfilms.

Holt, Claire. 1967. *Art in Indonesia: Continuities and Change*. Ithaca: Cornell University Press.

Howell, Julia Day. 2001. "Sufism and the Indonesian Revival." *Journal of Asian Studies* 60(3): 701–29.

Hutchinson, John, and Anthony D. Smith, eds. 1994. *Nationalism*. Oxford: Oxford University Press.

Jackson, Michael. 2006. *The Politics of Storytelling: Violence, Transgression, and Intersubjectivity*. Copenhagen: Museum Tusculanem Press.

Jameson, Frederic. 1983. "Postmodernism and Consumer Culture." In *The Anti-Aesthetic: Essays in Postmoden Culture*. Hal Foster, ed., pp. 111–25. Seattle: Bay Press.

Jones, Carla. 2007. "Fashion and Faith in Urban Indonesia." *Fashion Theory* 11(2/3): 211–32.

Kapur, Geeta. 1996. "Dismantling the Norm." In *Traditions/Tensions: Contemporary Art in Asia*. Apinan Poshyananda, ed., pp. 60–69. New York: Asia Society.

Keane, Webb. 2007. *Christian Moderns: Freedom and Fetish in the Mission Encounter*. Berkeley: University of California Press.

Kratz, E. Ulrich. 1986. "Islamic Attitudes toward Modern Indonesian Literature." In C. D. Grijns and S. O. Robson, eds., *Cultural Contact and Textual Interpretation (Verhandelingen van het Koninklijk Instituut voor Taal-, Land- en Volkenkunde 115)*. Leiden: Foris Publications, pp. 60–93.

Kratz, E. Ulrich. ed. 2000. *Sumber Terpilih Sejarah Sastra Indonesia Abad XX. (Select Sources from Twentieth-Century Indonesian Literary History)*. Jakarta: Gramedia.

Laffan, Michael. 2007. "'Another Andalusia': Images of Colonial Southeast Asia in Arabic Newspapers." *Journal of Asian Studies* 66(3): 689–722.

Leja, Michael. 1993. *Reframing Abstract Expressionism: Subjectivity and Painting in the 1940s*. New Haven: Yale University Press.

López, Sebastián. 1992. "Identity: Reality or Fiction?" *Third Text* 18: 32–34.

Mahmood, Saba. 2005. *The Politics of Piety: The Islamic Revival and the Feminist Subject*. Princeton: Princeton University Press.

Maier, Henk. 1987. "Chairil Anwar's 'Heritage: The Fear of Stultification': Another Side of Modern Indonesian Literature." *Indonesia* 43 (April): 1–29.

Maier, Henk. 2004. *We are Playing Relatives: A Survey of Malay Writing. (Verhandelingen van het Koninklijk Instituut voor Taal-, Land- en Volkenkunde 215)*. Leiden: KITLV Press.

Marcus, George E. and Fred R. Myers, eds. 1995. *The Traffic in Culture: Refiguring Art and Anthropology*. Berkeley: University of California Press.

Mathur, Saloni. 2007. *India by Design: Colonial History and Cultural Display*. Berkeley: University of California Press.

Memmi, Albert. 1991. *The Colonizer and the Colonized*. Expanded edition. Boston: Beacon Press.

Merrill, Christi A. 2009. *Riddles of Belonging: India in Translation and Other Tales of Possession*. New York: Fordham University Press.

Mintz, Sidney. 1989. "The Sensation of Moving, While Standing Still." *American Ethnologist* 16(4): 786–96.

Mitchell, W. J. T. 1986. *Iconology: Image, Text, Ideology*. Chicago: University of Chicago Press.

Mitchell, W. J. T. 2005. *What Do Pictures Want? The Lives and Loves of Images*. Chicago: University of Chicago Press.

Moosa, Ebrahim. 2005. *Ghazali: The Poetics of Imagination*. Chapel Hill: University of North Carolina Press.

Myers, Fred R. 2002. *Painting Culture: The Making of Aboriginal High Art*. Durham: Duke University Press.

Nandy, Ashis. 1998. *Exiled at Home*. Oxford: Oxford University Press.

Narayan, Kirin. 1989. *Storytellers, Saints, and Scoundrels: Folk Narrative in Hindu Religious Teaching*. Philadelphia: University of Pennsylvania Press.

Nasr, Seyyed Hossein. 1987. *Islamic Art and Spirituality*. Albany, NY: SUNY Press.

Ortner, Sherry B. 1995. "Resistance and the Problem of Ethnographic Refusal." *Comparative Studies in Society and History* 37(1): 173–93.

Ortner, Sherry B. 2006. *Anthropology and Social Theory: Culture, Power, and the Acting Subject*. Durham: Duke University Press.

Pamuk, Orhan. *My Name is Red*. Erdag M. Göknar, trans. New York: Vintage.

Pinney, Christopher and Nicolas Peterson, eds. 2003. *Photography's Other Histories*. Durham: Duke University Press.

Ricoeur, Paul. 1992. *Oneself as Another*. Kathleen Blamey, trans. Chicago: University of Chicago Press.

Roberts, Allen and Mary Nooter Roberts. 2003. *A Saint in the City: Sufi Arts of Urban Senegal*. Los Angeles: UCLA Fowler Museum of Cultural History.

Sabapathy, T. K. n.d. "Introduction to the Themes of the Exhibition." In *Contemporary Art of the Non-Aligned Countries: Unity in Diversity in International Art 1995* (Post-Event Catalogue). Anonymous, ed., pp. 33–37. Jakarta: DepDikBud (Department of Education and Culture).

Said, Edward W. 1978. *Orientalism*. New York: Vintage Books.

Sells, Michael. 1999. *Approaching the Qur'an: The Early Revelations*. Ashland, OR: White Cloud Press.

Siegel, James T. 1979. *Shadow and Sound: The Historical Thought of a Sumatran People*. Chicago: University of Chicago Press.

Siegel, James T. 1997. *Fetish, Recognition, Revolution*. Princeton: Princeton University Press.

References

Siegel, James T. 2000. *The Rope of God*. New edn. Ann Arbor: University of Michigan Press.

Silverstein, Brian. 2008. "Disciplines of Presence in Modern Turkey: Discourse, Companionship, and the Mass Mediation of Islamic Practice." *Cultural Anthropology* 23(1): 118–53.

Smith, Wilfred Cantwell. 1976. *Religious Diversity: Essays*. Willard G. Oxtoby, ed. New York: Harper and Row.

Smith-Hefner, Nancy J. 2007. "Javanese Women and the Veil in Post-Soeharto Indonesia." *Journal of Asian Studies* 66(2): 389–420.

Snouck Hurgronje, Christian. 1906. *The Acehnese*. A. W. S. O'Sullivan, trans., 2 vols. Leiden: E. J. Brill.

Soegijo, G. Sidharta. 1985. "Di Sekitar Pameran Retrospeksi A. D. Pirous" ("About the A. D. Pirous Retrospective Exhibition"). *Kompas*, November 3 (Sunday Arts Section).

Soemardjo, Trisno. 1954. "*Bandung Mengabdi Labortorium Barat*" ("Bandung is a Servant for the Western Laboratory"). *Siasat*, December 5, p. 26.

Spanjaard, Helena. 1988. "Free Art: Academic Painters in Indonesia." In *Kunst uit een Andere Wereld (Art from Another World)*. Paul Faber, Liane van der Linden, and Mien Tulmans, eds., pp. 103–32. Rotterdam: Museum voor Volkenkunde.

Spanjaard, Helena. 1998. "Het Ideaal van een Moderne Indonesische Schilderkunst, 1900–1995: De Creatie van een Nationale Culturele Identiteit" ("The Idea of Modern Indonesian Painting, 1900–1995: The Creation of a National Cultural Identity"). PhD thesis, University of Leiden.

Supangkat, Jim. 2005. "Tolerating the Intolerant: An Interview." *Broadsheet* 35(2): 85–7. ⟨http://universes-in-universe.org/eng/nafas/articles/2005/cp_biennale_2005⟩. Accessed May 16, 2009.

Supangkat, Jim. n.d. "Contemporary Art of the South." In *Contemporary Art of the Non-Aligned Countries: Unity in Diversity in International Art 1995* (Post-Event Catalogue). Anonymous, ed., pp. 20–32. Jakarta: DepDikBud (Department of Education and Culture).

Tambiah, Stanley J. 1992. *Buddhism Betrayed? Religion, Politics, and Violence in Sri Lanka*. Chicago: University of Chicago Press.

Taylor, Nora Annesley. 2004. *Painters in Hanoi: An Ethnography of Vietnamese Art*. Honolulu: University of Hawai'i Press.

van der Veer, Peter. 1994. *Religious Nationalism: Hindus and Muslims in India*. Berkeley: University of California Press.

van der Veer, Peter and Hartmut Lehman, eds. 1999. *Nation and Religion: Perspectives on Europe and Asia*. Princeton: Princeton University Press.

van Dijk, Kees. 1998. "Dakwah and Indigenous Culture: The Dissemination of Islam." In *Globalization, Localization and Indonesia (Bijdragen tot de Taal-, Land-, en Volkenkunde* 154, no. 2). P. Nas, ed., pp. 218–35. Leiden: KITLV Press.

Westermann, Mariët, ed. 2005. *Anthropologies of Art*. New Haven: Yale University Press.

Willford, Andrew, and Kenneth M. George, eds. 2005. *Spirited Politics: Religion and Public Life in Contemporary Southeast Asia*. Ithaca: Southeast Asian Publications Series, Cornell.

Williams, Raymond. 1977. *Marxism and Literature*. Oxford: Oxford University Press.

Winegar, Jessica. 2006. *Creative Reckonings: The Politics of Art and Culture in Contemporary Egypt*. Stanford: Stanford University Press.

Wolff, Janet. 1993. *The Social Production of Art*. 2nd edn. New York: New York University Press.

References

Wright, Astri. 1994. *Soul, Spirit, and Mountain: Preoccupations of Contemporary Indonesian Painters*. Oxford: Oxford University Press.

Wright, Astri. 2000. "Indonesian Artists Reflect on Past Horrors." *Jakarta Post*, January 16, 2000. Posted at ⟨http://www.javafred.net/rd_wright_10.htm⟩. Accessed May 15, 2009.

Young, Robert J. C. 2001. *Postcolonialism: An Historical Introduction*. Malden, MA: Blackwell Publishing.

Zaman, Muhammad Qasim. 2006. "Consensus and Religious Authority in Modern Islam: The Discourses of the Ulama." In *Speaking for Islam: Religious Authorities in Muslim Societies*. Gudrun Krämer and Sabine Schmidtke, eds., pp. 153–80. Leiden: Brill.

Zitzewitz, Karin. 2008. "The Secular Icon: Secularist Practice and Indian Visual Culture." *Visual Anthropology Review* 24(1): 12–28.

INDEX

Italicized page numbers refer to figures. Locators for plates are also italicized (as in *plate 10*).